STUDIES IN
COMPARATIVE ECONOMICS 1

Studies in Comparative Economics

THE ECONOMICS
OF LABOR

by E. H. Phelps Brown

NEW HAVEN AND LONDON
YALE UNIVERSITY PRESS

Copyright © 1962 by Yale University.
Fifth printing, November 1969.
Designed by Sally Hargrove.
Set in Baskerville type
and printed in the United States of America by
The Carl Purington Rollins Printing-Office
of the Yale University Press, New Haven, Connecticut.

Library of Congress catalog card number: 62–16231.

Distributed in Great Britain, Europe, Asia,
and Africa by Yale University Press Ltd.,
London; in Canada by McGill-Queen's University
Press, Montreal; and in Mexico by Centro
Interamericano de Libros Académicos,
Mexico City.

FOREWORD

Modern economics has been bred chiefly in Western Europe and the United States, and despite its aspiration toward generality it bears the stamp of institutions and issues characteristic of these areas.

But the economic world no longer revolves about London and New York. Dozens of new nations are struggling toward economic independence and industrial growth under institutional arrangements quite unlike those of the West. Economies of a novel type also extend eastward from central Europe to the Bering Strait and have been busily developing their own principles as a by-product of administrative experience. It is asserted that "Western economics" has only limited analytical value in these other countries.

The problem of the content and relevance of economics thus arises inescapably. Are the economic principles taught in the West really susceptible of general application? Or are they culture-bound and relevant mainly to industrial capitalist countries? Is it possible to create a general economics which would be as useful in Poland or India as in Canada or France? Or must we be content with several species of economics which will remain distinct in intellectual content and applicability?

"Comparative economics" has been regarded as a separate area of the economics curriculum, consisting of a botanical classification of national economies into a few loosely labeled

Foreword

boxes. But surely any course in economics is potentially comparative. A concern with comparative experience can profitably be infused into any of the standard branches of economic study. This series is inspired by the hope that a rethinking of particular branches of economics in world perspective, combined with a bibliography of available material from many countries, may help teachers to give their courses a broader and more comparative orientation.

In pursuing this objective, we deliberately chose autonomy over standardization. Each author was left free to determine his own approach and method of treatment. The essays thus differ considerably in length, analytical as against descriptive emphasis, geographical coverage, and other respects. How far the original intent of the series has been accomplished is for the profession to judge.

We are grateful to the authors who have struggled with possibly insoluble problems, to the Ford Foundation for its support of the enterprise, and to the staff of the Yale University Press for their helpful cooperation.

The Inter-University Committee on Comparative Economics: Abram Bergson, Arthur R. Burns, Kermit Gordon, Richard Musgrave, William Nicholls, Lloyd Reynolds (Chairman)

ACKNOWLEDGMENTS

I could not have undertaken this survey without the partnership of Mrs. Meyrick Browne of the London School of Economics. She has ranged over a wide terrain with a zest for reconnaissance and a keen eye for the significant feature. She has contributed not only information but insight. The materials she has gathered received from the first the imprint of her judgment and her grasp of the conception of the inquiry. The Bibliography is the product of her scholarship. If the reader should remark any apt instance or striking parallel in the text, that too will be her handiwork. Another benefit he will owe her in what he does not remark, for in reading the draft she has removed many blemishes.

Dr. Hilde Himmelweit of the London School of Economics and Dr. Walter Elkan, formerly of Makerere College and now of the Durham Colleges, have read parts of the draft and advised me on them; and the whole draft was typed by Miss Helen Beven. I wish also to record very gratefully my debt to them.

E. H. P. B.

London School of Economics
July 9, 1962

CONTENTS

Contents

Contents

THE ECONOMICS OF LABOR

1 THE ECONOMIST'S STUDY OF LABOR

   The tools of his trade that the economist applies to labor are the same as those he would bring to any other subject in his field. They consist of micro- and macroeconomic theory, and a stock of information about institutions and magnitudes. The theory gives the economist a framework within which to arrange his observations and direct his inquiries: it suggests where causes and consequences are to be looked for, it traces the network of interdependence, and it guards against pitfalls in reasoning. The information provides a diagram, roughly to scale, of the whole mechanism of which the particular element studied forms one working part.

   Applied to labor as a factor of production, these tools quickly yield an answer to a first question, why the rates of pay for different kinds of labor are what they are. These rates appear as one set of prices, simultaneously determined with all others, whether of factors or of final products, through the interplay between demand and scarce resources in the pricing system. Any one rate has to equilibrate the number of applicants coming forward for a job with the number of vacancies offered. There is a supply curve of applicants, whose form depends in part on what alternative demands there are for that kind of labor. The vacancies are given by a curve of derived demand, i.e. the demand for one of several collaborating factors, derived from the demand for their joint product.

But this is only common form: we may have called the factor "labor," but the argument would be much the same if we spoke of land or equipment. Only when we bring in more particular circumstances do we develop a theory specific to labor. We do this when, for instance, we allow that how much work a man will do depends on his relative valuation of monetary income and leisure; or recognize the imperfections of the labor market, and apply the theories of market forms such as monopoly and oligopoly; or ask what obstacles prevent some men from earning as much as others, and on what conditions some remain unemployed. In such ways as these the methods of economic analysis are applied to situations which, though still generalized, are specified in sufficient detail to be characteristic of labor markets.

Such applications yield insights, but into possibilities rather than actualities. There has to be a running interaction between analysis and field work. Analysis there must be to start with, for facts do not speak for themselves, and the meaning that those we gather have for us depends on the framework within which we arrange them. But given an informative arrangement, it is only through the patient study of the facts that we can reach the actual causes of particular

The Study of Labor

states of affairs. Much more than this, the framework of analysis itself bends or breaks as new facts are brought into it, and it has to be designed anew. Gathering information does not merely give body to established relations, but questions existing hypotheses and suggests new ones.

A great part of the economics of labor consists accordingly of information about those institutions and procedures through which the labor force is nurtured and trained, deployed between occupations and industries, and organized and directed at the place of work; and those through which its rates of pay are administered and negotiated. This information is not merely factual. It has life: it is physiology, so to speak, and pathology, as well as anatomy. It shows us how things seem to work; it suggests what can or cannot be done about them. It also reveals an amazing variety. Everywhere men have to work to get their living, but the arrangements they work under have been and are extraordinarily divergent: techniques differ, but also there is a range of striking contrasts in the relations between the worker, the community he lives in, the consumer of his product, and the hirer of his work. It is a main purpose of this essay to remark on some of these. They break up the insularity of our thought and challenge us to extend our speculation. When we find the day's work organized in so many different ways, when the same effect arises from different causes or the same cause is followed by different effects, we recognize the interplay of more factors than we had seen at first.

In the study of labor, these additional factors include some that lie beyond the usual beat of the economist. Labor is a factor of production—but the worker is a human being, and his work involves social as well as technical relations. Work is not merely the way to get a living, but a way of life, a game or a thralldom, a field of conflicts and loyalties, anxieties and reassurances, prestige and humiliation. The propensities of human nature that suffice to actuate a pricing system are limited, but the student of labor who does not go beyond the "economic man" leaves out much that is indispensable to his own etiology. The quality of the labor force depends on inheritance and upbringing. The occupational and social structures are interlocked. How much work any one man will do depends on his motivation—on his household, the standards of the group he works in, and the goals inculcated by his community. The application of labor requires direction: some workers are self-directed, but most come under management, and the relations between employer and employed affect both productivity and the satisfactions of the working life. They also affect pay. Though pay is arrived at in a market, it depends not only on the impersonal balance of supply and demand but also on custom, notions of equity, and the balance of power between groups and classes. At these and many other points the economist who has set out simply to study labor as a factor of production, and pay as a price, will find his attention drawn inescapably to matters commonly pertaining to psychology and sociology.

If this is true of the attempt to understand why things are what they are at any one time, it is even more true of the study of why things change. Such questions as why the differential for skill has generally diminished in Western countries over the last fifty years, or why real wages in Western Europe fell greatly during the sixteenth century but have risen greatly during the twentieth, can fairly be put to the labor economist; but when he tackles them he finds that what he has to try to understand is history. The growth of population, the stagnation of technique or its rapid development, the opening up of new natural resources and new channels of trade, the extension of literacy, the rise and fall of principles of public policy—he cannot explain what has happened in the labor market without going to some extent into such questions as these. In part, of course, he can take them as given, and look simply at what goes on within the setting that they from time to time impose. But he cannot ignore the interaction between his own subject matter and the setting. This is evident in questions of economic growth: in the setting of a given achieved technique and stock of capital a certain distribution of the product between labor and capital will work itself out, but this distribution will react on the rate of accumulation, and this in turn on the technique and capital stock of the future. There is a similar interaction with the social setting: a higher general level of real wages enables wage earners' children to defer their entry into full-time employment and get more training meanwhile; the consequent change in the supplies of different kinds of labor reacts on their relative pay; this in turn reacts on social structure and attitudes, and these affect trade unionism. The test of the labor economist's ability to stop short at the boundary of someone else's field is his capacity to advise. What will he point to, for instance, if he is asked how an underdeveloped country can raise the productivity of its labor force? If he seeks the understanding that is effective operationally, he must study the labor market in its setting of economic growth and social change.

But in the division of labor among the social sciences he does not cease to be an economist, and economics proper has its distinctive contribution to make. In some studies of wages, it is true, the influence of such factors as convention and bargaining power have seemed so paramount that economic analysis has been dismissed, its services no longer required. But this has been too hasty. What stands out in particular transactions is often peculiar to them: the course of events in the aggregate is influenced more by forces that may be secondary in any one case but work in the same direction in all. The forces of demand and supply are of that kind. The actual course of pay, country by country and period by period, shows uniformities that can be anticipated on the grounds with which the economist works, but would be surprising on others. Whatever their causes, the movements of the labor market are knit up with those of prices, incomes, and output generally, in a system whose static and dynamic connections have been explored only by economic analysis. If a textbook of that analysis is read as a description of what the investigator will find when he goes into the field, it will appear to leave out so much of practical importance that it may seem far removed from reality; but the forces it has lifted out for separate scrutiny are really at work, and policy will flounder if it neglects them. Nonetheless, the economist who studies labor needs to recognize that his own quest for causes leads him within the scope of other disciplines, from which he must get all the help he can.

The present essay follows the path of inquiry sketched here. It deals mainly with labor as a factor of production and with pay as a price and a distributive share, but it tries to appreciate influences that are the object of other sciences, and to set market processes in the context of history. The first question to be asked is what the place of the labor force has been within the economic system and the social structure —what arrangements have regulated the relations between those who direct work, or take its product, and those who carry it out. In a word, what has been the status of the worker?

2 THE STATUS OF THE WORKER

THE LABOR FORCE BEFORE THE CONTRACT OF SERVICE

Most of the work of modern economies is done by people who are under a contract of service: they put their skill and energies under the direction of an employer, who pays them wages or salaries. In man's previous experience, that is rare. The reason is not that the problem of how work is to be organized was very different in earlier economies: on the contrary, that problem arises in its essentials wherever there is division of labor, and economies in which the division of labor has been extensive have existed to our knowledge for four thousand years or more, and in the last two thousand years they have covered much of the globe. They have usually, it is true, contained at least some workers who earned their living through a contract of service with an employer, but only in the last two hundred years, and then

9

only in certain countries, has this type become predominant.

We can see several reasons for the slow growth of contractual employment. One is that men who can spend the hours of their working days at their own discretion regard it as an indignity to put themselves under the orders of another man. The issue is not how hard they shall work or how much they shall get, but whether they shall work as they choose or as they are told. The distinction most Greeks drew, M. I. Finley has said,[1] was not "between one kind of work and another, so much as between working for oneself, which was the mark of the free man, and working for another, working for hire, which was the mark of the slave. Hence, with the exception of domestic service, we find free and slave working side by side in every kind of occupation, skilled and unskilled. Even in the mines there were some free men who took small concessions and worked them themselves. What we rarely find is the free wage labourer, for such a man was 'under the restraint of another', in Aristotle's phrase, and even the poorest Greek avoided that position if he possibly could."

An evident way of keeping one's freedom is to work one's own land. Those who can stay on the land have seldom been willing, short of starvation, to leave it for employment as wage earners: the poorest peasants have been reluctant to commit themselves to work in the factory even though they can earn more there, and in Africa and Asia many of them still limit their commitment to a term of years. Wage earners who can get hold of land quit their employments—that was the experience of the colonists in America and Australia. In 1767 the Governor of New York, citing the case of the master of a glasshouse who had gone bankrupt because his servants, imported at great expense, had gone off to the land, remarked

1. "The Greeks and their Slaves," *The Listener* (London), September 10, 1959.

how such servants, "as soon as the Time stipulated for their Indentures is expired . . . immediately quit their Masters and get a small tract of Land in settling which for the first three or four years they lead miserable lives, and in the most abject Poverty: but all this is patiently borne and submitted to with the greatest cheerfulness, the satisfaction of being Landholders smoothes every difficulty, and makes them prefer this manner of living to that comfortable subsistence which they could procure for themselves and their families by working at the Trades in which they were brought up."[2]

But the attractions of the land are of no avail in a country where all the usable land has been taken up. That has been the state of many economies which nevertheless had few wage earners. It was not that they had few manufactures: on the contrary, they built cities, monuments, and ships; they carried out great works of irrigation; their workshops turned out clothing and furniture, harnesses, carts and ploughs, armor and weapons, knives and sickles, pots and pans. For this kind of production in a modern economy, most of the labor force is made up of wage and salary earners. If in many older economies that was not so, we have to look for circumstances that would inhibit the growth of wage earning even where the working population was greater than could live by farming, and a substantial part of it was in fact specialized to industry.

Those circumstances may be found in the absence of one or more of three conditions which are all necessary for the existence of the wage earner. The first is law and order. The second is the presence of a market, in which the wage earner can exchange his pay for houseroom and consumables. The

2. Report of Governor H. Moore to the Lords of Trade, quoted in E. L. Bogart and C. M. Thompson, eds., *Readings in the Economic History of the United States* (New York, Longmans Green, 1916), pp. 66–67.

third is the availability of free training for a trade. If the first is lacking, a man cannot live alone, but will have to put himself under the protection of another and pay for security by subservience, or else he may be captured and enslaved. If the second is lacking, a landless man can get a livelihood only by joining in some capacity one of the existing households; only here are supplies of the necessities of life accessible. If the third is lacking, men will be trained in a trade only in return for some lien on their produce thereafter. In the forms labor took where few laborers were wage earners, we can see the working of these circumstances.

The chief form was slavery. This comprised a great variety of arrangements whose common base was property in manpower: one man owned the skill and energies of another who could not end or vary that relation of his own volition. The slave's lack of freedom exposed him at the worst to ruthless exploitation and death itself, but it was also compatible with a relation of reciprocal obligation between master and man, and, until about a thousand years ago, it provided the working arrangements under which a great part of the labor force —including some of the most skilled—was organized and motivated. These arrangements ran through every field of employment.

One field more extensive then than now was the household. We have said that, in the absence of a market, men had to have a place in a landowning household in order to get food. Under the pressure of population in Japan, parents used to put their children out as perpetual servants to other families: these bondservants became, in a way, part of the family; they might marry, and their children also became servants in the same household. In Homeric Greece the free but landless laborer might have to undertake domestic service for life to ensure his keep. As the household grew bigger, it became an economy in itself—indeed the very word "economy" means household management—and the bondservants were occupied not in domestic duties alone, but in farming (especially the care of animals) and in all the arts and crafts practiced in the estate workshops. A rich household in Rome of the later years of the Republic would have a retinue of barbers, perfumers, tutors, singers, poets, actors, and gladiators; Tolstoy's grandfather, early in the nineteenth century, would walk under his lime trees of a morning to the music of his serf orchestra, whose flutist remained in the house as a footman when Tolstoy was a boy. It was in an imperial household that the crafts of the time would be most fully developed: some of the earliest teachers of the crafts in Japan were Koreans who had been presented to the emperor by the king of Korea; in Europe the Emperor Charlemagne had hundreds of industrial slaves in his villas—the goldsmith, the blacksmith, the miller, the weaver, and the embroiderer were the highest in the servile hierarchy of those days. In the early Middle Ages, in both Europe and Byzantium, the manors, the estates of the nobles, and the monasteries all had their workshops staffed by slaves. But here a move appeared toward more modern arrangements: these workshops did not supply their own communities alone but began to trade with the outside world; and sometimes in Europe the slaves were allowed to carry on this trade for their own profit, subject only to the payment of fixed dues to their masters.

The arrangement by which the household slave was assured of maintenance in return for taking his part in the household's division of labor has had a more recent counterpart in the Indian village, where those who follow different occupations live apart, but craftsmen or laborers have hereditary affiliations to particular farming households. A carpenter, for example, would repair a particular farmer's implements and supply him with new ones without immediate payment, but in return for a share of the crop twice a year; the blacksmith, the potter, the barber, the washerman would work for him in the same way. One or more families of untouchables would be affiliated to each substantial farming household, which would feed them once a day and give them a share in the harvest and one new cloth a year. Although the untouchable used to work under compulsion, there has otherwise been no slavery in the system. Yet it has resembled household slavery in two respects—its restrictions on the worker, who cannot rise above the occupations permitted to the caste into which he was born or go outside the service of certain employers, and its restrictions on the employing household, which must employ only its own affiliates and give them not a rate of pay fixed by bargain but a share in the crop fixed by custom.

But slavery used to prevail not only in the household but more widely in all manner of public works and private manufactures, and its wider sources lay in destitution, rapine, piracy, and war. Freemen whose crops failed or who fell into debt would sell themselves or their children, or be condemned to work their debt out in bondage. Raiders carried men, women, and children off as they might cattle, and shipowners specialized in human cargoes. War was lucrative for the victors: the generals could make a fortune by selling or leasing out their prisoners, and the citizenry could keep the captives to do their hard and dirty work for them. Where the slaves were allowed families, the children grew up as slaves, and slave-breeding might be profitable.

The victims were used first and foremost to do the kind of work that freemen could not be made to do, either because there was no landless surplus bound to look for work, or because they would sooner starve than do it anyhow. Slaves were used for the great works of civil engineering—irrigation, drainage, fortification; the backbreaking tasks in the raising of pyramids, palaces, and monuments; the toil of plantation and mine. Sometimes labor was found for these works as it is found for the armed forces today, by a draft or call-up or *corvée*, which rested on the freeman as well as the slave. In Babylon the irrigation system needed constant attention because of silting, and the obligation to work on it for a term of years was laid alike on some classes of freeborn labor and on slaves: when a slave was sold, the contract stated whether he had done his service. In China, before the time of Christ, ironworks and saltworks were carried on by the government with labor that was provided by compulsion but paid wages: we hear of a saltworks in the China of the Sung dynasty for which 380 families had each to provide two laborers, who were given a daily issue of grain, while the family received an annual payment in money. But where masses of laborers had to be brought together for hard work in bad conditions, most often they were slaves. In the Athenian silver mines at Laurium the number of slaves may have reached thirty thousand. The slaves died in thousands who dug the Great Drain of Tarquin the Elder. In the Spanish dominions of the New World, as the native Indians died out by disease and suicide, Negroes began to be brought in to take their place, and the importation went on at the rate of three thousand or more a year for some two centuries. The introduction of rice and indigo into the Carolinas set up an importation of Negroes there, until soon they outnumbered the whites. At their peak before the Second World War, the Russian labor camps, which provided the lumberyards and mines of the far North with an expendable labor force of kulaks and political prisoners, may have held as much as 6 per cent of the whole working population of the country.

The Economics of Labor

In better conditions and in more skilled tasks, slavery also provided much of the labor force for the factories, as we may call them, of the ancient world and its immediate successors in Europe. In the eighth century B.C., the Greek shipowners impoverished the free craftsmen by setting up factories manned by slaves for the mass production of jars to use in the export trade in wine and oil; the independent craftsman also had slaves working under him, and the larger workshops were manned almost wholly by slaves. As the Romans acquired slaves by conquest, in the second century B.C., the free craftsmen there too lost their customers to the slave workshops of potters, smiths, tailors, and armorers. Some of these workshops were part of the establishment of wealthy families, but sold to outsiders as well as serving their own household. The seignorial or abbey workshop in the time of Charlemagne traded in the same way.

Slavery and skill went together because slavery filled a gap in the system of incentives. Alfred Marshall pointed out how, on a comparison of the earnings of the educated and uneducated man in the Britain of the 1870s, the rate of return on education made outlay on it a highly profitable commercial investment; but the outlay was not made, because the investor had no guarantee of getting his annual return thereafter from the boy he educated. In our own day some firms and branches of the public service advance the cost of training to selected candidates in return for an understanding that the candidate will work for them for at least a certain term of years thereafter, but the understanding is not enforceable by law. Slavery did carry with it this sort of enforcement, and the training of slaves in the arts and crafts was a widespread enterprise. The neo-Babylonian contracts of apprenticeship for slaves contained a clause for the compensation of their owners if the master craftsman failed to teach them the trade. Cato, the Roman Censor, educated slaves and hired them out or sold them at a profit. In Japan, even after slavery had been nominally prohibited in the thirteenth century, apprentices were bought and sold, and they might be bound to work for a long term of years—even for life—for their masters.

The effect was that many slaves were not only more skilled but less oppressed than those whom the name of slavery raises first to the mind's eye. The spectrum of servitude has extended from the captive worked to death under the lash to the craftsman who lived on his own, carried on his own business, possessed property (which in Babylonia may even have included other slaves), and was obliged only to pay an annual rent charge to his owner. Far from always carrying the connotation of the coarsest and most exhausting toil, slavery in the ancient world was specially associated with skill: not only the mason, the goldsmith, and the armorer, but the ship's captain, the civil servant, and the bank manager were slaves. Those whom we call today the white-collar workers were particularly likely to be slaves or to have been trained as slaves before gaining their freedom. In Athens during the fifth and fourth centuries B.C., the state slaves served as police, inspectors of weights and measures, registrars, and accountants; and slaves were made managers of workshops, banks, and estates, and captains of ships. In China under the Former Han dynasty (206 B.C.–25 A.D.), government slaves were educated to serve as clerks, accountants, entertainers, and teachers. In Rome, in the early imperial fleet, the common seamen were freemen; the captains, slaves; and the admirals, freedmen. It was slaves and freedmen who provided the civil servants of the Roman empire, in the imperial administration and the municipalities.

We have stressed the difficulties that beset the independent wage earner, and the wide extent of slavery; yet the independent wage earner was generally to be found working alongside the slave, and in Hellenistic Egypt, at least, he was predominant. The foremost freeman in the labor force was sometimes the farmer working his own land, and he was the archetype of human dignity and sturdy citizenship: he demeaned himself if he became a "base mechanic." Yet some freemen did become mechanics and the like: it was difficult to be a landless freeman, but not impossible. The freeman might work as an independent craftsman who sold his product direct to the customer. He might undertake particular commissions for the customer at an agreed price for the job, or move one step more toward the status of the wage earner and be paid by the day as he worked on the customer's materials. The independent craftsman might overcome the limits of the local market by becoming itinerant; workers in wood, metal, leather, and pottery did so in Homeric times, shoemakers and tailors did it in the American mainland colonies. In building, where the function of the contractor was specialized, the free craftsman came near the position of the wage earner working under the direction of an employer, at least for the time of the job. Those craftsmen whom we have heard of as suffering from the competition of slave workshops in Greece and Rome may likewise have been working for an employer.

But where there was room for the employment of a permanent body of wage earners, most often the workers were slaves. Wage earners of the modern kind could not appear in any number until the growth of population created a body of landless men and until those circumstances arose, which we have already noted, that alone allowed the landless man to live, as a freeman, by his trade: that is, sufficient law and order to save him from looting and kidnapping; a market sufficiently wide to give him enough work in his trade and provide the necessities of life for him to buy with his earnings; and the means of first learning his trade.

THE BREAK-UP OF SLAVERY AND DECLINE
OF THE SELF-EMPLOYED

The transition to the arrangements of the modern labor market required two great changes: slavery had to go, and the employee working for wage or salary had to gain a numerical preponderance over the self-employed worker.

Slavery came to be opposed as immoral. But as long as the slave was kept in a brutish state, his bondage seemed part of the natural order of things: only as he became like other men in his work and accomplishments did it come to appear outrageous. Slavery was undermined by training.

We have seen that there was a profit motive for training the slave, but training was in any case made necessary by the narrow limits of the work in which the untrained slave was worth his keep. Kept like a horse, with fodder but without incentive, he would work only under close supervision and the threat of the lash. That would suffice for much of the toil in the plantations of tobacco, rice, sugar, and cotton; in the mines; and on public works. But even in the work that the chain gang could do, the slave-owner might see that he had to house and feed his laborers all the year round irrespective of the work he got out of them, whereas if he required them only to render certain limited services, and left them for the rest to raise their own food from holdings of their own, he might get as much work from them at less cost and trouble to himself. In that way outright slavery gave way to serfdom. In ancient Greece slaves working away from their masters, especially in vineyards and fruit farms, were given grants of land; the slaves of the great Roman estates were succeeded by the serfs of medieval Europe. It was found that the convicts who made up the first labor force of New South Wales got more done if their forced labor was confined to limited hours, after which they were free to cultivate a plot of their own, or work for wages paid in rum.

If this was so in heavy toil, even more was the need for incentive felt in work that required thought and initiative. If a slave was to do work of that kind he must first be made a more capable sort of man by being trained for it, and then be given both the measure of freedom without which he could not set about it effectively, and the prospects of reward for working well. The slave who learned a craft worked alongside other craftsmen who were free—so it was in the building crafts of Athens in the age of Pericles, and of the American South before the Civil War. In the South, as in imperial Rome, slaves might live apart, running their own works or shop, subject only to making a weekly payment out of their profits to their owner, to whom they were hardly more subordinated than to a landlord who must have his rent. We saw that in Babylonia slaves who had set up in business might own other slaves: in the American South slaves might hire other slaves to work for them. The Sung dynasty in China paid regular wages to artisan slaves such as their swordmakers. These slaves whose powers were trained and used for skilled work were still tied to the employer they worked for, or obliged to pay a tribute to their owners, and they were still liable to be sold and uprooted and, with their families, shifted bodily to a strange place; but ordinarily they went about the day's work just like the wage earners or small employers who were freemen. The barrier that remained between them and their freedom was not high.

Sometimes it crumbled, sometimes it was swept away. In imperial Rome the slave obtained his freedom most often by buying it with money he himself had saved from his earnings as a wage earner or his profits in trade. His owner might require a full market price, or take something less, out of respect for his qualities and as a reward for services prospective as well as past. It was a powerful incentive to promise a slave his freedom if he could show he deserved it. The trouble of holding a serf on the estate when he wanted to abscond, and exacting day-labor from him that he gave sullenly, made its cost felt when the growth of markets and the use of money gave the owner the alternative of commuting labor services for a rent paid in money, and hiring wage earners instead who could be discharged if they did not work well. Where there was already a market for free labor, the slave might run away and get his living in it, unless his speech or color made him a marked man. Whether the slaves and serfs that remained were few or many, moreover, a force was working for their general liberation. If they were relatively few, their bondage stood out in indefensible contrast with the status of the citizen beside them who, now that they were no longer newcomers made outlandish by speech and faith as well perhaps as by color, must increasingly accept them as fellow countrymen. If they were numerous, they spread into skilled work, and then slavery had against it the unrelenting opposition of many of the most capable and indispensable workers—the slaves themselves. Whether by some considered measure of emancipation or in the upheavals of irruption and revolt, the institution was abolished.

The second great change needed to make the transition to the modern labor market was the extension of the relative numbers of those who worked for an employer over those who worked on their own account.

The Economics of Labor

There had usually been some wage earners among the free workers, but as long as markets were local and technique was simple, those who worked under the direction of an employer were in a minority. To call the others independent would imply too much: they might not own the land they tilled or the houseroom they worked in, and the way they worked or the prices they charged might be closely prescribed and circumscribed by the authorities, by custom, or by a guild of their fellow workers. But they had this in common: they did not work under a contract of service. On the land, the peasant or smallholder or farmer, though he might have to hand much of his product over to a landowner and keep his work within the traditional pattern of the village, worked for the rest in his own time and for his own profit. As long as markets were local, the craftsman was typically his own master. He bought his materials with his own funds, worked them up in his own way in his own workshop, and sold the product directly to the consumer. He had helpers in the workshop, but they were learning the trade and working their way up, as apprentices first and then for some years as workers paid by the day or *journée*, and therefore called journeymen, with a reasonable prospect of becoming their own masters in due course. Other craftsmen, like the mason and the woolcomber, had no settled workshop of their own, and not having a material product to sell took a price for each job they did that came near being a piece rate or time rate in the modern sense; but those who paid them remained customers rather than employers, and they themselves, as they moved round from one job to another, were more like contractors than wage earners. Besides these producers, there were small traders and shopkeepers.

The self-employed worker remains with us to this day. In Japan the sector of unincorporated enterprise generates more than 40 per cent of the national product. But the extension of markets and the development of technique, as they have come about from time to time and place to place since the Dark Ages in Europe, have acted to reduce the relative number of the self-employed and raise that of the employees, and their action has been powerfully reinforced by the growth of population.

The extension of markets broke down self-employment in several ways. It meant, in the first place, that the producer would now find his customer at some distance: he would need an intermediary to arrange for the transport and sale of the product, and finance it in the interim. The raw material, too, might now be brought from a distance, and this also required contacts, transport, and finance. The merchant who provided these functions might conceivably have been in effect only an agent working for the producer on commission, or a trader competing with other buyers and sellers in the markets for raw materials and the product; but in fact he tended to gain control, and set the producer to work for him at piece rates.

The reason must lie in restriction of competition between merchants. It is not enough to point out that once the market was no longer local the producer could not buy or sell except through a merchant; for if he could have played off one merchant against another, he could have dealt at the ruling market price and been no more dependent on any one merchant than he had been before on any one customer. If that was not so, it must have been because the merchants were not numerous enough, or did not compete effectively with one another: their numbers might be restricted by scarcity of the knowledge, connections, enterprise, and capital that their calling required, and they might combine tacitly or in a guild to maintain a local monopoly or monopsony. Improvements in transport made the product travel farther, but did not, like bus, bicycle, and car in our own day, bring the worker into potential touch with more employers. It is because his market changed that the craftsman is held to have lost his independence when he ceased to own the materials he worked on, and began to work at piece rates on materials furnished and owned by the merchant: previously his living had depended on the prices at which he could buy and sell in the markets for commodities; now it depended on the price he could get for his labor in a market where competition between dealers gave him less protection against the hard bargain. Sometimes the worker lost his independence by getting into debt. Free miners had worked together in companies with "parts," which could be handed down from father to son; but they got into debt to those who supplied them with materials or made advances on their produce, and then their creditor became their employer and they worked for him as wage earners—so it came about by the sixteenth century at Liége in Belgium and at Newcastle and Nottingham in England.

Whatever the reason, the tendency of the merchant to become the employer of the craftsman has been widespread. We learn that in thirteenth-century England the dyers, who brought in essential supplies of dyestuffs from the Mediterranean, took on the functions of enterprisers, employing weavers and fullers and organizing production and sale. In the United States toward the end of the eighteenth century, the merchant-wholesalers were becoming small contractors employing outworkers for wages. In Osaka in the 1930s the production of silk thongs for sandals was organized by merchants, who bought the silk and employed workers to cut it up, then passed it to "manufacturers" who put it out to be processed in the workers' own homes and did only the finishing in their own workshops, after which they returned the completed article to the merchant who had financed the whole process.

This last example illustrates a second way in which the extension of markets has broken down self-employment: it has increased the division of labor. This division may grow up spontaneously between a number of specialists who work on their own and finance themselves, and coordinate their work simply by buying from and selling to one another; but often the function of coordination has been undertaken by an agent who at the same time finances the whole process and comes to employ, rather than trade with, those who carry out the different parts of it. The division of labor lengthened the time taken for materials to move from the primary producer to the final buyer, and created a need for a large capital even when the equipment used at each stage remained simple. It was partly because the production of woolen cloth required so many different processes that its manufacture in medieval Europe tended to fall under the control of the capitalist.

Thirdly, the extension of markets increased the size of the unit of production, and in the bigger units most of the workers could only be wage earners. Already in the thirteenth century, where international trade had developed in Europe, cloth was manufactured in the Low Countries and northern France, copper at Dinant, silk at Venice, by workers who (though they might still be working in their own homes) were taken on and laid off as wage earners. Advancement from apprentice to journeyman and from journeyman to master craftsman could be general only if the ratio of apprentices and journeymen to masters was low, but larger units raised the ratio, and stopped advancement, creating a class of permanent wage earners: so it was in Europe in the fifteenth century; and in Japan in the sixteenth and seventeenth centuries apprentices too numerous to have prospects of advancement became a form of indentured wage labor, and many journeymen lost all hope of becoming masters.

The workers to whom work was put out by the merchant suffered some of the disabilities of the wage earner, but kept one element of independence, in that they worked in their own homes and their own time; in fact they would often play for the first day or two of the week, and then toil long hours by rushlight to complete their task and earn their money by Saturday morning. Those who worked at the employer's place of business had to be there at set times and work under discipline. While most equipment was still simple there had always been some kinds of production that brought men together in that way—shipbuilding, for instance, and the manning of the ship, some building and public works, the offices of the scribes and tax collectors, mining, smelting, brewing, and the making of glass and pottery. Sometimes also workers like weavers, whose equipment could be and usually was dispersed cottage by cottage, were brought together under one roof to save transport of the materials and prevent their embezzlement. But it was the development of the central power plant and costly machines to be driven by it that brought in the factory. Undercutting the independent craftsmen, and bringing more young entrants immediately into wage earning, the factories whose growth started two hundred years ago carried further and faster the supersession of the self-employed by the worker who owns neither the materials nor the equipment he works with, and who cannot set about his job in his own place, his own way, or his own time.

The influences we have been considering all flowed from the extension of markets, and the division of labor and development of technique which it fostered. But the predominance of the employee was advanced by another and distinct factor—the growth of population. Labor that is surplus to the current requirements of work on the land has always been a source of wage labor, even when those concerned remained attached to their holdings: especially in India and China, where animal husbandry has played a small part relative to crops whose labor requirements are highly seasonal, the peasant has provided wage labor for towns and factories during the slack seasons on the land. When the population of the villages grows beyond the number who can get land to work within the existing pattern of holdings, the excess may be absorbed for a time by subdivision, or receive a subsistence as members of underemployed families. But if the growth goes beyond a certain point, the excess must starve or take themselves off to find a living somewhere else. These landless men appear as vagrants and migrants. They have nothing but their labor to sell, and if they are to find a livelihood, it can only be as wage earners. In Western Europe since the Middle Ages we know of two great upsurges of population: one, inferentially, in the sixteenth century; the other, on more direct evidence, from the middle of the eighteenth century onward. Meanwhile, the population of the territories settled by Europeans overseas has generally grown past the point at which the last free land was taken up; and, more recently, Western methods of hygiene and pest control have brought to the underdeveloped countries a rapid fall in the death rate and an explosion of population. The overspill from the countryside forms cities and. conurbations. These can exist only with the wide market, the division of labor, and the large units of production that promote the transition from self-employment. But the labor force of the cities and conurbations of today does not derive from that transition so much as from the newcomers who, being surplus to the establishment, could not succeed to any holding of land or capital, and, having only their labor power to offer, must find an employer to give them a job.

THE GUILD

We have just seen how, as slavery receded, the labor force came to be made up mainly of two types, the self-employed and the wage earner, and that the self-employed predominated at first. Each type has formed its own characteristic organization. Down to the eighteenth century the leading and usually the only form of association among workers was the characteristic organization of the self-employed, the guild.

The one name of guild covers many forms and functions. There have been guilds of merchants, of craftsmen, of porters. Some guilds have been concerned mainly with religious observances or fraternal junketing, some have been organs of local government, some have been trade unions of wage earners. In the ancient world, in Babylonia, Hellenistic Greece, and republican Rome, there were guilds whose members were solely the tradesmen who sold to the public—the millers, the pastry cooks, the goldsmiths, the butchers, the ropemakers—and those who worked for them or learned the trade under them had no place in their membership. But we are concerned here with the guild whose typical member was a self-employed craftsman, with simple equipment but high manual skill, who sold his product to consumer or merchant, and whose workshop was so small that those who worked with him were few enough to expect to have workshops of their own in time. He had learned his trade as an apprentice, then served for some years as a journeyman for a daily wage. The structure of the guild thus held three tiers which were also rungs on a ladder of advancement—apprentice, journeyman, master.

Perhaps that structure was seldom found for long in its ideal form: the merchants who bought the product might reduce the masters to pieceworkers, or the journeymen might be taken on in such numbers that they became permanent wage earners and formed their own combination to keep wages up. But the main traits of the association of small masters, living by the sale of their product and working with apprentices and journeymen, appear over a wide expanse of space and time. Guilds of that kind can be traced in Japan from the eighth century, though the apprentices are said to have been often so numerous and bound for so long that they were little better than slaves. The written records of the Chinese guilds go back only to the seventeenth century, but those of the Korean guilds go back a thousand years, and refer to contemporary guilds in China. In India, guilds of craftsmen were general; they may have preceded the formation of castes—which may be in part a hardening of the separation and association by occupation that the guild itself provides, especially when membership is hereditary. The craft guild can be traced from the tenth century in London, and from the eleventh in Western Europe. The craft guilds of Byzantium enjoyed privileges such as a monopoly of the local market, and sometimes exemption from military service, in return for a strict supervision by the state of admissions, techniques, and prices. Their descendants, the Esnafs of Turkey, Bulgaria, and Serbia, in the early years of the present century, were said to bear "the closest resemblance to the medieval gild of Western Europe."[3]

So widespread an appearance suggests that the guild met

3. G. Unwin, *The Gilds of London* (3d ed. London, 1938), p. 3. But Unwin also remarked that the Esnafs differed from the medieval guild because they had not broken themselves up by engendering changes of technique.

needs common to the self-employed worker in very different societies. One of those needs was for the preservation of his art and mystery, for a way to transmit to the young entrant the skill that had been handed down to him in all its magic, rigor, and beauty. Another need was for security. The earnings of the worker who sells his product may be safeguarded by the competition of buyers in his market, or by custom that assures him a minimum price. His earnings are threatened by weak selling when demand falls off, by the entry of more neighbors into his trade, or the invasion of the local market by products made elsewhere. He is therefore prompted to stand shoulder to shoulder with his neighbors already in the trade. The French say, "craftsmen like to feel each other's elbows." The objectives of that united front are to regulate entry into the trade, to keep interlopers and "foreign" wares out of the local market, and to maintain agreed prices for the product and wages for the journeyman. These purposes are restrictive: but the student of the labor market soon learns that the pursuit of self-interest leads to combination as well as to competition, and that security is a goal sought no less ardently than profit.

CONNECTIONS BETWEEN OCCUPATION AND SOCIAL STATUS

Our sketch of how the modern labor force took shape has shown how the job a man does carries with it relations with other people that include but also go far beyond the relation of buyer and seller. Wherever there is division of labor, the worker must sell his product or his labor, and so he has to deal with buyers, and agree with them on terms that will decide how beneficial the transaction is to each party. But over and above that, the work a man does is likely to carry with it particular ways in which he behaves toward other people, and they toward him: there is at any one time a more or less systematic connection between the occupational structure of the labor force and the social structure of the community.

This is at its clearest when the social structure is made up of hereditary castes. A boy born into a certain caste can enter only a certain range of occupations: he will not be allowed to enter higher occupations at all, and should he enter a lower one, he loses caste. The terms "higher" and "lower" call our attention to another feature: the castes, and their permitted occupations, are arranged in a hierarchy of prestige and respect. The members of the higher castes are socially superior: they do not speak to men of the lower castes as they do to one another; they may keep them at a physical as well as at a social distance; they abhor the thought of intermarriage. The men of the lower castes for their part must know their place, keep their distance, and approach their betters with every obsequious mark of respect. The essentials are that a range of jobs is linked with each stage of a social hierarchy; that this hierarchy is hereditary, so that each range of jobs is also hereditary; and that the gradations of the hierarchy appear not so much in income as in prestige, in acknowledged nobility or baseness, and in men's manners toward one another.

Much of this consciousness of rank still persists in societies that have repudiated the hierarchical principle. They have proclaimed the democratic principle instead—equality before the law and in the franchise, parity of esteem in the speech and bearing of citizens toward one another, and, so far as the nature of things allows, equality of opportunity. But even where castes are unthinkable, there still are classes: there are gradations of prestige, and there is segregation by grade. The gradation is partly a scale of income, partly a scale of education shown also in manners and speech, and partly a scale established by consensus of esteem, which in European societies may contain vestigial venerations such as those for hereditary title and landownership. There is segregation by grade in that people tend to associate in their work, their place of residence, their recreations, and their schooling, mainly with members of their own grade. Though many people move out of the grade into which they were born, the majority do not, and most marriages are between members of the same grade. With this social gradation, again, there is linked a gradation of jobs. Architects and miners, shop assistants and bank clerks, truck drivers and school teachers— all tend to hold positions in the social scale that we can predict from knowledge of the jobs they do. People who do certain kinds of work feel themselves assimilated to one another thereby, and segregated to some extent from those who do other kinds, whether it is the job that makes the social distance, or the social distance that enforces the choice of job. In particular, the manual wage earners, who in a contemporary economy may make up as much as two-thirds of the whole labor force, may feel themselves to constitute "the working class," with its own distinctive manners, grievances, and goals.

This feeling is strengthened by some disabilities that having to work for an employer inherently imposes on the worker. The contract of employment is not simply a contract of sale, but carries particular relationships with it between the employed person and the rest of society, particularly with the employer himself. On several grounds the employed person has reason to fear that these will be relationships of inferiority for himself.

One ground is that in the fixing of his pay he is liable to

be exploited. If he has access to a number of employers, and they compete with one another, then he is unlikely to have to sell his labor below the value that the market puts upon it: if his day's work is worth $20 to employers, in the sense that they would reckon it just worth having even though they paid $20 to get it, then if one of them will not pay $20 for it, another will. But if he has access only to one or two employers, or if the potential employers, however numerous, maintain an understanding that they will not pay more than so much, and not poach labor from one another, then his case is very different. He is liable to meet this situation not infrequently in practice. We saw how the worker who sells his product can get into trouble if the market is narrow: for the worker who sells his labor, narrowness of the market is a threat even more imminent. So Adam Smith saw it in the eighteenth century: "We rarely hear, it has been said, of the combinations of masters, though frequently of those of workmen. But whoever imagines, upon this account, that masters rarely combine, is as ignorant of the world as of the subject. Masters are always and everywhere in a sort of tacit, but constant and uniform, combination, not to raise the wages of labour above their actual rate. To violate this combination is everywhere a most unpopular action, and a sort of reproach to a master among his neighbours and equals."[4] It is true that against the intent of the employers to maintain a certain maximum the worker can pit his own will to maintain a minimum, but here he comes up against another disability— he is generally less able to hold out. Adam Smith again recorded this as a fact of observation in his own day: "A landlord, a farmer, a master manufacturer, or merchant, though they did not employ a single workman, could generally live

4. *Wealth of Nations* (1776), Bk. I, chap. 8.

a year or two upon the stocks which they have already acquired. Many workmen could not subsist a week, few could subsist a month, and scarce any a year without employment. In the long run the workman may be as necessary to his master as his master is to him; but the necessity is not so immediate."[5]

So the worker who makes his own bargain has reason to fear that he will have to settle for something less than his work is worth to the employer, who will thus be able to make a profit by withholding part of his due reward. This is the basic notion of exploitation. It tends to be extended in practice so as to tar with the same brush the quite different kind of profit that is the return to enterprise and risk capital after labor has been paid its full market value.

The disability that the worker is liable to suffer in this way is the more threatening the bigger are the firms. When each employer has many workers, each worker is likely to be in touch with fewer alternative employers than if the same labor force were spread over a larger number of smaller firms. The disparity between the resources, and the ability to hold out, of the employer and any one worker will generally be greater when firms are large. The worker's alternative possibility, of setting up in the trade for himself, will amount to little when the existing firms have great capitals.

There is another major ground for the worker's apprehension that his relationship with his employer may be one of inferiority for himself: it is, in a word, that he must put himself under the employer's orders. The independent craftsman works in his own home, in his own time, in his own way, subject only to the restraints that he must make the kind of thing that will sell, and make enough of it to get his living;

5. Ibid.

those restraints extend a little further when the customer commissions a particular piece of work, but the worker is still selling his *product* and not his *labor*. When he enters instead into a contract of employment, it is his labor that he sells: in return for his pay, he agrees to undertake the tasks that, within certain assigned limits, the employer will set him from time to time. This can be perfectly acceptable, a part of the arrangements for the job as necessary and natural as the provision of materials and tools. But it may seem quite otherwise: it may be felt and resented as a loss of freedom so great as to mean a loss of pleasure and pride in the job, of spontaneity and the will to work, even of manhood itself. The worker has to go to the employer's place of work, which has been laid out by the employer, and whose amenities or inconveniences, safeguards or dangers, the worker has to take as he finds. He cannot indulge his own inclination about when to start work and stop, but must attend through appointed hours, or be penalized. Nor can he always follow his own mood in the pace at which he works: the pace may be set by the machine, or kept up by bonuses and fines, or the rough side of the overseer's tongue and the threat of discharge. There have to be rules in the work place, and rules must have sanctions: so the worker in taking the job puts himself under discipline. Generally, though not necessarily or always, the work of a firm is more subdivided and more repetitive than that of the man who is self-employed; and the firm's employees lack to that extent the relief of variety, the interest of problem-solving, and the pleasure a man finds in setting about his work in his own way.

To represent resentment of these constraints as the invariable or even the general state of affairs would go much too far. There are work places where the prescription of tasks is undertaken and accepted not as the assertion of authority over subordinates but as part of the organization of a team with whose purposes the individual worker identifies himself. There are temperaments to which directions, rules, and discipline are not irksome: rather they meet a need and provide reassurance. But the record of unrest, protest, and proposed reforms leaves no doubt that many men have felt and still do feel it irksome to be compelled, if they are to get a living, to put themselves under the orders of an employer. His authority appears arbitrary, and a way of exploiting the power that is his by reason of his relative wealth and his control of the access to livelihood. The parties once accepted in English terminology as master and servant have been renamed, in merely functional terms that imply no subordination, employer and employed; but the employed in practice may still speak of the employer as the boss. The issue is one not of amenity, or pay, but of power. The trade union leader Ernest Bevin, speaking in 1934 on an occasion that recalled the repression of the early attempts of English farm workers to form a union, declared: "The landlord does not fight to retain his land merely because of the money it yields him, but because of the power it gives him. The capitalist is the same. He will give you sport, welfare and charity and everything but one thing, and that is power. He will hold on to that, the power to give you the sack, to impose his will and withhold from you the means of sustenance. Such power is unwarrantable."[6]

So there seem to be two main sources of the worker's sense that his status is inferior: his liabilities to be exploited and to be subordinated. He may connect both with another aspect of that status—the fact that he and his employer are commonly at some distance from each other in the social scale,

6. A. Bullock, *The Life and Times of Ernest Bevin* (London, Heinemann, 1960), pp. 551–52.

that with their difference of occupation goes a difference of class. Those who are doing his kind of work share certain disabilities, certain habits of life and ways of speech: he recognizes them when he meets them, and marks the difference in the bearing, the interests, the very facial expression of those whose work is different. To the extent that he feels drawn toward his fellows and separated from the rest of society, he will see the disabilities of his working life as those of his class, and the conflict of interests between employer and employed as those of a class struggle.

Karl Marx, surveying the advance of industrialism in Western Europe in the 1840s, concluded that as it went on it would increasingly divide all men into two and only two classes—those who owned capital and controlled production, and those whose livelihood could come only from working for the capitalist—and that in the end the working class would expropriate the capitalist and establish a communist society in which they were their own masters. The belief that this is the mainspring of history remains the creed held and taught throughout the Soviet world, from the Oder to the Pacific. But the actual course of events has not borne it out. Where communist societies have been set up, it has been through the seizure of power by a minority. The social structure has proved too complex to allow the division of interests and loyalties into only two camps. Power has been dispersed through the checks and balances of a pluralistic society. The equality of men as citizens before the law and in the franchise, and the extension of educational opportunity, have mitigated the continuing inequalities of the working life. A rise in the standard of living has diminished the contrast between the incomes of men in different occupations.

Nonetheless, the conflict that in Western countries in the nineteenth century was called the conflict of capital and labor remains as a stress and strain within those countries today, and appears wherever industrialism develops in the emergent economies elsewhere. Ways of accommodating it within an orderly society have been worked out: only rarely does it break out in violence, and though peaceful disputes still cause losses, these bear a minute proportion to the national product. But it remains as the unsolved problem of industrial relations. The employed feel a common interest in being able to resist the employers. Where agreements are reached, or relations are harmonious, they are still between "the two sides." When we speak of "the men's leaders," we do not mean the captains of industry.

THE RISE OF TRADE UNIONISM

It is the generality of the disabilities inherent in the status of the employed worker that must account for the generality of the institution he has created to offset them: wherever a permanent class of wage earners has appeared in substantial, locally concentrated numbers, and combinations are not broken up by the authorities, there has appeared the trade union. What the guild was for the worker who sold his product, the trade union has been and is for the worker who sells his labor. We hear of strikes in the ancient world, and these must have meant at least a temporary combination of workers. In the thirteenth century, where manufacture was already organized on a large scale in the Low Countries, northeastern France, and Tuscany, and though most of the workers remained outworkers large numbers worked for the same employer, years of bad trade brought unemployment: here strife was endemic, and unions enforced strikes and boycotts. But the concentration of employment was not general enough as yet, and the authorities put down combinations with too rough a hand for a continuing unionism to grow up.

The roots of modern unionism are rather to be seen in the seventeenth and eighteenth centuries, when some members of the guilds began to find themselves in the position of permanent wage earners. In the early guilds the craftsman had united in his own person the functions of merchant, shopkeeper, employer, foreman, and worker. As markets extended and capitals grew larger, these functions became separated—singly or in pairs—and there appeared merchants, merchant-shopkeepers, merchant-employers, employers, small masters who worked themselves and also acted as foremen in their workshops, and, lastly, the journeymen. Within the industries that the guilds controlled it was from the last two types that the modern wage earner was formed. The small masters were reduced to the condition of wage earners when they came to depend for their work on what merchants put out to them. The journeymen found their numbers increased when restrictions on apprenticeship broke down; at the same time the amount of capital a master needed grew with the market, and the journeyman thus had less and less prospect of becoming a master in his turn and owning his own stock in trade. Employers also began to take on "foreigners" and "serving men" who had not been apprenticed. By 1776 Adam Smith could report that "in every part of Europe, twenty workmen serve under a master for one that is independent, and the wages of labour are everywhere understood to be, what they usually are, when the labourer is one person, and the owner of the stock which employs him another."[7] But small masters and journeymen alike had a tradition of asso-

7. *Wealth of Nations*, Bk. I, chap. 8.

ciation within the guild that helped them now to form combinations against it. It is in the efforts at organization of the small masters in seventeenth-century England that "the immediate antecedents of the modern trade union are to be sought."[8] The journeymen might already have had their friendly societies, for sick and funeral benefits, and now they formed "clubs" for bargaining. In 1682 the journeymen clothworkers of London took advantage of an export order to refuse to work for less than twelve shillings a week. In 1777 the journeymen hatters of London had a congress, probably eighty years old at that time, that drew up bylaws, limited apprentices, and threatened a strike unless fifty journeymen who had refused to pay dues to it were sacked.

The conditions that broke combinations of wage earners away from the guilds worked to form trade unions in industries that had no guilds. They have also given rise to unions as they have appeared at different times in other countries—in the United States, as in Britain, toward the end of the eighteenth century; in most other countries, later.

We have noted some of these conditions for the development of unions: there must be a class of permanent wage earners sufficiently numerous and concentrated to be able to keep in touch with one another and to get together in some force; and efforts at combination must not be repressed by the authorities absolutely. To these conditions we may add some others. The great protection of the wage earner, in the absence of a union, was custom, which prescribed a customary wage and made it seem unjust to take advantage of the worker's need for a job by paying less. Whatever broke down custom, therefore, heightened the felt need for a

8. G. Unwin, *Industrial Organization in the Sixteenth and Seventeenth Centuries* (Oxford, 1904, republished London, Cass, 1957), pp. 200–01.

union, whether it was the improvement of communications exposing once sheltered local markets to the vicissitudes of wider competition, or a time of rising prices, very likely in wartime, that made it urgent to seek rises in pay. If unions are to maintain themselves from their own resources, two other conditions are requisite: the wages of their members must already be high enough for them to be able to pay their dues regularly (it is a great source of stability if the dues can be high enough to finance a scheme of "friendly benefits," that is, of insurance against, for example, sickness, death, and unemployment) and there must be at least some among the members who are educated enough to be able to keep accounts, write minutes and correspondence, and administer the business of the branch or head office. In the underdeveloped countries these last two requirements have hitherto been met by only a minority of the employed workers; and if unions were to be kept going for the rest, they have had to be administered, and often subsidized, by outsiders—a political party, or selfless men devoted to the workers' cause, or politicians in search of publicity and lawyers in search of briefs, or adventurers and sheer gangsters.

Until the end of the nineteenth century trade unionism was largely confined to the manual wage earner: the twentieth century has seen its extension among the white-collar workers in clerical, administrative, and technical occupations. That these workers had not felt the need to combine before may be explained by the social distance that separated them from the manual worker who typified the unionist of those days, by their working in smaller units than he and with more personal contact with the employer, and by their having more prospect of personal advancement. In recent years these factors have been broken down or offset by the extension of education and the rise (relative as well as abso-

41

lute) in the standard of living of the manual worker, the increases in the relative number of white-collar workers and in the size of offices, and the need in times of inflation to move salaries up with less lag than under individual bargaining. Unionism extends among the more highly paid or educated employees in proportion as they cease to regard it as beneath them socially and come to feel the same needs as the manual worker in their own working life.

We saw that these needs were mainly two—for support in bargaining about the terms and conditions of employment, and for keeping one's own end up despite having to put oneself under another man's orders at the place of work. The functions that the union performs for its members correspond with these needs. Through collective bargaining it enables them to hold out for a certain rate, despite their own lack of resources and their need for a job, by ensuring that they will not be undercut by other workers, and by amassing strike funds and building up a common purpose. The same sanctions it brings to bear on bargaining can be applied, through the bargain itself or outside it, to make its members' views on the arrangements of their work felt by management, to set limits to the executive discretion of management at the place of work, and within those limits to protect its members against any use of the executive power that they may feel arbitrary or unfair. It may negotiate a detailed code of working rules to govern the day-to-day administration of the firm, or it may only set itself to uphold customary practice and make its wishes known on fresh issues as they arise; but in either case it will generally resist what it sees as victimization or favoritism, seek a rule for or a voice in promotion, obtain safeguards in disciplinary procedure, and try to limit or regulate redundancy.

The checks and balances through which the union exercises these last functions do not work without some friction and, from time to time, some strife. Nor do they satisfy those who wish not merely to offset the disabilities inherent in the status of the employed worker but to change that status altogether, and who may contrast it with the status of the same worker as a citizen in a democracy, where he has the right to be informed and consulted about all matters of common concern, and has as much voice as any other voter in the ultimate choice of the executive and its policy. They may also contrast it with that of a working partner, who has an equal voice in the councils of the enterprise, does his work in it neither as one who gives orders nor as one who has to take them but as a member of a team, and draws his income as an agreed share in the product. Both contrasts enforce the difference between existing arrangements and the ideal of industrial democracy. This ideal has obtained only very partial acceptance, if effort in pursuit of it be the test, among trade unionists, but it is persistent: it has survived the small success or outright failure of various experiments in profit sharing, employee shareholding, joint consultation, and workers' control, and since the Second World War it has inspired attempts to build an element of self-government into the very constitution of the firm. Notable among these have been the statutory provision for *Mitbestimmung* or codetermination in the coal and the iron and steel industries of Western Germany, under which the Works Council of employees appoints one of the three executive directors of each firm and half the members (other than the chairman) of the supervisory Board of Directors; and the scope given by the Yugoslav decentralization law of 1952 to the Workers' Council of each enterprise and the Management Board it appoints.

STATE ACTION TO REMEDY THE DISABILITIES OF THE WAGE EARNER'S STATUS

The disabilities that attach to the status of the employed worker have been offset not only by the trade union but by the state.

In part the state has acted along the same lines as the unions, fostering the growth of voluntary unionism, providing statutory bodies and rules to fill the gaps that unionism leaves, and supplementing collective agreements by general regulations. When unions first appeared in Western countries they were often treated as seditious conspiracies, or at least as being against the public interest because they were combinations in restraint of trade. In the course of the nineteenth century their functions began to be better understood, and the law was changed—at first by the removal of prohibitions, and later by the working out of a code that gives the unions protection and may lay on the employer an obligation to accept and work with them. The growth of unions, meanwhile, was still partial, and left wide tracts of employment without collective bargaining. In these tracts some states have set up boards to arrive at terms and conditions of employment, in much the same way as in collective negotiations, by discussion between spokesmen of employers and employed; but the boards also contain spokesmen for the public interest, and their decisions may be made legally binding on all employers. In other countries the legislature has provided for a general minimum wage—either fixed in dollars and cents in the law itself, as in the Fair Labor Standards Act (1938) in the United States, or adjusted from time to time according to the cost of living, as in the French S.M.I.G. (1950).[9]

States that have provided for the compulsory arbitration of labor disputes were usually moved to it originally by the wish to ensure a settlement and keep the peace, but it has had the effect in practice of enabling trade unions to enforce rates on employers who would not voluntarily negotiate, to uphold a national minimum wage, and to extend local advances over adjacent sectors; in Australia and New Zealand it has come to determine the main proportions of the national wage structure. The state entered another wide field in which protection by unionism was inadequate or nonexistent when it began to build up a code of factory law, as it is still called, though today it applies to much more than the factory. The hours of work, and the design of equipment and processes so as to guard the worker against accident and disease, can be and are the subjects of collective negotiation, but the workers who suffered most from exhaustion by long hours in the early days of modern industry were the unorganized women and children; and though the miners and the seamen had their unions, these were far from being able to protect them from the hazards of life and limb to which the day's work exposed them. "Is it not optional with the miners to go into the pit?" an English mine-owner asked, when a miners' leader was describing the dangers of work underground. "Certainly," the miners' leader replied, "but it is also optional with them to starve if they do not."[10] The

9. Salaire Minimum Interprofessionnel Garanti (guaranteed minimum rate of pay for all occupations).

10. Royal Commission on the Organization and Rules of Trade Unions, 1867–69, Seventh Report, Q.15485, *Parliamentary Papers* (1867–68), 39.

common purpose of the wide range of regulations in the factory laws of today is to ensure that the worker's need of a job shall not oblige him to undergo any risk of accident or disease that can be warded off by measures within the power of management.

In all these ways the state has acted to offset disabilities whose source is the dependent status of the employed worker, and especially the urgency of his need for a job. But there are other ways in which what is remarkable in his status is its independence. Here, too, there are disabilities, and the state has taken action to offset them.

The employed worker is independent in this sense: it is he who must look after himself and his family day in and day out, and all that his employer has to provide him with under the simplest form of the contract of service is a payment for particular pieces of work. But he can do those pieces of work only if he, or someone for him, has incurred certain costs. He has had to be reared as a child, given some general education, and trained for the particular job. To be in health and strength for the work he has had to provide himself with a certain standard of consumption. Where there is slavery, these costs of maintaining the labor force fall on the employer, but when the worker is independent, they fall on him, both in his own capacity and as the parent of workers to be. There is no presumption that his pay will cover these costs. Because the cost of training for a particular occupation restricts entry into it, the pay will be higher, but it does not necessarily go to those who have borne the cost of the training, nor does what is being spent out of today's pay on rearing and training future workers bear any necessary relation to the price that the trained ability is going to command. There is not even any presumption that the rate of pay a worker can command will at least be enough to provide him and his household with the bare essentials of physical efficiency: as recently as in the years just before the First World War, a third of the households of British towns were getting less than that, and in the emergent countries today very generally the worker's pay is low because of his low efficiency, and his efficiency is low because of his low pay. The obstacle to the employer himself investing in the building up of a stronger work force is the independence of the worker.

But there are still other ways in which the worker's independence makes him responsible for provisions that are needed to make labor available to the user. There is a familiar example in the docks, where the amount of work to be done fluctuates, and if a man is to be available on the days when there is work for him, he must somehow be maintained through those when there is none: if he is treated as independent, then he must bear the cost of that himself. The function of a scheme of decasualization is to transfer the cost to the user of his labor. But the same principle arises in all unemployment that is not the worker's own fault. This includes his absence from work through illness, which reminds us in turn of the cost of medical care, quite apart from absence: it is because of the independent status of the worker that (short of organized provision to the contrary) this cost is borne by him, whereas the cost of care and maintenance of a machine is met by the employer. A like consideration applies to the cost of accidents suffered in the course of employment. At the last, there is old age. Most of today's workers are bound to need maintenance later on when they are too old for work: should provision for that be their responsibility alone or be treated as a current cost of employing them?

In the last half-century the feeling that the user of labor should bear more of the costs of supplying it has joined with the generally increased willingness to transfer income to those who are worst off, and changes have been made in two directions. In the first, trade unions have widened the collective agreement to include sick pay, unemployment pay, and pensions; and governments have set up schemes of social insurance against the same contingencies, financing them, in whole or in part, through a payroll tax. The state has also laid greater liability on employers for the cost of accidents to their workers. The general effect of these measures is to transfer the cost of this sort of provision from the employed worker to his employer in the first instance, and through the employer to the buyers of the product, who include the employed worker himself; there may or may not be some endeavor to vary the charge laid upon different sectors of employment according to the different incidence of given contingencies, such as unemployment, within them. The second direction of change is to lay the charge for such provisions on the community as a whole, which meets it out of its general tax revenue. The difference from the first method may be more in form than in substance, for the objects may be the same, and the first method of financing may be only a form of the indirect taxation that is part of the second. But the second has been used to assume charges that are not so closely connected with current employments, and not only to meet the cost of provision already being made but to make much greater provision: through the maintenance of a minimum standard of living, especially for children, through assisted housing, medical care, and, above all, through education.

3 THE QUALITY
OF THE LABOR FORCE

ADAPTATION OF LABOR TO REQUIREMENTS
OF ECONOMIC GROWTH

Economists, noting that the equipment used in current production is itself the product of earlier activity, have sometimes tried to trace all output back to ultimate factors of production that make, but have not themselves been made. They have found these factors in labor, waiting, and land, or the gifts of nature. It is hard, however, to imagine what labor in that unshaped shape could be like. Every man is what he is, and works as he does, through nurture as well as nature: what sort of producer he will be depends on what sort of product he is. This is true not only in the obvious sense that to do most jobs he has first to be trained: much more important, his capacity to be trained, his whole attitude to work, the kind of economy he can tolerate and develop—

all these depend on the way he has been brought up and the imprint that family, society, and culture have set upon him.

This is manifest when modern techniques are brought into a primitive society. Labor there cannot simply be trained to use them. The difficulties that arise at many points show that the whole way of life of the worker—his customs, values, habits of thought, his ties of kindred and his notions of obligation and authority—must undergo deep changes if he is to serve the uses of a developed economy.

This appears in the very pattern of the day. We can understand that those who have no clocks find it hard to keep good time—but more than that, they may lack the very idea of punctuality and of allocating time at all. It goes with this that they start and stop according to the feeling of the moment, moving spontaneously, enjoying variety in their activity, making great exertions and enduring great strains sometimes, but only between long spells of ease, and generally being indefinite about what they are going to do next. The steady, regular pattern of the day's work, the week's and the year's, which the worker of the developed economy for the most part accepts as part of the nature of things, is strange and repugnant to them.

One reason is that where regularity of work is accepted, it is as the means to an end, namely, a regular income; but the categories of means and end, cause and effect, are alien to a more intuitive habit of mind. True, life can go on nowhere without action that is instrumental in effect: weapons must be fashioned for the hunt, seed planted for the harvest. But such action need not be seen and felt as instrumental: it may be traditional, and performed without men asking themselves, "In order to attain this object eventually, what measures shall I take now?" still less, "What measures can I devise to attain the object best?" Where much activity is spontaneous, or not directed beyond the immediate task in hand, the very distinction between work and play may be absent, and both alike be rites. Men from such communities will find it hard to understand machinery, not just because it is new to them but because it is made and used not for its own sake but as a means to an end. Operating it efficiently means understanding it in that way—running it at its operational speed, not racing it for the fun of seeing the sparks fly. When it goes wrong, what it needs is diagnosis—that is, observation and inference that will find the cause: it cannot be set right by love or anger. This is a strange approach; when the tractor stops, the natural remedy is to beat it. The same unfamiliarity with the categories of cause and effect brings a difficulty in understanding the division of labor. Where this division has been pushed far any one man's work does not yield a product that is directly useful to himself or indeed has necessarily any use that is apparent to him at all, but has its place in a complex design, as a means to a remote end: as such it may be incomprehensible to those whose purposes are generally immediate. In the same way the payment of wages by time is harder to understand than payment by task or piece. The latter is like a sale in the market place: hand so much over to the employer, and he will pay you so much for it. But when he pays by time, he requires you to attend for certain hours and do what he tells you, and after a while he will give you some money. This is intelligible only if you can see how your work can be a means to the employer's end of output and your own end of pay, even though it has no immediate connection with either.

Part of the difficulty here may lie in the size of the employer's business. The firm in the developed economy, though its working in each particular instance depends much on personalities, is inherently an impersonal system of administration, with its structure that sets positions, not persons, in their due relation to one another, and its working code that assigns authority to offices and is binding upon all. This is confusing to those for whom authority is inherently personal. It is hard for them to see their place in an organization chart when the question they are asking is, "Who is my father here, who is my chief?" When rules are applied to them, they see this only as the exertion of someone's power, and so capable of being changed if he will show favor. They come too easily under the sway of the foreman, or the sirdar through whom they have been recruited.

The problem of finding personal relations within the impersonal firm is graver when the worker deprived of such relations is far more bewildered than he generally is in Western societies. In these, for all the ties of kindred and locality, men have become accustomed to standing by themselves, not much restrained in their activities or supported in their difficulties by ties beyond those of husband and wife, parent and child; even this last tie may be strong only in the early years of life, and children are brought up in the expectation of going out into the world, of getting married and setting up for themselves. In the last century the word "individual" came into use for what had been divided as far as division would go. But in other societies family or tribe or village permeate the being of their members, who, when separated from them, are not just lonely or homesick but lose much of their capacity for action. The analogy of the hand that can no longer grasp when it is cut off from the body is needed to bring home to Western man, with his custom and virtue of independence, how the one lifeblood of feeling and judgment suffuses the veins of all the members of such a group. It is not so much that they depend on the group as that there is no "they" apart from it. One manifestation of this is the propensity to carry grouping by family or tribe into the place of work, and to refuse to work alongside those who do not belong: workers whose very being is in kindred and affinity find it harder to shake down together than the more separated, self-contained individuals of the West. But this is only one form of the more general difficulty: a developed economy requires its workers to be units who can be variously combined and assorted, whereas in much of the emergent world men are not units.

From these characteristics of the people of that world there follow some features of the labor force. Foremost is the reluctance with which men enter the labor force at all. The fruits of economic development may be desired, but the way to win them does not attract those who have not been in the habit of acting to better their own condition. Often the impulsion into the new forms of work has had to come from behind. Sometimes government has supplied it, either by imposing taxes that force men to go out at least for a time to work to pay them, or by some form of forced labor on public works. But the main propellant has been the pressure of population. When this pressure is not too high, it may make itself felt only at certain seasons, and provide a reversible migration. Animal husbandry needs attention throughout the year, but in arable farming there may be a big difference between the labor force needed in seedtime and harvest and at other times—it was reckoned that on the average farm in northeastern and central China there used to be work for about 190 man-days in the course of the year, but this was performed by two men, capable, say, of 600 man-days. So a rural people may gain an habituation to industrial work through seasonal migration; and the other side of the same penny is that industry has a seasonally fluctuating labor force. But where population pressure becomes higher, separation from the soil must last longer or become permanent. Sons and daughters may be sent away to work long enough to earn bride-price or dowry; men who can earn more in industry than from their share of the yield of the family holding may spend most of their working years, with some interruptions, in the town, but return to the village at the last; some will move their whole being to the town. But in India and Africa these last are still few: men may have a right to share in the family produce or tribal land that they cannot sell outright or draw on to bring them revenue while they are in the town, and their only way to use it is to go home.

The labor force thus provided to industry remains unstable. Beside a minority of long-service workers is a majority that works only intermittently. Those coming to town for the first time change their jobs in their quest for the work that they dislike least or that pays best. Almost all, including those who have settled in a job, withdraw after a time to go back to the village. They often return, and to the same employment, so that many of a firm's workers will have long years of service with it, but these years are not continuous. There is also much absenteeism for shorter visits home, or through sickness, which is frequent among the undernourished. So it comes about that just where labor is in excess supply it is hardest to retain.

The reason for this paradox is ultimately the reluctance of men and women to enter into a way of life quite alien to their own habits of thought and social ties. In noting some of the sources of this antipathy we have by implication noted some of the qualities that the labor force of a developed economy requires. It needs to accept regular and steady work through fixed periods of time. It must use the categories of means and end, cause and effect, in its own thought, both to be able to operate machinery and to understand the contract of employment under the division of labor. It must be accustomed to the distinction between personal authority and the executive authority vested in an office under a constitution or administrative code. Its members should be sufficiently independent of the ties of the extended family or tribe or village to make their way on their own and to be capable of being variously combined with one another. Though in this way mobile, they must at the same time be settled, in the sense that they have no ties to pull them back into another way of life.

These are not the prerequisites for all and any industrialization: even where they are still largely lacking, firms whose technique or markets enable them to carry high labor costs do operate modern plants; Kenya and Egypt, for instance, have attained in this way a considerable industrial development. Nor can countries and phases be readily classified or contrasted: there are many mixed conditions and intermediate stages. But the labor forces that attain technical skill and a high material standard of living do seem to need such qualities as we have noted. Let us go on to ask how they can be acquired.

RAISING THE QUALITY OF THE LABOR FORCE IN EMERGENT ECONOMIES

To form from the peoples of a primitive society a labor force capable of high output means helping men and women to find a new way of life. The main responsibility rests on management, whether public or private. It is on the manager as a man that the worker accustomed to personal authority will fix his hopes and fears. But the manager cannot simply take the social setting as given, bring in equipment, and train men to operate it: he has also to help them get used to living in a different place and to following a different pattern of work, leisure, and expenditure. His technical knowledge will avail him little unless he also knows how to handle people. "The impression is recorded that the efficiency of East African natives depends first on the quality of the European administrators, business executives and foremen who control them."[1] Not least in influence is the foreman, who is likely to combine the functions of recruiter, fitter or machine-setter, and overseer. It is he who is in direct touch with the workers and can make the day wretched or cheerful for them; but too often he has had no training in man management, and, even if he is trained, he is often preoccupied with too diverse responsibilities.

Though good management is specially needed, it does not necessarily have to use special methods. Of course it must take account of local circumstances, such as the tribal or religious differences that limit the allocation of tasks and the ability of men to work together. But there is evidence that the labor force of emergent societies can respond to the methods that are considered good labor management in an advanced society. Though the newcomer to industry is in many ways so different from the Western worker, he can still respond in much the same way to the same treatment. Indeed, what sort of man we take him to be may depend on what sort of treatment he receives. The local and traditional employer's view of his workers may be borne out by the way they behave under treatment based on or rationalized by that view: their behavior under different treatment might warrant different inferences about their attitudes and potential. Some at least of what seem to be inherent and specific characteristics of the

1. U.K. Colonial Office, *African Labour Efficiency Survey*, ed. C. H. Northcott (London, 1949), p. 34.

labor forces of the emergent societies may only mark the kind of handling they have been getting.

Though in emergent societies good managers are a more productive asset than good equipment, they are far harder to acquire. Where these societies have armies in the Western tradition, the training of the young officer not only to take executive control of his men but to consider their comfort and well-being provides a possible source of managers schooled to see understanding of the worker and care for his welfare as a foremost part of their job. But that approach is unlikely to be general. Where labor is cheap, there is no immediate incentive to get the best out of it, or to consult its feelings. Higher education may be valued traditionally as setting one apart from manual toil and toilers. Managing labor may be regarded as a subsidiary matter to be subcontracted to the sirdar who can work in the local vernacular and must be left to do his job in his own way. "It is fair to say . . . that a great many Indian managements still remain unconvinced or unaware of the value of in-plant supervisory and management training programmes."[2]

Experience has suggested various measures that good management can employ or the government promote to help build up a strong and settled labor force. Within the firm a principal part may be played at an early stage by provisions for welfare such as have appeared only late in the course of development of Western economies: there is no presumption that the sequence in which industrial relations and conditions of employment have evolved in those economies is either necessary or desirable in the economies now emergent. Amenities at the place of work make more difference to labor

2. C. A. Myers, *Labor Problems in the Industrialization of India* (Cambridge, Mass., 1958), p. 114.

that is housed squalidly than to the worker who returns to a comfortable home. Selection according to aptitude may help the raw even more than the seasoned entrant. Workers may understand joint consultation and be able to make something of it before they are capable of collective bargaining. There are also grounds for believing that workers whose response to wage incentives is uncertain do appreciate opportunities for advancement. Sometimes men shrink back from it because of an inbred fear of arousing envy; but when that does not inhibit them, they value the chance to work their way toward the more desired jobs. In Uganda, for instance, they will for that reason take work at low pay as cleaners and greasers in a garage; and a racial bar to advancement beyond a certain point, as when the Asian wage scale begins where the African leaves off, or the more qualified work is reserved for Europeans only, discourages the aspirations that might otherwise energize the worker.

Outside the place of work, much depends on housing. The migrant from the country who can find quarters only in a shantytown will not want to commit himself to work in industry. There is little incentive to earn more if you have no thief-proof house in which to keep what your earnings would buy. A decent house is not only a great part of a higher standard of living in itself but a prerequisite for much of the rest; and it enables the women, who will be pressing for more household amenities, to join their men in town.

If public agencies can foster the growth of an independent trade unionism, this will do something not only to negotiate better terms for the worker and protect him from abuses but to develop his own caliber and provide him with amenities outside the place of work. Thus in Mexico the unions have built houses, helped the newcomer from the village to find his feet, and combated his illiteracy by providing adult education. The very maintenance of a union, moreover, gives its members self-respect and training in citizenship. Reflecting in the 1890s on the effects of trade unionism in its early days in Britain, Alfred Marshall reached a conclusion that has application to the emergent societies of today:

> The power of Unions to sustain high wages depends chiefly on the influence they exert on the character of the workers themselves . . . Trade-unionism . . . found even the artisan with but little independence and self-respect, incensed against his employers, but with no well-considered policy for compelling them to treat him as an equal who had something to sell that they wanted to buy. This state of things would in any case have been much modified by the increase of wealth and of knowledge; which . . . would have taken away much of that want and fear of hunger which depressed the physique and the moral character of the working classes. Unions have been at once a chief product and a chief cause of this constant elevation of the Standard of Life: where that Standard is high, Unions have sprung up naturally; where Unions have been strong, the Standard of Life has generally risen.[3]

We touch here upon that progressive interaction of higher output on personal quality and higher personal quality on output that reverses the vicious circle of poverty and weakness within which the labor force of undeveloped economies is initially locked, and provides the main way out of it. Higher earnings improve physique. There is great scope for this, and sometimes the effect can be rapid. An English

3. *Elements of Economics of Industry* (London, Macmillan, 1892), Bk. VI, chap. xiii, par. 16.

engineer who had had experience in railway building in many parts of the world a hundred years ago concluded that

> with regard to unskilled labour men seem to be like machines: the work given out bears some relation to the food consumed. A good illustration of this occurred on the French railways executed by Mr. Brassey . . . He began by largely employing English navvies, paying them much higher wages than would have been required by French labourers, but the larger amount of work done by the Englishmen compensated him for the higher wages. After a time . . . the Frenchmen, gradually receiving higher wages than previously they were accustomed to receive, were enabled to live better and do more work, until ultimately the French labourers came to be chiefly employed.[4]

But a yet more powerful effect on physique comes as a new generation grows up that has had more to eat in childhood, where malnutrition does most harm. Better physique brings better health, which means less absenteeism and a longer span of life. This, a gain in itself, also brings an indirect gain by extending the return on investment in training: in Uganda, for example, only 11 per cent of the population have been living beyond the age of 45, and apprenticeship is lengthy in comparison with the span left to apply it in. A rise in the standard of living also promotes an improvement of personal quality, because it tends to bring a reduction of the birth rate where that has been out of balance with the rate of mortality. Overpopulation, it seems, is not self-correcting: the misery it brings imposes an ultimate check through the death rate, but the remedy of a lower birth rate is likely to be

4. Sir Arthur Helps, *Life and Labours of Mr. Brassey* (London, Bell and Daldy, 1872), letter from John Hawkshaw, p. 364.

reached only when economic development first brings a relief from misery. There remains to be noted a linkage through management; as labor comes to cost more, relative to equipment, and to be at once more capable of good work and more resistant to rough treatment, management is put under pressure not only to be more considerate but to organize work more efficiently and economize on labor—that is, to raise output per man yet further.

Our survey of the means of raising the quality of the labor force of an emergent economy has left to the last the means that, given the right social setting, acts most directly—namely, training. This includes education, both general and vocational. An effective system of only elementary education makes a great claim on resources (in India a plan for it is expected to take forty years to carry through), and noticing how well the illiterate can be trained for certain jobs, some observers have doubted whether education can be given priority in a still poor economy. But it is not only that once the light of learning is at hand you cannot deny it to men without deliberately shutting them in the dark: an elementary education seems also to be prerequisite for most industrial training, not only because so many jobs require the worker to read, write, or figure, but basically because the illiterate man is less able to reason, to communicate, and above all to adapt himself to fresh requirements. A distinction may be attempted insofar as general education exists to develop the pupil and enrich his life, and so is an end in itself, whereas vocational training is only a means to the end of production. But this does less than justice to vocational training; and in any case the economist, concerned with the effect on the potential of the pupil as an agent of production, can draw no dividing line, but sees the general and the vocational alike as part of the formation of the labor force.

The Economics of Labor

We proceed to consider this process of formation as an activity of developed as well as emergent economies.

TRAINING FOR THE WORKING LIFE

One would have thought that any ruler concerned with perpetuating his house's sway would have found his surest means in the training of a cadre of officers and administrators; and still more that any father of his people would have sought their continuing strength and prosperity by ensuring that the young folk would be trained, generation after generation, in skill, discipline, and purpose. But governments until quite recent times have made singularly little provision for training. Some, it is true, have taken care to recruit their servants from among the best qualified of their young men; the armed forces have had their ways of instructing and seasoning; Sparta had a plan for the exercising of its children, and ancient China for the training of its mandarins. In most ages, too, governments have been attracted by autarky, and have wanted their people to be able to make at home whatever others were making abroad: so they have sent for foreign craftsmen to come and impart the secrets of their trade, have offered settlements to industrially qualified migrants, and welcomed refugees who brought new skills with them—as the Huguenots brought silk-working to England. Yet what is remarkable, on a wide survey, is how small the provision is that governments have made for raising the quality of their peoples—for imparting knowledge to them, and the ability to read and write, reason and calculate; for their instruction in the arts and crafts, in agriculture and industry; and, not less, for causing them to learn by experience the rules of self-discipline and respect for others. On what a people in any generation have taken in as they grew up depends their stability, their capacity for growth, the full-ness of the life they lead, their very survival in a dangerous world. The philosopher of history, seeking causes for the rise and fall of empires, might well ask what arrangements they have made, or failed to make, for training.

One reason for the lack of provision is that education, whether liberal or technical, has often been regarded as a function of the religious orders, and a matter proper to the members of a cult. Homer's carpenters and shipwrights were guided by the goddess Athena, and when Odysseus built a raft, it was Calypso who brought him the augers, the axes, and the drills. The practice of a craft was associated with worship of a particular deity, and the temple was a training center. The early guilds of Japan began in services to shrines. Later it was the monasteries that were the schools not only of letters but of the industrial arts: so it was in Europe under Charlemagne, and in Japan, where from the seventh century A.D. the Buddhist monks were being sent to China to learn shipbuilding, bridgebuilding, and the ceramic arts, which they taught on their return. To this day, we are told, "for the traditional Indian craftsman his trade is a way of life sup-ported by religious sanctions and expressed in religious themes and objects. His knowledge and skill are a divine revelation which he must carefully guard and transmit to his disciples; and his tools are inspired instruments which will do his bidding if he shows them the appropriate reverence." [5]

Another reason for the neglect of training by governments may be that the upbringing of children in all its branches was felt to be solely a matter for the family. Perhaps the most

5. M. B. Singer, "Changing Craft Traditions in India," in W. E. Moore and A. S. Feldman, eds., *Labor Commitment and Social Change in Developing Areas* (New York, Social Science Research Council, 1960), p. 269.

widespread of all methods of industrial training has been the training of sons by their fathers in the father's trade. That crafts should be hereditary in this way was sometimes made a principle of law, or of custom no less binding. Under the Roman empire the "colleges" which the workers in various trades had formed were made corporations in which membership was both compulsory and hereditary. In the state factories of Byzantium, the sons of workmen had to follow their fathers. In the caste system of India, a boy born into a craftsman's caste must become a craftsman himself. More generally, the father was held responsible for the training of his son, though the training did not have to be in his own trade: in Athens if a father failed to have his son trained, the law exempted the son from the general obligation to provide for his father. This law calls attention to a lack of incentive: even the father's identification of himself with his son may not suffice to make him provide a training whose cost will fall upon him immediately, but whose benefit to him will accrue only uncertainly and remotely. We have seen how this led at one time to the industrial training of slaves rather than of freemen. The long interval between outlay and return may also be part of the explanation of the lack of outlay by governments, whose preoccupation has been to meet the day's problems with the day's resources. But where industries have been carried on in the home, parents have had all too strong a motive to press their children into its service early and to habituate them to its processes: of some English clothmaking districts in the sixteenth and seventeenth centuries, it was recorded with pride that every child above the age of five could earn his own living. This often meant cruel drudgery and a stunted body. But where manufacturing was carried on as a family affair, perhaps as a part-time occupation in the farmer's slack season or as the woman's part in the earning of the family's living, generally the children would learn by watching and helping. Industry apart, moreover, this was how girls learned the craft of housekeeping, and how the boys, and many girls too, learned how to farm.

But the means of formal training in earlier days was apprenticeship, and this belonged not so much to the family as to the guild. The essentials of apprenticeship are that a boy is placed under an obligation to work for a fixed term of years for a master, who on his side undertakes to have the lad taught a trade, not one or two processes only but the whole range that the craftsman commands; the boy gets little pay or none; someone may even have to pay a premium on his behalf. The term of years is long enough for his output meanwhile to become of value to the master, who is compensated thereby for the time and trouble of teaching a beginner. This sort of arrangement has been extraordinarily widespread. In Babylonia contracts for the apprenticeship of slaves provided for the compensation of the owner if the master failed to teach them the trade. In Greece of the fifth and fourth centuries B.C. formal contracts of apprenticeship—indentures, as we would call them—were drawn up, and high premiums were paid to sculptors and painters, though we are told that the treatment of apprentices was harsh and they were not always allowed to learn trade secrets. The papyri of Hellenistic Egypt include indentures, some of them of slaves, to a wool carder, a fuller, a stenographer, a flutewoman. In Japan, the first apprentices were bought, and were bound for life, and this variant of slavery continued until after 1600, when an endeavor was made to limit the contract to three years in the crafts and ten in commerce: in Tokyo a patriarch was appointed in each guild to keep the masters to their agreements. In Europe of the eleventh and twelfth centuries, apprenticeship, we are told, was thorough and effective: "the working classes have never at any time had a better technical preparation for the fulfillment of their function."[6] In Byzantium apprenticeship was enforced strictly. In India, though apprenticeship is rare today, the guilds of craftsmen have maintained it. In China, until recent years, apprenticeship to a trade was a prerequisite for any employment in the towns except as a coolie. In a word, apprenticeship seems to be found wherever the craftsman had a status, for there it seems to have met needs both of the parent and of the craftsman himself. The parent who could not endow a boy with land could still set him up with a stock in trade if he could enable his son to become a craftsman. The craftsman got some useful work out of the apprentice before his time was out, and as a member of a guild he himself had an interest both in maintaining the numbers and skill of journeymen and in restricting competition by insisting that only those who had served their apprenticeship might practice the trade.

With the rise of modern industry, apprenticeship has had its vicissitudes. It has been open to abuse: some masters have used it as a supply of cheap labor and failed to give the apprentice a training in all the branches of his trade; some unions have used it as a means of creating an artificial scarcity. It has been attacked, moreover, as inadequate to the needs of the day—as being spun out for longer than is needed to shape a workman by intensive training, and as ill suited to the trades where the learner must be instructed in an advancing technology. It has become costly, and only the bigger firms can maintain it. But it has held its own, and in

6. P. Boissonnade, trans. E. Power, *Life and Work in Medieval Europe, fifth to fifteenth Centuries* (New York, Knopf; London, Kegan Paul, Trench, Trübner, 1927), p. 213.

contemporary discussion of vocational training as a means to economic growth it appears to have gained acceptance as a major agency. This may be attributed to two considerations. First, it is a form of training on the job, in which the schoolroom is an actual workshop and the teacher a craftsman such as the pupil himself aspires to be; it is therefore likely to keep more closely up to date, provide more equipment, and above all motivate the pupil and keep his interest more surely than would courses in the classroom alone. Second, though apprenticeship is a cumbrous method of teaching particular operations, it provides the range of experience that alone will give the pupil the versatility that is the hallmark of the true craftsman.

It is this aim of versatility, with the independence and initiative which make it possible, that marks off apprenticeship from the other forms of training on the job whose only aim is to practice the pupil in particular operations that will be carried out under supervision. But such training as this is all that most workers in contemporary industry have ever had. Even to call it training may be to claim too much, for often there is no explicit provision for practice or instruction, and the newcomer is left to pick up the work from the example of the older hands, with a word or two from the foreman here and there; and what experience even of this kind any one man may get depends on what new job he happens to find, or how senior he is in his existing employment. But the bigger firms of today are likely to provide carefully for the training of their semiskilled workers. They may have vestibule schools, to orient and equip the entrant before he goes into the workshop. They train the trainers, whether these are specialists or the first-line supervisors. For young people, they may combine training on the job with some further schooling: in Western Germany, the learners spend five days a week in the shops and one in a vocational school, and they are prepared for a trade test.

The need for management to plan for training on the job is great in the emergent countries, where such training encounters special difficulties if it is left to itself. The pupils have a greater adaptation to make than in countries where industry is familiar. To be able to receive instruction they may have to learn something of another language; Swahili, for instance, has no words for engine parts and cannot express fractions. They may be herded into occupations according not to their aptitudes but to the caste, village, or tribe they come from. The trainer may be unwilling—in East Africa Asians are said to be reluctant to teach the African; in Egypt the experienced hands fear being replaced by newcomers if they make good workers of them. Too much depends on the foreman, who may himself have had no training in how to train, who is in any case likely to be overworked, and who may advance the pupils because of their race or the bribes they give him instead of for their proficiency. To overcome such obstacles, some big firms have developed training programs with their own schools. The linchpin of such programs is the training of trainers who will not be required to act as supervisors at the same time; thus in the Johannesburg mines, "boss boys" are given a two months' course to teach them how to teach, even though their own contract may be for only six months, and they serve as intermediaries between the European foreman and the African worker.

As governments have become more willing to take responsibility for the condition of their peoples and more aware of the possibility of raising the standard of living by raising productivity, we should expect them to make increasing provision for the training of the labor force. Insofar as that training depends on a general elementary education, they have done so: it is a distinctive mark of modern societies that they provide general and compulsory schooling, and this has brought about a "silent social revolution"[7] within the last hundred years. But the more technical training that prepares the pupil for a specific occupation has been less developed by governments. This is partly in the nature of things—schooling that is much the same for all boys and girls can be provided by public agencies more readily than the many and various courses required for myriad diverse occupations. These occupations, however, fall into groups with common processes and problems, and so the question arises whether young people cannot be helped by a phase of preparatory training between their general schooling and their entry into paid employment—by courses in mathematics, the physical sciences, and the use of basic tools, for example, for those who are going into industry, or in accountancy and stenography for entrants to commerce. Much has been done in some countries to diversify the courses open to those who stay at school after about the age of thirteen, with this aim in view. There has also been some setting up of technical schools, but hitherto their effectiveness has been limited. Often they have lacked up-to-date equipment and teachers of sufficient caliber. They have sometimes gained the reputation of setting a low standard for a day's work; employers may find their products harder to fit in than the complete novice. The more academic side of their teaching may be over the heads of many of their students. We have seen how they are likely to lack the practicality and the incentive that go with training on the job. But this is not to say that their

7. The title of a history of English public education by G. A. N. Lowndes (London, 1937).

work cannot be developed. Experience has already shown the value of combining training on the job with some periods of work in the classroom, whether in the firm's own school or in a center that serves the neighborhood. Some central provision is in any case necessary to train the labor force of firms too small to maintain efficient programs of their own.

The training of the labor force has naturally found a place in the programs of the centrally planned economies. In the first years of planning in Russia, it is true, the vast numbers of entrants to industry had to pick up a partial knowledge on the job, and a system of factory training schools was introduced only under the Second Five-Year Plan, which began in 1932; training on the job remains the main channel, and the ways in which it is provided in the workshop and combined with classroom work in or out of the plant are very similar to those of Western countries. But a distinctive feature appears in the Russian system of State Labor Reserves. In 1940 this took the place of the factory training schools. In the schools of this system the discipline is quasi-military; some give a six months' course in preparation for factory work, others a two-year course for craftsmen and railwaymen. At first many of the students were drafted, but now all are believed to be volunteers. These schools open the door, especially for young people from the villages, to better paid jobs in the towns. In China most of the universities have become "technical and political labor schools," whose function is to turn out technicians, and many of whose students are on leave from wage-earning employment; the graduates must go where they are posted. Schemes of apprenticeship that provided at first for courses of only a year or eighteen months proved inadequate, and in 1957 the courses were extended to three years, beginning at not less than sixteen years of age.

Quality of the Labor Force

Our account of training so far has applied mainly to the manual worker and the junior technician. The approach to the higher technical and professional occupations runs naturally through the subjects that are taught in schools and universities on their academic merits—the future doctor studies physiology, the lawyer jurisprudence, and so on—though some additional provision may be needed for more vocational training. Generally, a greater output of the higher skills has been achieved by the expansion of schools and colleges of existing types, though with many changes in the relative sizes of faculties. But many of the students who acquire these higher qualifications will in practice be concerned with management, and this has been increasingly recognized as a specific function requiring a distinctive course of training with its own body of information, principles, and problems. In particular, a manager needs a conspectus of types of organization, an awareness of the issues of principle in administration, and insight into human nature and human relations. In recent years, increasing provision for such training has been made through graduate schools of business administration, sandwich courses for managers already in positions, and executive development programs within the firm. "There are no bad soldiers, only bad officers": that is only part of the truth, but it is an important part, and no other form of training seems to offer greater prospects of raising not only productivity but the whole quality of the working life of people in production.

THE LIMITATIONS OF HUMAN POTENTIAL

Training schemes commonly come up against limitations of ability: not every applicant has the capacity to learn the job. When there is a shortage of men who fit the jobs, firms have to adjust the jobs to fit the men. In several ways the pattern of the work to be done is constantly being adjusted to the pattern of the abilities available, and though in one way this does not raise those abilities, it does enable people to make the most of them, and so raises the quality of the labor force as that is measured by performance.

The limitations of ability may be illustrated by the intelligence quotient, though this is a measure of only one kind of proficiency. In the tests commonly used, the scores people make prove to have a normal distribution: the Stanford-Binet scale assigns a rating of 100 to the average performance, and most of the individuals tested lie between 70 and 130, less than 5 per cent lying outside each of these points. Though the proficiency that the I.Q. measures forms only part of any man's capacity to work, it does seem to limit the range of occupations open to him. If a boy's I.Q. is less than 115, say, he cannot really hope to become a doctor, for whatever his drive and determination, he will fail his exams. Though requirements for admission are less formalized outside the professions, it seems likely that other occupations have their effective thresholds of I.Q. too—a man will not be able to do satisfactory work as a maintenance fitter, for example, unless his capacity includes an I.Q. higher than will suffice for a machine-minder on repetitive work; or a girl may be able to become a good shop assistant while lacking the capacity to become a good stenographer. If this is so, then the frequency distribution of I.Q.s provides one set of limits to the potential of the labor force: if jobs that require more capacity to acquire knowledge, communicate, and solve problems than do the manual and simpler clerical occupations can be performed effectively only by those whose I.Q.s are not less than 115, the frequency distribution of I.Q.s tells us that only one-sixth of the population is able to fill them.

The illustration shows a basic problem of all economies,

but it lies in disputable ground, and is in any case partial. Performance in one kind of test is no sure measure of the proficiency that will be displayed in other settings. When tests of I.Q. are designed, they are adjusted as necessary until the scores yield a normal distribution, and this is not necessarily the form of all the relevant qualities. Height is one human attribute that is distributed normally—but there are others, like weight, whose distribution is highly skewed. Men's earnings depend on the conjunction of personal attributes and the economic environment: we shall see later (below, pages 153–56) that the distribution of personal earnings is generally skewed.

But though the forms it may take are various, at any one time there exists a distribution of capacities that assigns certain proportions of the population to each part of the range of attainment. We need not suppose that the capacities are all innate: some may be precast genetically, but what a man can learn to do depends also on his upbringing, on the influences that have come to bear on him in home, neighborhood, and school; these influences, however, will have their own distribution, so that were they all-powerful, there would still be a dispersion of capacity about the mean. Nor need we suppose that the average level of capacity is impervious to education and the processes of social improvement generally: the experience of Africa already runs to the contrary. But wherever the average lies at any time, there will be a dispersion about it, and only a limited part of the labor force will be available for work requiring capacity above any but the lowest threshold.

This would not matter if the threshold was low for all the jobs there actually were to do. There may have been some Arcadian economies in which this was nearly so: in them anyone who could work at all could learn to do pretty well any work that was going on, and men who had the capacity to become surgeons and architects, had such jobs existed, might have passed their days as fishermen and plaiters of straw. But part of the secret of economic growth is that it differentiates tasks and finds some to occupy the highest abilities exclusively and fully. It is as though, in some primitive task of excavation, people were carrying the earth away by the basketful, and there was one size of basket for everybody, small enough for a child to carry: but then baskets of different sizes were brought in, and now while the child carried the same as before, the grown man carried far more. In this kind of way the division of labor raises the quality of the labor force that is actually applied and engaged.

But in practice the baskets are not simply adjusted to the strengths of the laborers: their design proceeds under influences some of which take no account of what labor is available. At any one time a given firm or industry will be using different occupations in proportions which are fixed within a narrow range of discretion by the nature of its plant and processes. The proportions will differ from one industry to another—the ratio of manual workers to technicians will be higher in coal mining, for instance, than in pharmaceuticals. Taken together, the jobs to be filled industry by industry compose a certain pattern of jobs in the economy as a whole. What assurance is there that this pattern will agree with that of the capacities available in the labor force? Since the pattern of jobs depends on the relative size and the techniques of production and administration in different industries, it tends to change as demand in the market shifts and as technology develops: but these pressures are independent of the current availability of different sorts of labor and the way this may itself be changing.

What happens when the tendencies diverge? In considering training we have been looking at one of the processes of adjustment. But if training is fitting the worker to the job, there is also the possibility of fitting the job to the worker. When war brought an excess of demand for the skilled man, especially in engineering, it was found that his work could often be broken down: some parts of it did not themselves need skill at all, others newcomers could learn to do fairly soon if each had to learn only one of them. Sometimes the semiskilled could do skilled work if they had more jigs, or women could do men's work if they were supplied with power for lifting. In recent years the name "ergonomics" has been given to the studies whose object is to improve the design of the work place and process so that the operative can work with less strain, discomfort, and fatigue and so with greater speed or precision. These studies can help to bring jobs within the reach of those who were not up to them when they were more exacting. Years of full employment have led management to adapt the conditions of work so as to tap additional sources of labor. Another recent minting, "geriatrics," denotes studies of aging, and of the kind of work that the elderly worker can do; and part-time work, or short shifts and evening shifts, have been organized to enable married women to combine paid employment with work in the home. It is in making more use of the abilities of women that thought given to the design of process and system seems specially promising. Intelligence tests have gone far in settling a long argument by showing that, whatever it is that these tests measure, women have as much of it as men: what seems remarkable by contrast is the small proportion of working women who are found in the more highly qualified occupations, and there may be changes in the conditions of work and in men's attitude to women that will help to make fuller use of women's abilities.

The Economics of Labor

We have been dealing with ways in which the pattern of the labor force and the pattern of the jobs to be done are adapted to one another by the training of labor and the re-shaping of jobs. But mingled with these adaptations are other processes of adjustment, to which we now turn.

4 THE DEPLOYMENT OF THE LABOR FORCE

MIGRATION

The broadest form of deployment is that which distributes mankind over the face of the globe and allocates a labor force to the resources of each region. The growth of numbers within any one region depends partly on the rate of increase of those already there and partly on migration. The forms of migration range from the eruption of armed and ravening multitudes who raid, seize, and settle, through the broad but peaceful currents that have flowed to lands of opportunity from those where soil and jobs were scarce, to those unchanneled movements of this man and that in search of employment or betterment, which on balance bring gradual but extensive changes in the labor forces of different regions.

Two periods of the movements of multitudes over long

distances have shaped the modern world. The first lies between the heyday of the Roman empire in the second century A.D. and the end of the ninth century. Coming, some of
them, from Central Asia ultimately, and then from the
steppes and the German forests, the Huns, Goths, and Van-
dals poured across Danube and Rhine. Angles, Jutes, and
Saxons crossed the narrow seas to occupy England and the
Scottish Lowlands. The Norsemen sailed the Atlantic as far
as Greenland and Vineland the Good, penetrated the Mediterranean, harried the coasts of Europe, pressed inland, and
settled. They followed Volga and Dnieper to the Caspian and
Black Seas, and colonized Kiev—"Russians" means "rowers."
Meanwhile an explosion of energies, and perhaps of numbers, occurred among the Semitic peoples of the Near East:
the Arabs spread through North Africa and Spain, and con-
quered northwestern India. What the impelling forces of
these outpourings were, we can only conjecture. There is
evidence of a change of climate, a desiccation of central Asia
that would have driven whole peoples from the dust bowl:
the Huns, being thrown back by the Chinese, recoiled upon
India and Europe. Perhaps, too, it was because the seventh
century was a time of drought that Arab tribes were on the
march even before Mahomet gave them their fighting creed.
But we also have reason to believe that populations can
begin to grow rapidly without any apparently connected
change in their environment or way of life, perhaps through
a decline in the virulence of their endemic diseases: so it
seems to have been in Western Europe in the sixteenth and
again in the eighteenth centuries, and so it may have been
too in some of the overspills of the first millennium.

Whether these migrations were of whole tribes or only of
the younger sons, they had come to an end by the tenth century. There followed nine hundred years without movements

of great masses: only the Turks pressed their conquests west; the Germans with sword and settlement advanced eastward beyond the Oder; the Russians spread slowly north and east from their heartland on the Dnieper. But in the sixteenth century a rise of population sufficient to about halve the real wages of artisans in Western Europe still did not drive men far afield. There were now no unclaimed lands, no abandoned forts and cornlands open to rapine: those who sought a new settlement would have had to go far overseas. A few did begin to go: the Spaniards sent settlers to South America and the Caribbean, and the Portuguese to Brazil; the first English colony on the American mainland was attempted in 1606, and soon a slow but general migration set in across the Atlantic. The labor force of the New World was further augmented by the slave trade: it has been estimated that some twenty million Africans were carried off in all. But when one considers the vast territories to be opened up, and the great disparity between the New World and the Old—not in prospects only but in the earnings that came to be immediately available—it is remarkable how few people moved. The obstacles lay in transport: by sea, in the small, slow, storm-beaten sailing ship; by pack and wagon on the further shore.

Those obstacles were removed in the first half of the nineteenth century by the steamship and the railroad. At the same time the population of Western Europe, which probably had not changed much since 1600, was bounding up again. There set in the second period of the movement of multitudes. This time the movement did not depend on conquest: though British rule was extended over much of India between 1770 and 1850 and most of Africa had been divided between European powers by the time of the First World War, settlers followed the soldier only in Kenya and Rhodesia, and there only in small numbers. The new movement of multitudes was rather to lands where only a thin peopling of aborigines resisted the newcomer: the vast hinterlands of the United States and Canada, and Australia and New Zealand. Before long, the immigration was serving to reinforce an already developed economy in the coastal regions, from which the pioneers were pressing up-country, to farm, ranch, and mine. The rate of migration from year to year now began to depend increasingly on the momentary state of the demand for labor in the new economies, rather than on that of the pressures driving them out of the old. The turning point, at least for the United States, may be set about 1870. Before that, the potato disease in Ireland in 1846 had driven starving families in hordes down to the shore, to go wherever ships would take them: here was a tragic set-piece of Malthusianism, a country which in the next half century was to halve the population that had expanded so precipitately in the seventy years before. There had also been an expulsive force at work in the emigration of the liberals after the repression of the European revolutions of 1848. But from about 1870 onward the annual rate of immigration into the United States is closely correlated with the cyclical variations in the economy's path of growth: in earlier decades the great bursts of railroad building and house construction had followed after the years of greatest immigration, so as both to use and to provide for the newcomers, but now the lag was the other way round: more newcomers arrived only after more jobs had been offered. But though the time at which the emigrant set out seems to have depended on the advices reaching him, whether ultimately he set out at all may still have been determined by the state of his difficulties and prospects at home.

Basically, the great migrations of the nineteenth century were from regions where the pressure of population upon natural resources was higher into those where it was lower. This holds not only of movements from Europe to America but of the other major movements of the time: the Russians spreading over Siberia; Italians, Poles, Belgians, and Spaniards moving into France; the Chinese settling around the Pacific, whether in Malaya or California; and the Indians, moving in only small numbers to any one place but in large numbers in total, to Trinidad and British Guiana, Fiji, Mauritius, and East Africa.

After the First World War a number of changes combined to reduce migration across frontiers. In the European countries of origin, the natural rate of growth of population had generally diminished. Some of these countries restricted emigration for political reasons. In the receiving countries, most if not all of the free land had now been taken up and the great tasks of primary construction completed: so the unskilled immigrant no longer found a job waiting for him as a laborer, and if he were to be used he would have to be trained—the "coolie trade" could flourish no longer. Instead of being complementary to the skilled worker of older stock, therefore, the immigrant now appeared as a competitor likely to undercut the rate for the job. The "new immigration" of the twenty years before the war had brought to the United States increasing numbers of southern Italians, Russians, and Poles, and these had been less easily assimilated to the American way of life than the British, Germans, and Scandinavians who had predominated before. In all the receiving countries, had there been no restrictions, a greatly increased proportion of the immigrants would now very probably have been Asians, who aroused even more sharply the anxieties concerning undercutting and assimilation. Organized labor therefore gained the assent of public opinion and of government to its demand for limitation of entry. By 1939 it appeared likely that migration would continue only insofar as governments found an interest in providing for it by mutual agreement.

Since the Second World War, however, some forces have been making for greater freedom of movement. Full employment decreases anxiety about the competition for jobs and the undercutting of rates, and through the "promotion effect," which shifts shortages of labor to the lowest grades, it specially increases the vacancies for the kind of labor the unskilled immigrant can provide. At the same time the receiving countries have entered on a conscious course of economic development that goes far toward taking the place of the advancing frontier of old, and sets up a demand for the skilled man and the specialist, who may be attracted by a sufficient difference of pay. As standards of living in the less developed territories are raised, the reduced pressure of want may be more than offset by men's increased capacity to qualify themselves for work in another land and pay their fares to reach it. Better education and broader channels of information give more adaptability and greater knowledge of other countries, and make migration less of a leap in the dark and more likely to be considered as a step in a career. Generally, the combination of full employment, economic development, and wider knowledge seems likely to make for some reductions in the restrictions on migration, as on trade, and to guide the movement of labor across frontiers by much the same influences that play upon the changing deployment of labor within any one country. But this tendency continues to be resisted by the difficulties of assimilation.

DEPLOYMENT OF THE LABOR FORCE DURING ECONOMIC GROWTH

Any one job requires a man to help make a particular product by applying a particular proficiency in a particular place, and the changes that occur in the deployment of the labor force in the course of economic growth can be examined in these three dimensions of industry, occupation, and region.

The relative size of different industries evidently depends in part on how people apply their incomes: the proportion they choose to save bears on the division of output between consumers' and producers' goods, and within their consumption the relative sums they spend on different articles bear on the relative quantities of those articles that will be made. In part, the pattern of outlay depends on custom and fashion: at any one time households of much the same real income in different countries divide their outlay differently—French wage earners, for instance, generally spend a larger part of their income on food than do the British—and similar differences can come about in the course of time within any one country. The invention of new products will also divert outlay, not to these products alone: in Western societies the automobile is changing the whole way of living. But the pattern of outlay also depends on the total spent. Studies of the budgets of households with different incomes at any one time suggest that the sums spent on each article vary systematically with the household's income. If we take any one article, say meat, we can plot the sums spent on it household by household as a function of the income; and we often find that this function, known as the Engel function, is approximately linear. But the slopes of the lines for different articles vary: as we move from households of lower to those of higher income, outlay on rent, for example, will commonly rise faster than that on food; and within food, outlay on potatoes will not rise as fast as that on meat. Some lines may even slope down: as we move away from the poorest households, outlay on bread may actually diminish. These observations suggest that as the standard of living of a whole community rises, the pattern of its outlay will change, and a higher proportion of its production will be devoted to the comforts and luxuries of life, a smaller to the bare necessities.

What inference we draw for the industrial deployment of the labor force depends much on the classification we use, for one industry broadly defined may produce necessities and luxuries alike—agriculture, for example, provides strawberries and cream as well as bread. But we can at least see that as output per head rises, the composition of that output will be altered by changes in the allocation of income, and generally we may expect that the industries that wrest the primary foodstuffs and raw materials from nature will not grow as much as those that work them up into more elaborate forms or provide intangible amenities.

Even this conclusion, however, needs qualification, because the division of outlay depends not only on tastes and the standard of living but on the relative prices of the different products available. It is for this reason that we may find, in an economy whose standard of living is relatively low, a large part of the working population engaged in providing those services of retail distribution and household amenity whose increase is usually a mark of the continued advance of societies where real incomes are already high. Thus in Japan the "tertiary sector," as it is called—which includes the small shopkeeper, the odd-job man, the servant, and the craftsman working directly for the consumer—expanded from about a quarter of the labor force in 1920 to more than a third in 1955, because, we are told, it offered the only outlet for people with very small capital, working with unpaid family help; and of Mexico one observer remarks that "much of the increase in the so-called service and white-collar industries . . . simply reflects the fact that the population of working force age has increased more rapidly than have the job opportunities in industries producing physical goods. This is implicit in the fact that so many of these service and white-collar industries pay lower than average wages."[1]

Thus an industry may be big because those who crowd into it for lack of anywhere else to go press their products on the consumer at very low prices. When more capital becomes available and better techniques are applied with it, the numbers in such industries may diminish at the same time as the output greatly rises. Transport has provided a notable instance. "The statement that 20 per cent of the population of China is engaged in transport," an observer remarked in 1932, "is no doubt an exaggeration: but it is not wholly unplausible," and he went on to tell of the "almost unbroken procession of human beings moving bales and packing cases" in a large town.[2] The change to be made here by the coming of railroad and motor truck exemplifies the effect that advances in technique take by simultaneously increasing an industry's output and decreasing the numbers occupied in it; the agriculture of Western countries in recent years has provided another instance. Changes in technique also affect the industrial deployment of labor because they change the division of labor between industries: thus the rise of the automobile and truck has caused a relative decline in the reported number of transport workers, because more transportation is now carried out by other industries and by consumers for themselves. This reminds us that the outcome of any statistical inquiry into industrial deployment depends on the prevailing division of labor: in the underdeveloped economy the peasant, whom the enumerator can only assign

1. A. J. Jaffe, *People, Jobs and Economic Development* (Glencoe, Ill., 1959), p. 265.

2. R. H. Tawney, *Land and Labour in China* (London, 1932), p. 120.

exclusively to agriculture, may in fact spend much of his time in delivering and fetching, buying and selling, and—he or his family—weaving and building. As the division of labor develops, the numbers reported as occupied in these other activities rise faster than the proportion of the working hours of the labor force that is actually devoted to them.

So far we have been assuming a self-contained economy. To the extent that the people of a particular country take part in the division of labor in the world economy, the connections between the stages of their economic growth and the industrial deployment of their labor force are transcended. In the extreme, some sheikdom where oil is struck may attain one of the highest incomes per head in the world, through the same forces as concentrate its labor force in the one primary industry. It is because both New Zealand and Britain participate in international trade, and not because their standards of living are so very different, that in recent years more than a quarter of New Zealand's labor force has been in the primary or extractive industries as against less than a tenth in Britain, whereas for manufacturing the proportions are about a sixth in New Zealand but two-fifths in Britain.

This survey of the course of change in industrial deployment has denied us any generalizations about the outcome but has brought to light the chief forces that go to shape it. These are: the tastes and customs of consumers, the changing division of their outlay as their standard of living rises, the relative numbers seeking employment in different industries, the division of labor between industries, and the techniques they use. There is a continual interplay between changes arising on the side of supply and of demand.

A similar interplay governs deployment by occupation. In part this is locked into deployment by industry: indeed, in the simplest form of the division of labor, when each man makes only one product but himself performs all the processes that go into making it, occupation and industry coincide; even today the miner, for instance, cannot work as such outside mining, and mining cannot be carried on without miners. As soon, however, as men specialize in processes, a difference appears. The occupation is defined by the process, not the product: a given occupation can often be carried on in more than one industry, and any one industry can be carried on with some different blends of occupations. The forces that govern deployment by occupation can therefore be considered separately.

Here, in the course of economic growth, three major changes appear on the side of demand. One is the extension of the division of labor already noticed: men attain a higher proficiency when they learn to perform only one or two of the many processes that go into making a product. In part this is because practice makes perfect, but only in part, for training up to the highest level of performance of which he is capable in one process usually leaves a man time to attain as high a level in another. The major gains when men specialize by process are rather that the proportion of their working life they spend in training is reduced; that since versatility is rare, most men can reach and maintain a higher level if they have to perform only one process; and that a man who has more aptitude for one process than another can, if he has been well guided, give all his time to what he can do best. The last consideration has an important bearing on the contention that specialization by process is degrading because it denies men variety and initiative and holds them to a dreary repetition. The charge holds when the process in which a man has specialized is below his capacity, and indeed there is no assurance that the range of specializations will match that of capacities, or that everyone will find his way into the specialization his own capacity matches; but the greater the range, the greater the opportunity for each man to give all his time to what fully extends him, and not have to do work he finds dull.

The second major change is an outcome of the growing size of enterprises. When a great part of production is carried on in small enterprises, many people will be employers, or self-employed, and combine with their daily work in a particular trade some functions of initiative, risk-bearing, and administration; and many of those who work for them will be members of their own families. As recently as in the 1950s, about a quarter of the whole labor force of both Japan and Italy consisted of employers and self-employed, and in Italy a further sixth, and in Japan a third, was made up of unpaid family workers. But agriculture, in which the small unit generally prevails, commonly loses ground to industry in the course of economic growth, and in industry itself the unit of enterprise expands. The proportion of the labor force that is occupied within the household consequently tends to fall; and so does that which is occupied at least in part in functions of management. This last tendency, however, has later been offset by the discovery of the high potential productivity of an expansion of management beyond those minimal requirements of quantity and quality that must be met if a business is to be carried on at all. In part this productivity arises from the need to make the best use of elaborate equipment and the technicians who serve it. A recent comparative study of management found that the large Egyptian textile mills "are among the most up-to-date if not the most modern in the world. Furthermore, they are equipped with the most advanced labor-saving machinery that money can buy." Yet "in the best Egyptian factories four to six workers may be employed for every one in comparable establishments in the United States. But, managerial resources are scarce and managerial methods are quite primitive."[3] The need is for quantity as well as quality. The same study compared a German and an American steel plant, each employing seventeen to eighteen thousand people. It was largely because the German plant had old machinery that its output was only half that of the American; but it was also notable that "in comparable steel making and rolling departments, the American company used three foremen to every one in the German mill," and for senior technical staff the ratio was ten to one.

This tendency to increase the relative size of managerial occupations at an advanced stage of economic development may be looked on as part of that general expansion of the clerical, technical, and administrative occupations which forms the third major change in the occupational structure of the demand for labor. This has been the most strongly marked development in the labor forces of Western countries since 1914. Its origins are in part social and political: the activities of central and local government have extended, partly under the pressure of two great wars, but also because people generally, whatever their abstract philosophy, have come to find a concrete advantage in using the machinery of government to control and promote more activities and provide more benefits. But the origins are also industrial. Part of the technique of "scientific management" was "to take the brains out of the job," that is, to extend the division of labor between manual operations and the tasks of designing prod-

3. J. D. Brown and F. H. Harbison, *High-Talent Manpower for Science and Industry* (Industrial Relations Section, Princeton University, 1957). See also F. H. Harbison, "Steel Management on Two Continents," *Relations Industrielles* (Revue Trimestrielle, Laval University, Quebec, Canada), March 1955.

ucts, solving problems, and organizing processes. At the same time the agencies of research, planning, communication, and control have been developed as part not of the dead weight or top-hamper of the factory but of its essential equipment: according to traditional nomenclature the labor in them is "unproductive," but in that sense the aim is now a factory without a single "productive" worker in it. So industry has come to employ more and more people at desks for every hundred at the bench; and within industry as well as in the community around it, more and more people have come to be occupied in designing products and processes, planning output, and collecting, analyzing, and communicating information.

In occupational as in industrial deployment, there have been changes initiated on the side of supply as well as of demand. Of these the most extensive has been the increased provision of general and technical education by public agencies, which was discussed in the last chapter. This has diminished the relative number of entrants to the labor force who are capable only of muscular exertion, and increased the relative number of those who have already reached the standards of education that are prerequisite for the attainment of manual skills and of proficiency in the clerical, technical, and administrative occupations.

The third dimension of deployment is regional. Some production must be located near the source of raw materials or power, some near the consumer, and some can be carried on at various points between, with its actual location a matter of accident or of the availability of labor. Little, therefore, can be said in a general way about the changes that occur in the regional deployment of a population in the course of economic growth. But one tendency seems to be a function of growth, namely urbanization. A high density of population naturally occurs where raw materials are concentrated or the channels of trade converge, but the urbanization with which we are concerned arises when the reason for one man's working in a given place is only that others are working there too. This reason may make itself felt in various ways. For firms there are external economies in proximity, through the common services that will grow up and the breadth of the common labor market. For many types of activity, moreover, aggregate costs of transport are reduced by location near the customer: electricity has removed some of the limits formerly set by the cost of carrying fuel; and the more highly fabricated products that enter into higher standards of living tend to be more costly to move than are the raw materials they are made from. So the mere fact that there is already, for whatever reason, a concentration of production and therefore of consumers in a certain place tends to bring more production in: save for zoning by public authorities, there seems to be no reason why a new plant not tied by its nature to sources of raw material or water should not always come in to raise a density already high, unless it be the deterrent of high land values there or the attraction of untapped sources of labor elsewhere. Hence an urban concentration of the demand for labor. But there are also factors at work to concentrate the supply. The worker in the large town feels he has some greater security and opportunity through the greater number and variety of jobs within his reach—a man seeking a job or a fortune commonly moves from the country to the town, and not the other way round. Some amenities of residence are available only in the countryside, but others, especially of entertainment and society, are available only in the town, and these are more attractive to many, perhaps most, people. All these reasons help to account for the fact that population does not grow evenly

throughout a country in the course of its economic development, nor concentrate only on the veins and nodal points of
natural resources, but agglomerates wherever it was densest
to start with. In Japan, in 1920, less than an eighth of the
population was in towns of more than 100,000 inhabitants,
but by 1940 the proportion was approaching one-third, and
of the total increase in numbers in the five years before 1940,
about three-quarters went into the six big cities. In the United States in the 1950s nearly two-thirds of the whole population was classified as urban.

When we ask whether industry has settled in the towns
because the people were there, or the people have settled
because industry was there, we raise again the problem of
the mutual adjustment between vacancies and applicants
that has run through all our discussion of changes in deploy
ment. In the tracts we have been surveying, the problem has
seldom been solved on any scale by planning and direction.
Within any one household or farm or firm, it is true, the head
may decide what jobs are to be done by an existing labor
force, and allocate its members to them. But over most of
the economy there has been no such plan, and various forces
have played upon the allocation independently: consumers
have generally been free to spend their money on what they
choose, managers to make changes in methods, workers to
take what jobs they prefer among those within their reach.
One might suppose that these freedoms are incompatible
with one another: how can consumers be entitled by switching their outlay to direct production into this or that particular line, when producers are entitled to take what line
they choose?

We know that there has been no clear-cut solution, but a
rough adjustment has gone on from day to day in a world
of immobilities, predilections, incentives, and tolerances. The

processes of this adjustment have been threefold. First, workers have been trained to fill jobs, and job requirements have been trimmed to the capacities of workers: this we discussed in the last chapter. Second, the choices made by consumers, managers, and workers react upon one another, and are shaken down together, through the interplay of supply and demand in the pricing system: we will go on to look at this in the chapter following. At any one time the adjustments of these first two kinds will have provided one pattern of jobs available for workers and another of workers available for jobs: the two will match each other largely but not completely, and where they overlap they call for a movement of workers to jobs and of jobs to workers. The workings of this third kind of adjustment through the labor market we will consider here.

THE WORKINGS OF LABOR MARKETS

The function of a market is to bring buyers and sellers into touch with one another. The fulfillment of that function by labor markets has never been more than partial and imperfect.

A general meeting of buyers and sellers of labor used to take place in some parts of Britain where farm servants were hired for a year at a time; in the fall a fair was held, at which those seeking engagement stood each with an emblem of his trade in hand, and the farmers walked round and discussed terms with them. In the nineteenth century in Scotland those terms rose and fell with the trade cycle and the demand for labor in the towns. In North China in more recent years, "for extra men, to work by the day at harvest time, spring and fall, the employers went to the 'man market' which usually was held before sunrise at some central place in the village. The employers would circulate among the waiting workers quoting the price they would pay. The 'condition of the market' would naturally push wages up to a peak at the height of the harvest and drop them rapidly thereafter."[4] More often it has happened that those seeking work present themselves together, and an employer who wants labor will take his pick, but the applicants have little chance to play off one employer's offer against another's. In the manufacturing towns of medieval Europe, the journeymen wanting work went to the market place in the morning, to hire themselves out by the day or the week. In India, to this day, craftsmen walk the streets with the tools of their trade, or sit each at his door, waiting to be engaged. Casual labor, so called because at each hiring the applicant has only a chance of being taken on, has commonly had to appear in a body at the hiring point. So it has been throughout the docks of the world, until decasualization schemes have been applied and the enrolled docker has been assured of some payment for attendance even when there is no work for him that day. In Britain before 1914 groups of casual workers could be found waiting in many other places where the work load varied from day to day—at the railway yards, the warehouses, the butchers' and bakers'. In the textile mills of India a substantial proportion of the workers are nominally substitutes for absentees: a crowd of such *badlis* waits at the gate each morning for the foreman or sirdar to take those he chooses, whether by rotation, seniority, or favor, for the one day's work. Where countryfolk come in to seek employment in a new factory, whether in Egypt or the southern United States, they will very likely stand in a throng to be hired. "When a company opens a new plant

4. S. D. Gamble, *Ting Hsien: A North China Rural Community* (New York, Institute of Pacific Relations, 1954), p. 221.

in rural Georgia or Tennessee, five to ten thousand applicants may be lined up at the gate when hiring starts, and some may have come five hundred miles."[5]

But more often the applicants do not present themselves together to an employer; still less do employers meet in one place to hire. The market is defined rather by potentialities of individual access. For a given employer there are a certain number of workers who could possibly work for him, and with whom he is in touch or can get in touch. For a given worker, similarly, there are a certain number of potential employers within his reach and his actual or potential knowledge. Where a set of employers and a set of workers exist so that each member of one set has potential connections with a number of members of the other, and relatively few with outsiders, the two sets may be said to constitute a market. But the members may see little of each other; their knowledge of each other may be vague and fragmentary; and they may meet only as one employer and one applicant at a time, without either having much immediate opportunity to compare alternative offers.

Some markets, so defined, are nationwide, and even in part international. Generally, in the more technical occupations and the professions, the main features both of the position offered and of the applicant's qualifications can be presented initially on paper; though personal qualities must be tested by interview, the cost of the required journeys bears a small proportion to the annual salary of the post; and the members of these occupations have not only the resources to move, with or without assistance from their new employer, but also the expectation of moving from time to time in the course of their careers, and the greater adaptability given by higher

5. E. Ginzberg, *Human Resources: The Wealth of a Nation* (New York, 1958), p. 48.

education. The main means of communication for changes of job in such a market as this is the advertisement in the newspaper or trade journal. The terms offered in these advertisements will have their influence on the adjustments being made from time to time in the terms of existing engagements throughout the market.

But more often the effective labor market is restricted to one locality, whose bounds lie within a radius of less than a day's journey from where the workers are living. The limits are set partly by the difficulty of making contact over greater distances, partly by the reluctance of the worker to move far away from the place and society with which he is familiar. A study of histories of workers in a factory city of New England in 1947 found that 60 per cent had not worked outside the area, and 75 per cent had not worked outside the state.[6] A similar inquiry in Britain in 1949 found that "geographical change is largely a change from one town to another within the same region. Even so, nearly half the population has worked in one town only and a further quarter in two towns only. Three quarters of the population have worked in one region only. Few have worked in more than two regions."[7] Shifts in the preponderance of population across the whole length and breadth of a country, such as the growth of northwestern England in the Industrial Revolution, and of southeastern England since the First World War, have been brought about mostly by the cumulation of short intermediate movements, with few people moving all the way between the opposite poles of growth. Women are even less ready or able than men to take a job that means a change of

6. L. G. Reynolds, *The Structure of Labor Markets* (New York, 1951), pp. 77-78.

7. U.K. Social Survey, Report 134, *Labour Mobility in Great Britain 1945-49* (not printed, c.1952), Pt. I, 3.C.

residence. Workers may be reluctant to move far in space even where, as in the United States, they show "a surprising propensity to make drastic changes in their work status," and move readily from one occupation or industry to another.[8]

The limiting factor is not strictly distance in miles but the cost, time, and trouble of the journey; and the improvement of roads and the coming of railroads did much to throw together markets that were once separate. This has been associated with some of the origins of trade unionism, for it exposed the worker to more competition for his job. More recent changes in transport, however, which have shortened distances not so much between markets as within them, have worked the other way. The improvement of local travel by subway, streetcar, and train, by bus, and, in some countries, by the workers' own motorcycles and cars, has increased very greatly the number of jobs accessible to the average worker from his present house. The consequent reduction of the imperfections of the market shows itself as a major change in the working of Western economies whenever unemployment is low, for employers must now find themselves in more effective competition with each other than they used to be at that level of aggregate demand. The short distance between alternative employers and the availability of local transport may have been part of the reason why earnings in cities have been generally higher than in regions of lower density. As more and easier transport reduces the effective distances within these regions too, we may expect that the flash point at which the aggregate demand for labor begins to make earnings rise will be generally lowered.

But however easy the communications within the local market, the information on which its members act is still

8. W. Haber, et al., eds., *Manpower in the United States: Problems and Policies* (New York, 1954), p. 151.

likely to be rough and meager. Most workers who are old enough to have settled down and found by trial and error a job that is "not too bad" have no intention of leaving it in quest of something better, and do not keep themselves posted on alternatives. Those who do want to change, or being out of work need to find a job, can by their own efforts learn about only part of the field, and in any case can hardly tell what a new job will be really like until they have tried it. This does seem bound to make the market very imperfect. "The typical worker," Lloyd Reynolds has concluded, "has no sensation of being in 'a labor market'. He has no idea of the full range of jobs, wage rates and working conditions prevailing in the area; nor does he have any realization of the hundreds or thousands of job vacancies available on a particular day."[9] He does not do much window-shopping before he takes a job, but is guided by tips from friends and relatives, and by the chances of propinquity. The employer, for his part, it is true, can advertise his vacancies to a wide range of readers, but in practice he is likely to recruit mostly from those who are brought along by his present workers and those who live nearby.

Yet we must not overestimate the effect of these imperfections of knowledge. Most workers are not desirous of moving, but neither do they want to stay where they are and watch other men's pay rise relative to theirs: the sensitiveness of pay claims to changes in differentials suggests that actual immobility may be conditional upon the market having provided no sufficient inducement to move. In times of peace employments seldom expand or contract so rapidly that their changes cannot be accommodated by the movements of a fringe of workers already in jobs, and some diversion of the

9. Reynolds, *The Structure of Labor Markets*, p. 85.

young entrant. Here as elsewhere in human behavior—notably in the consumer's reaction to a change in price—movements that individually are rough and ready, hit or miss affairs, but at the same time are subject to some common influence, may compose in the aggregate the curve of a functional relation.

Nonetheless, it is greatly in the common interest to raise the level of information in the labor market, and this has been attempted by two kinds of agencies—vocational guidance and the employment exchange.

The object of the first is to inform young people about the requirements and rewards of different occupations, and to help each to choose one that will suit his own tastes and aptitudes. Without such guidance young people, and their parents, are apt to give too much weight to the pay offered in the short run, or, insofar as they take the longer view, to be influenced by current notions that accord prestige to some occupations and industries and dismiss others as unfashionable; they may also have no very clear appreciation of what doors are opened and closed to them by their own attainments. Vocational guidance therefore tries to provide young people with a picture of the prospects that various occupations and industries offer them throughout a working life, to set out the training required before and after entry, and to help them make a realistic assessment of their own tastes and aptitudes, which they can then compare with the requirements and prospects of different callings. Early in the present century there were vocational guidance centers in various towns of France, Holland, and Switzerland, but the first legislative provision seems to have been the setting up of Juvenile Advisory Committees under the British Labour Exchanges Act of 1909. The prevailing contemporary administration in Britain is by a partnership between the Ministries of Education and Labour—the first entry into insured employment is a natural point at which to make sure that every entrant has been offered guidance—and the Ministries work through local committees that include representative employers and trade unionists. But however good the system, there will be many young people who will pay little heed to it, and some of those who do use it will make mistakes nonetheless. So there still has to be much learning of what jobs are like by trial and error, and that means much chopping and changing by young people. It is important accordingly that entry to organized training within industry should not be confined to the school-leaving ages but be open to some who are making a fresh start later on. Here British apprenticeship, which generally can be entered at not more than sixteen years of age, is at a disadvantage in comparison with the United States, where the usual age of entry is from eighteen to twenty-five.

The second agency is the employment exchange. Its object is to inform each applicant of the range of vacancies for which he seems eligible, and each employer of the applicants who might suit him. Some exchanges have long been operated for particular occupations by private enterprise—for actors, secretaries, nurses, and domestic servants, for instance. Trade unions, especially craft unions, often serve as an exchange for their members: the employer with a vacancy calls the union office, and the members seeking work attend in a hiring hall, or wait for a message at home. The union network may cover more than the local market, and it has long been the practice of some unions to inform their branches of the towns in which there are jobs vacant, and help their unemployed members to reach them. In France in the seventeenth and eighteenth centuries there were two nationwide unions, the Gavots and the Dévorants, each of which kept an inn in the chief towns for its itinerant members and had its *capitaine placeur,* who maintained liaison with the capitaines of other towns, so as to keep his members informed of the state of the market. But today the exchanges that cater for all comers are those maintained by governments. Potentially, these exchanges might give every employer and worker a far wider view of the opportunities offered him by the market than his own contacts can provide: employers could then use the exchanges as their channel of recruitment for vacancies at all levels; and workers of all sorts, though in good jobs already, could keep in touch with the exchanges for the same reason that the professional worker casts his eye down the situations-vacant column in a journal. In this way the employment exchange would fulfill the purpose of general information and contact served by the floor of the produce or stock exchange from which it draws its name. But such a perfecting of the market requires a general agreement to make use of the exchanges that has never come about. Some firms do make regular use of them, most firms use them occasionally; but among the workers there is a feeling that the good jobs are filled directly, which has its counterpart in a presumption among employers that only the weaker applicants are left for the exchange to place. So though the activities of the exchanges have widened, their principal function remains to help those who cannot find a job by direct application, which is still the chief procedure of the labor market.

Inadequacy of information does not inhibit a great deal of movement. Between 1947 and 1950 almost all hirings in Britain had to be registered with the Employment Exchanges, and they proved to be running then at the rate of about one in five of the working population each year. This was a time of full employment, and what evidence we have suggests that the rate of turnover falls when employment falls, and was much lower in the interwar years. The British inquiry of 1949, already mentioned, attempted to find the motivation of the high rate of change by interviewing a sample of those who had made at least one change in the past four years:

> 24 per cent of all those interviewed had left their previous job because they were dismissed or declared redundant. 39 per cent had left because of bad pay, prospects or conditions, or because there were better pay and prospects elsewhere. 35 per cent had left for personal reasons associated with health, family, or desire for a change, or, alternatively, to set up their own business or find work nearer home. . . . A greater number of men and women thought their present wages, hours and conditions were good, than had thought their previous wages, hours and conditions were good. Similarly, a higher proportion of informants liked their present job than had liked their previous job.[10]

Even at the lower rate of the interwar years, this kind of movement was enough, together with the allocation of the new entrants to employment, to change the industrial deployment of the British labor force radically in a short span of time: between 1927 and 1937, for example, the numbers of workers in coal mining and in cotton both fell by more than a quarter, but the numbers in entertainment and sports, and in electrical cable, apparatus, and lamps, more than doubled, and those in electrical wiring and contracting came near trebling.

10. U.K. Social Survey, *Report on Labour Turnover in Great Britain, 1945–49* (not printed, c. 1952), p.2.

Deployment of the Labor Force

Nonetheless, new or growing firms have often found no sufficient supply of labor presenting itself to them, and have had to rely on subcontractors for labor, or develop their own recruitment agencies, or locate themselves specially where labor was available.

After the end of the slave trade a form of recruitment of coolies from abroad, usually for plantations and mines, was devised in "contract labor." In return for free transport and perhaps a cash advance, the coolie agreed to work in a given undertaking for a term of years. Large numbers of Chinese and Indians migrated, particularly to the East and West Indies, under these arrangements. The contract laborer's condition varied widely in practice, as did the extent of the protection that he came to be afforded by public regulation, but his contract could be enforced in a way that brought it near slavery; and even when his term was up, he might be held in bondage for debt.

Where recruitment is difficult in the underdeveloped countries today, many businesses pay subcontractors a lump sum for the labor of a gang, whose members' own pay comes from the subcontractor; or, though they pay the workers themselves, they leave recruitment and discharge in the hands of their foremen, the sirdars or *maistrys*. In either case there is a "squeeze": the gangmaster pays out less than he receives; the foreman takes bribes from workers desperately in need of jobs. But if that need is so great, why cannot firms recruit directly? It looks as though they could pay their workers more while reducing their own labor costs, simply by cutting out the middleman, or transferring engagement and discharge to their own employment office; but, despite some endeavors, generally they have not yet done so. Why? For some firms the reason lies in their having to work in places where there is an insufficient supply of labor locally, or their having to bring labor from a distance to meet a seasonal peak in the work load: the coffee plantations of south India and the tea gardens of Assam use local recruiting agents to bring bands of workers with them from their own districts—perhaps hundreds of miles away—and take charge of them on arrival. Again, where the managers are expatriates or, though nationals, do not speak the local tongue, they have to rely on foremen who do.

But the system prevails even where these things are not so. The basic reason may be found in the poor quality of the available labor, and its lack of adaptation to the factory. Underfed, accustomed to underemployment, unfamiliar not only with machinery but also with the continuity of attention it demands, this labor will work only in fits and starts unless it is under close control. So the foreman has to be held responsible for getting the work out, and must be armed with the power to hire and fire. Managers cannot take that power back from him until they have workers to employ who will perform their tasks under supervisors who have no such whip hand.

This explanation may be supported by the limited use made of the subcontracting of labor in more developed countries. It was once common in mining, as in the "butty system" in Britain; it is used in some "labor only" contracts in building; and under full employment it is extending in catering. The problem in mining was to provide effective supervision of scattered groups whose tasks were hard. In building, the "labor only" contract has been used in practice to get a higher rate of output—for example, in bricklaying—than could be obtained under normal supervision. The shortage of labor in catering, and the high turnover of what there is, has made it worthwhile for institutions in which catering is only ancillary to pay specialists to bear the responsibility of maintaining a staff. The common elements are a need to give first-line supervision more driving power, and a lack of staying power, in both senses of the term, in the workers. These seem to be the reasons that induce or compel management to delegate recruitment and discharge.

Even where long years of economic development have formed a labor force habituated to steady work in industry, some firms do not rely for recruitment solely on what the market can offer from day to day, but develop their own agencies and programs. Industries planted in undeveloped countries may have to send far afield for their technicians and craftsmen, and governments have long taken a hand in this, welcoming religious and political refugees who brought their trades with them, offering weavers land for settlement, or— as in fifteenth-century Spain and even earlier in southern India—exempting the immigrant craftsman from taxation. When Britain had a technical lead in the early days of its Industrial Revolution, its skilled men were sought overseas —so much so that from 1782 to 1824 they were forbidden by law to leave the country. As science is increasingly applied to industry, firms come to need technical specialists of kinds not provided through the broad channels of professional training, and must seek them either at the few schools that exist for them (at certain university laboratories, for example) or in younger recruits of a caliber to warrant the firm's paying for their perhaps lengthy training, which may include general education. A wider inducement lies in a growing awareness of the productivity of talent and training, not in technicians only but in managers generally, that leads firms to send out their scouts, make the prospects they offer known in the schools, and generally try to tap ability at the source, and program its development. Even for unskilled labor, full employment leads firms to send its prospectors far afield to find new sources.

An alternative is to take the job to the worker, and locate new plants where those sources are. Gaining access to less restricted or cheaper labor has long been a motive promoting the dispersion of industry. In medieval Europe industry moved into the countryside to be able to hire men who were not journeymen under the restrictions of the guilds, and to take advantage of the peasant's seasonal lack of work; and again in France in the eighteenth century, manufacturers were bypassing the wage rates for which journeymen held out in the established textile centers, by setting looms up in the countryside where there was unemployment or underemployment. Similarly in Japan before modern industrialization set in, a growth of rural industry was promoted by the restrictions of the guilds in the towns and the lower wages due to the lower cost of living and the plentiful supply of partially occupied labor in the country: the silk industry, once the virtual monopoly of the artisans of one district in Kyoto, spread out through the villages. When much later, in the interwar years, this industry fell on evil days, munition factories were set up in the countryside. The movement of industry into the southern United States, and especially the displacement of much textile output from New England, provides a counterpart. More generally, the sheer unavailability of further supplies of labor in established centers in recent years of full employment has forced firms to place new plants where labor was available, even though the location imposed higher costs in other ways. The main reserve of labor now consists of women as yet occupied only in the home, and these can go out to work only if jobs are provided close at hand. Their numbers vary with the industrial structure of the district: a smaller proportion of the women will already be going out to work in a mining than in a textile district, and in Britain the mining districts of Yorkshire, for instance, have attracted light industry because they could offer more women recruits than the adjacent towns which were woolen textile centers.

Despite all the adjustments between applicants and vacancies that we have been considering, some part of the labor force generally remains unengaged. There may be underemployment, or outright unemployment.

One form of underemployment arises when the work load fluctuates seasonally, as in cereal cultivation. The farmer who specializes in cereals is busy when he is ploughing and sowing and harvesting but has little to do in between, so that he is not employed for all the working hours that he could readily put in during the year. But the number of men occupied in this kind of cultivation could not necessarily be reduced without loss of output, so that we can speak of underemployment only if we can assume the possibility of employment in some other line of output during the slack season. In the rice fields of China and Japan one such possibility has been found in a winter migration, of the peasants' sons at least, into the towns, and into such industries as mining, lumbering, and brewing. A better remedy is to bring in industries that either, like sericulture, can be dovetailed with work in the fields, or provide a separate and more continuous occupation for members of the farming family who otherwise would be occupied only at the times of seasonal pressure. During the Second World War "subsidiary occupations" were bringing the Japanese peasantry about twice as much income as did agriculture. "In many parts of the country," it has been said of the United States, "farming is becoming a part-time occupation. In 1955, only one in every four families living on a farm supported themselves solely from agriculture."[11]

Whether there is much seasonal fluctuation or not, there may also be underemployment on the land when more persons share the cultivation of a given area of land than would suffice to raise the same output from it if each put in a normal annual sum of working hours. The picture is familiar of rural overpopulation, with a growing number finding a subsistence from the same family holding and sharing as much work as its limited acreage allows to be done. Yet how much underemployment there is, by the strict criterion of the possibility of withdrawing labor without loss of output, remains a matter of some controversy. For technique adapts itself to the relative plenty and scarcity of the factors of production: holdings, for example, will be subdivided, and draught animals given up; a withdrawal of labor, without an immediate change of technique, would then cause a fall in output. The case can be important for the emergent economies, for it means that they cannot draw a labor force from the countryside to man their new industries while raising the agricultural surplus available to feed the towns, unless at the same time they improve the technique of agriculture.

Though farming methods are adapted to absorb more labor, if population goes on rising there will be an overspill. Some of this enters into the casual and intermittent employment of coolie and badli, and makes up that semidestitute mass of labor in the towns where, as Tawney remarked of China, there is "no sharp division between the workers and

11. Ginzberg, *Human Resources: The Wealth of a Nation*, p. 48.

the workless":[12] the same could have been said of as much as a quarter of the labor in the cities of Britain before 1914. In Japan we have already met the other outlet of the overspill: the service trades, where men can make jobs for themselves by setting up as shopkeepers and handymen—and wait for customers most of the day. Where they provide domestic service, they insist on demarcations of duty that result in more servants being used than there is work for. Though usually unorganized, they combine spontaneously to resist any reduction in the number over whom tasks are spread.

Short of emigration, help for the underemployed of this kind can come from economic development, to provide the equipment, direction, and training with which alone they can produce as much as an adequate standard of living would require them to consume. When in Italy about 1950 there were nearly two million unemployed, it was reckoned that there were even more underemployed, and a main object of the Vanoni plan was to take up some of this slack.

In outright unemployment, a man who expects to be in full-time work is not working at all because he cannot find a job. We can make an approximate distinction between causes general and particular. The general causes operate through the movements of aggregate effective demand, and affect many trades and regions at much the same time; the particular causes result in an excess of applicants over vacancies of a specific kind, at this specific point or that. But the distinction can be only approximate, because when the level of aggregate effective demand rises or falls it changes for different products in different degrees, and so alters the disparities point by point. We cannot say that the unemployment of certain men is part of general unemployment simply

12. Tawney, *Land and Labour in China*, p. 121.

because a rise in aggregate demand would end it, for that rise might at the same time carry the demand for labor at other points well above the supply, and in that region, at least, be inflationary. A sufficient inflation will wipe out practically all unemployment; if aggregate demand, on the other hand, is kept down to the level at which the demand for labor does not more than match the supply in any part of the market, a volume of unemployment will probably remain such as we normally associate with a slump. But though in this way the workings of general and particular causes are intertwined, we can make a rough distinction between unemployment that can be removed by raising aggregate demand to a level at which local inflationary pressures are only just beginning to be felt, and that which then remains. This level will be higher in a country where the prevailing pattern of demand is closely congruent with current capacities than in one where there are structural disparities, and the rate of unemployment that remains when the level is reached will differ accordingly from one country to another. The numerical value of this rate will also vary with the way in which statistics of unemployment are compiled: but we may say that at present it seems to be about 1.5 per cent as unemployment is reckoned in the United Kingdom, and perhaps 4 per cent as it is reckoned in the United States. In our present study of deployment it is this residual unemployment with which we are mainly concerned.

It has four main components. First, at any one time some people are in the midst of changing jobs, and there may be some interval between the old job and the new, even though the possibility of finding a new one was never in doubt. When covered by insurance, this transitional unemployment raises few problems. Second, there are defects of personal quality that do not stand out enough to prevent a man from ever getting a job but generally prevent him from holding it for long, whether it is he who quits or the employer who cannot put up with him. With some people, again, illness recurs so frequently—it may be psychogenic—that they cannot keep at work for long. Some defects of mind or body are consistent with steady work if the right job can be found; but it seems that the sources of instability can be reached only in the clinic, if at all. A third component is due to fluctuations of demand in the short period—the irregular rush and pause of work in the docks, or the rhythm of the week, the month, and the natural and conventional seasons of the year. In the past this sort of unemployment has fused with the second because it was the poorest human material that had to take the most irregular work: since then, the disappearance of much of the supply has starved out much of the demand. Much has also been done in recent years, through the pressures of trade unions, public opinion, and, above all, full employment, to even the work load where that is possible, bring in complementary enterprises that will utilize labor in its off season, and keep men in steady employment even where the work load still fluctuates. But difficulties persist where the seasonal trade is regionally concentrated: British seaside resorts, for instance, are trying to attract light industry that will provide employment for some members of the family throughout the year and, if possible, be able to take on more during the winter.

There remains the fourth component, and it makes up the hard core: it is the unemployment that is caused jointly by a permanent withdrawal of demand, and the inability of some of those whose jobs have gone to find new ones. Falls in the demand for the product of particular industries and regions are inevitable in a world of change and international trade, and the cause to attack is the immobility of the victim.

In British experience this arises in part from age, in part from a lack of adaptability and a sense of insecurity that make some men shrink from the unknown; but the greatest difficulty is the need to move to a strange place. If the general level of employment is not high, a man who moves to a new job may lose it before long and find himself with less support than if he were still out of work at home, whereas if the level is high, housing will be scarcest where jobs are most plentiful. Not many people choose to move to a strange neighborhood, once they are married and settled and have a family about them, and the ties of kin and neighborhood mean even more to those whose self-confidence has been undercut by their being discarded. So though public employment agencies can help many men to move by rehabilitation and retraining, by grants toward the cost of moving and help in housing at the destination, those who use the aids will mostly be in the categories which are generally mobile. The remainder may be numerous. Public policy can help them to find jobs only by amplifying or diverting those forces, already noted here, that direct new plants to available labor. The government may be able to locate some of its own activities in the regions of higher unemployment. Private enterprise may be pushed or drawn there, by refusal of permission to build where employment is already high, by forms of subsidy—such as the provision of capital, or of industrial estates with buildings ready to lease at low rents, and houses for the cadres that must be moved in—and by the directors' public spirit or wish to stand well with the government. These things may tilt the balance when the availability of labor, set off against the costs of transport to and from the site, do not leave it at much disadvantage with alternative locations. But, in general, the higher the rate of unemployment, the more remote will the locality be, and the higher will be the differential cost of operating there. The strong tendency of recent years to reduce and eliminate regional differentials in pay removes a former offset to costs of transport. It is hard to determine how far the gain of national product from using labor otherwise idle, and the gain to human welfare and self-respect through ending unemployment, can go in each particular case to offset the continuing loss of product through the dispersion and displacement of production that they require.

COMPULSION IN THE ALLOCATION OF LABOR TO JOBS

So far we have been considering the movements of workers to jobs and jobs to workers on the general assumption that people are free to make their own arrangements. In the expanse of human history this state of affairs is rare and recent. What work a man shall do has commonly been delimited or prescribed by custom and class interest. Rulers have conscripted men for specific tasks, and held them to particular callings as their life's work. Any plan for economic development implies changes in the deployment of the labor force, and governments that make such plans have put workers under various degrees of pressure and coercion. Let us now examine some of these constraints and directions.

One of the oldest is the rule that the son must follow his father's calling. In Homeric Greece the craftsman's calling was hereditary: masons, carpenters, smiths, and potters were known as *demiourgoi*—those who serve the people—and had something of the status and obligations both of public functionaries and of a hereditary priesthood. In this they have been compared with the caste of the Sudra in India. The Indian caste system itself is changing now under political and economic pressures, and it has never coincided entirely with division by occupation, but it has included some narrowly occupational castes—most children born into it have been precluded from entering certain callings, and some have been allowed to enter only one. A village of the Deccan, for instance, even in recent years, might have its *komtis* or traders, its *gollas* or shepherds, its *vaddars* or stoneworkers, and its untouchable *madigas,* who disposed of dead cattle, worked up the hide, and played the drums and pipes at ceremonies: and all these occupations were hereditary. We hear[13] of one village that has gone without fish, although it needs the food and has a well-stocked lake, because it happens to have no fishing caste.

But one purpose of a hereditary system is to ensure that there shall be no such gaps; and the requirement that the son step into his father's place, which we have seen enforced by custom here, has been made a rule of law by heavy-handed governments that seek to keep up the output of industries without letting men earn enough to stay in them of their own free will. The Roman emperors laid obligations on the "colleges" of traders and manufacturers—the shipowners were required to devote three-quarters of their earnings to new construction, the butchers were fined if they did not keep up the supply of pork—and it followed that the members of these "corporations," now compulsory, were forbidden to leave their calling, and that their sons were required to follow them in it. Similarly, in the enterprises that the state itself conducted—whether these were the manufactures of vegetable oil and papyrus in Hellenistic Egypt or the workshops making arms for the Roman legions or the great factories of Byzantium—if the workers were forbidden to leave, and their sons were compelled to follow them in their trades,

13. S. C. Dube, *Indian Village* (Ithaca, New York, 1955), p. 85.

we must suppose it was because the pay was not good enough to attract and retain a force of volunteers.

But the most widespread use of compulsion to keep a labor force together has been on the land. Rulers unable or unwilling to use the workings of the market and the self-interest of the farmer have always had a problem of the agricultural surplus—of deliveries, as it has come to be called: how can the farmer be made to produce more food than he needs himself, and hand it over for the support of the ruler, his fighting men and governors, and the folk in his towns? One way has been to plant men on the land, make them work for "the estate" as well as for themselves, and flog them if they try to run away. The Roman emperors, at a time when land was going out of cultivation while the plebs of the town needed corn, settled slaves, prisoners of war, debtors, and beggars on the state lands as *colons*. The Eastern Empire was to do the same, and here the colons included a class of settler that recurs in history, the heretic getting away from his orthodox persecutor. The colon was "tied to the soil," but part of the soil was for practical purposes a holding of his own, and he could pass it on to his son; in return, he worked for so many days in the year on the acres that the overlord kept for his own use. There was a rough equivalence here, and an incentive for the colon; he gave his labor services to keep his holding. So the arrangement worked—better than slavery, the Roman owners of the great private estates found when they went over to it; and in various forms of serfdom it was to govern the deployment of the greater part of the labor force throughout Europe. It prevailed also in some form in Japan: here the *nago* held land, and was supplied with irrigation, in return for labor services that might amount to as many as two hundred days in the year. One variant, here as in Europe, was that the occupier paid a rent in kind—half or

The Economics of Labor

three-fourths of his rice crop, it might be—instead of giving day labor. The common elements were that he had land to work for himself, and that he was forbidden to leave it. As markets and manufactures developed, he did often see the chance of a better living in the town. The Black Death, which carried off perhaps a third of the labor force of England about 1350, increased that unsettlement, and a statute of 1388, endeavoring to contain it, provided "that he or she who is employed in labouring at the plough and cart or other labour or service of husbandry until they be of the age of twelve years shall remain thenceforward at that labour without being put to a mistery or craft."[14] In Japan the government tried to stop the peasant from moving into weaving by repeatedly forbidding merchants to buy silk in the villages, and from the sixteenth century onward it tried to keep the peasant tied to his holding under penalties of law.

Rulers have not only had the problem of squeezing out an agricultural surplus: in economies where they cannot raise much revenue by taxes in money they have also had to use forced labor for various public works and services. In Babylon from the earliest times there was a royal corvée for works of irrigation; in Japan we hear of eighty thousand men being assembled for such works in the eighth century A.D., and some were maintained by corvée until the Second World War. Roads have long been built and maintained, after a fashion, by the forced labor of those who live near them—whether under the direction of the legionaries of Rome or of the tribal chiefs of Uganda in our own day. Transport, too, has been provided by compulsion: in ancient China we hear of sixty thousand men being used for carrying grain to the

14. Statute of 12 Richard II, cap. 5, in A. E. Bland, P. A. Brown, and R. H. Tawney, *English Economic History, Select Documents* (London, Bell, 1914), p. 174.

capital; in British territories in Africa the corvée was continued for carrying after it had been given up for other work. The Japanese port of Kobe was built in the fourteenth century by the forced labor, it is said, of fifty thousand men. There has often been conscription for military service, and this continues in democratic societies to our own day, alongside the provision of terms of service sufficiently attractive to maintain forces by voluntary enlistment. A cognate corvée is for military works. Japanese farmers were taken off the land to build castles. The English kings of the Middle Ages blended the corvée with the workings of the free market: craftsmen would be ordered, on pain of imprisonment, to proceed to the site of some castle, chapel, or palace the king was building, but when they arrived they were paid rather above the rate prevailing for free engagements.

Though we have seen compulsion used to keep men out of industry, it has also been used to get an industrial labor force together. When we hear of the workers for state manufactures being impressed, as in Hellenistic Egypt, we may surmise that the state was not paying enough to attract voluntary recruits. When the government of the Commonwealth in England in 1655 ordered young men and maids not to stay at home but "with all convenient speed betake themselves to service," it said explicitly that it did so because they were refusing to work at the rates of pay the authorities had fixed. Sometimes a labor force has been found by impressing vagrants: Justinian gave the vagabonds to the bakers of Constantinople; and an Act of 1606 in Scotland gave "power and commission to all masters and owners of coal-heughs and salt-pans to apprehend all vagabonds and sturdy beggars to be put to labour."[15] When industries are introduced to a so-

15. R. P. Arnot, *A History of the Scottish Miners* (London, Allen and Unwin, 1955), p. 4.

ciety unaccustomed to them, they may find it hard to get labor, even in the midst of underemployment, and governments have used or delegated various forms of compulsion to bring labor in. Down to the seventeenth century the English government tried from time to time to apply the principle that any unoccupied person must take work offered, or go to the stocks or the house of correction. In France in the eighteenth century manufacturers were given the exclusive right to collect labor, possibly by force, in one district, and children and paupers were drafted into industry from orphanage and almshouse. In parts of Africa, under European administration, the imposition of taxes to be paid by the native in money had as one of its objects and effects the bringing in of labor to earn the wherewithal by a spell of wage earning. Of Portuguese East Africa in 1960 it was reported that "every male African over 18 is compelled to work for at least six months in the year,"[16] on the ground that this is the only way to habituate him to the work and rewards of industrial development; he could not be compelled to work for a particular private employer, but found his job through a contractor, who recruited up-country and provided transport.

As the modern course of economic growth took its rise, from the eighteenth century onward, governments in the growing economies generally gave up the attempt to restrict and direct the movements of labor. Many did continue to act indirectly on the deployment of jobs by protecting particular industries, and one motive of protecting agriculture was to keep manpower on the land, perhaps as a source of sturdy soldiers. But to act directly on the deployment of applicants was another matter: it ran contrary to contemporary reliance on personal initiative and to the principle of per-

16. *The Times* (London), June 21, 1960.

sonal freedom, and in times of growing population and rapid economic change it was in any case impracticable.

In time of war, however, countries normally averse to the direction of labor have had to push through vast changes in the size and deployment of their labor force within two or three years. In the Second World War, for instance, the employed labor force of the United States grew from 47 to 64 million; and in the United Kingdom 10 million people—as many as half the whole prewar working population—learned new jobs in industry or the armed forces. Changes of that extent and speed could not have been made without intervention by government.

In the United States, however, that intervention was to control jobs rather than men. There was, of course, a draft for the armed forces, and the national employment service helped in many ways to bring job and applicant together; but otherwise the applicant was left free to take jobs and leave them, and it was the pattern of jobs that the government molded. It did so by issuing contracts for war needs, cutting back supplies of materials for nonessential products, and locating new plants where labor was available. Without having been directed to do so men and women moved into the new deployment because they wanted to help the war effort, they could take jobs only where jobs were going, and earnings on war work were raised by piece rates and overtime to levels that a widely effective control of wages prevented other employments from matching.

The United Kingdom went further, and brought pressures to bear on particular men and women. One reason was that the employed labor force as a whole could be increased by well over a third in the United States, but by less than a sixth in the United Kingdom, which therefore had to do more to ensure that what manpower there was went where it was most needed, and that everyone who could work did work. There were three further motives: the control of hiring reinforced the other means of restricting unessential activities; when many people had to suffer hardship it was fair that no one should escape doing his bit; and the movements of wages could be left to the normal processes of bargaining, as in fact they were, only if raising wages would not serve to draw labor in. The principal means of control were: a general registration of potential as well as actual labor; an obligation on employers to report hiring of personnel to the employment exchange, which could withhold its consent; an obligation on workers already in essential employments to remain there unless specially permitted to leave; and a power vested in the Minister of Labour to issue directions to particular men and women to take up particular work. This power of direction, however, was not used in practice to move civilians as troops are moved, but only to bring the rare recalcitrant into line with the general willingness to move, over not too wide a range, under guidance. Granted the willingness and the guidance, the main influence on deployment remained the availability of a not too uncongenial job that could be taken without too great a displacement; and the supply of labor with which the planners of the war effort had to reckon was not a total of bodies but a congeries of particular capabilities, preferences, and ties of locality. As such, however, the labor supply became the ultimately scarce resource, on whose allocation depended the whole balance of strategy. In the early stages of planning, the obstacle to the extension of this form of output or that was some limitation of existing equipment or supplies of materials; but in time it became the marginal loss of other outputs that switching manpower into that extension would involve. "At the end of the war, the manpower budgets were the main force in determining every part of the war effort from the numbers of the R.A.F. heavy bombers raiding Germany to the size of the clothing ration."[17]

It may well be inferred that any government administering a comprehensive economic plan, albeit in time of peace, will need equally to budget its manpower and apply some sanctions to carry the budget through, but this is not so. There may, it is true, be a stage of "military communism," in which a revolutionary government treats the whole labor force as subject to mobilization. Again, where the prospects of construction newly fire the popular imagination, there may be a general readiness to work wholeheartedly at whatever tasks are prescribed, and an overwhelming disapproval of the nonconformist: "all one can suggest," an observer of China in 1960 has remarked, "is that the distinction between directed labour and voluntary labour can hardly matter any more in a country where the pressures are so great. Society is indeed strong."[18] Where—as in China again—men are used to working not on their own account but as members of a family or tribe or village, they may take their part in whatever tasks are allotted to that cooperative without feeling themselves forced. We do not know whether such lack of awareness of a separate self will not recede as education and the standard of living increase, or whether collective work will prove compatible with high productivity, which seems to require a greater division of labor and a separating of particular persons for recruitment into particular jobs. We know at least that when central economic planning has been adopted by societies with a greater initial tincture of individualism, after the first years of crisis and devotion men have shown that

17. W. K. Hancock and M. M. Gowing, *British War Economy* (London, H.M.S.O., 1949), p. 452.
18. *The Times* (London), July 11, 1960.

they valued the freedom to choose jobs and leave them. Once that is so, constraints and compulsions on the deployment of labor do more harm than good to output and the fulfillment of the plan.

Probably this is why the planned economies of the Russian sphere have now tacitly abandoned most forms of the direction of labor and rely mainly on the same incentives and deterrents as guide the deployment of labor in the market economies. The Russian communists did not in fact set out to control labor, and freedom of engagement was inscribed in the statute book. In the 1920s the major practical problem was to stem the inrush of peasants to the towns; but about 1930, when the First Five-Year Plan brought inflation and widespread shortages of labor, controls were mounted to check excessive turnover and to mobilize manpower and steer it into essential tasks. It was made a grave offense to leave work without permission, and in 1938 work books were introduced that would show what previous jobs an applicant had held and left—a system of leaving certificates such as had been enacted by the English statute of 1388, already mentioned here, at another time of labor shortage and too high turnover. Unemployment benefit was ended, and the unemployed had to take whatever job was offered them in whatever place. Kulaks joined political prisoners in labor camps. The Commissariat of Labor was empowered to comb skilled men out and reallocate them. Collective farms had to fill quotas of recruits for industry. The graduates of the factory trade schools had to go for three years where they were sent, and in the name of vocational guidance school leavers were sent where bodies were needed rather than where the work was most suitable for them. By the time of the Second World War the instruments of a thorough-going control of the deployment of labor had thus been brought into play, though they had not been coordinated under any central plan. The war itself brought a general mobilization. Yet in the years since then the controls have mostly lapsed. Those who receive a technical training must still go initially where they are sent, but otherwise since 1956 the worker has generally been free to leave if he gives two weeks' notice, and this implies that he will no longer be drafted into a job he would not take voluntarily.

The reason is far from being that there are no more shortages of labor; rather it must be that the fulfillment of the plan has been found to suffer less if managers are allowed to attract volunteers instead of being sent conscripts. The readiest attraction is higher pay, and though all rates of pay are prescribed centrally, managers have gone above them by setting loose piece rates, devising bonuses for time workers, and upgrading (the two lowest grades in the eightfold national classification have for some time been virtually uninhabited). The state banks cannot cash checks for wages in excess of the wages fund provided in the plan unless higher authority permits, but higher authority is concerned more with output than cost, and generally has permitted, though there are recurrent attempts to tighten the control. This sort of competition for labor has naturally resulted in a "wage drift" (between 1940 and 1953 basic wage rates rose by no more than a quarter, whereas the wages actually paid out doubled) and in a jumbling of the wage structure. When in 1955 the State Committee on Labor and Wages began to formulate more orderly differentials, it based them upon unpleasant or exacting condition of work, skill required, remoteness of location, and "relative economic importance." These are precisely those drawbacks of the job or scarcities of qualifications that set up differentials so as to maintain supplies of labor point by point throughout a free market.

This is a strong case of a general experience. Though any partial or total plan for economic development implies some planned change in the deployment of labor, it does not seem practicable to promote that change by restraints and directions applied to the worker, except in such times of national peril or enthusiasm as for a while turn conscripts into volunteers. Controls can be applied effectively to stamp the shape of a plan on consumption or production, but the deployment of labor, it seems, must depend on inducements. There are two essential reasons: forced labor is sullen and careless, and the right man for the job and the right job for the man are more likely to be found by free choices than by posting orders. Where freedom is not an end in itself, it is still a necessary means to higher output.

5 THE FIXING OF RATES OF PAY:
CONVENTIONAL AND MARKET FORCES

We come now to pay and its movements, and first to the forces that bear upon the rate of pay for any one job. These forces are many and various. In some countries the most prominent are the bargaining power that is applied in negotiations between employers and trade unions, or the authority of the state as that is exerted through minimum-wage laws or the arbitration of wage claims. These procedures we shall deal with in the next chapter. This one will survey forces that prevailed before collective bargaining or the modern forms of state regulation arose, and that still remain powerful today. They are the forces of convention and of supply and demand.

By convention we mean opinions about what is the right thing to do that are reinforced because most people agree in holding them. There is a general opinion that pay should be proportioned to deserts. The Bible says that "the wages of sin is death"; to pay a man out means to serve him right. Pay is not thought of as a price: "the price of any thing is as much as it will bring," but the pay of any man is seen as the recompense and reward due by society to his exertions and qualities. That a pound of apples should sell for more than a pound of potatoes we generally accept as a fact of the market—here are two different commodities, each with its price, and the fact that the unit for both is the pound weight does not make us wonder whether the difference in price is fair. But if we went back to the earnings that the growers derive from the prices, we should see some point in asking about fairness, for now we are dealing with human beings. When people consider how much a given man should be paid, they usually look not for the rate that will balance supply and demand in his part of the labor market but for the rate that will be fair, just, and equitable. One notion of the fair rate is that it shall be commensurate with the requirements of the work the man does: people try to arrive at it by comparing these requirements with those of other jobs whose rates they take as given.

But measuring work is exceedingly difficult. Sometimes the product can be measured—the number of yards of cloth woven, or of bricks laid. But that helps little, for the product is usually due to equipment and materials as well as labor; and in any case we cannot reduce cloth and bricks to a common unit. What is needed is a direct measurement of the effort and the abilities that the worker puts into the job. But we have no means of recording any but the merest muscular form of his exertion: we have no measuring rod for the ability, training, experience, and care that he is applying.

Nonetheless, the endeavor is made, if not to measure any

one man's work by itself, at least to give a quantitative expression to the observed difference between one man's work and another's. This is done in two stages: in "job evaluation," comparison is made of the requirements of different jobs; but men have qualities over and above those they need to meet the minimum requirements of a job, and these personal qualities are assessed by "merit rating."

Job evaluation begins by drawing up a list of the qualities jobs require of those who are to do them; these qualities include the willingness to tolerate any unpleasant conditions of the job. Commonly there are five main headings: skill, training, and experience; responsibility; mental requirements; physical requirements; and working conditions.

Each of these will have its own components—responsibility, for example, may comprise responsibility for materials, for tools and equipment, for operations, and for the safety of others. To each component a certain range of points is assigned: responsibility for the safety of others might be given a range of from 0 to 20 points, for example, with the intention that a cashier's job should receive 0 points whereas a bus driver's would receive 15 and a locomotive engineer's the full 20. A panel of assessors now studies the jobs, and assigns to each component of a given job the number of points it seems to rate in comparison with the same component in other jobs. The points so assigned build up a certain total score for each job. Some way must now be found to turn points into cents. One way is to take the present rates for certain jobs as bench marks: if the rate for the turner is $2.50 an hour and that for the laborer $1.75, and if the turner's job scored 410 points and the laborer's 260, then the difference of 75 cents might be equated with that of 150 points, at the rate of two points to a cent, so that a job that scored 300 points would be held worth $1.95.

Merit rating proceeds in the same way, except that the list is now of personal qualities like reliability, energy, and co-operativeness, and it is the individual workers and not jobs that are assessed. The outcome is a plus rate which a given worker can receive as the recompense of his personal merits, in addition to whatever is the rate for the job he is doing.

It is a basic assumption of job evaluation that the varied requirements of each job can be combined and expressed as a single total, at least for the purpose of comparing one job with another. Some of the early economists accepted this assumption in an extreme form, and treated different kinds of work simply as embodying different quantities of a common stuff of labor—if the laborer received only two-thirds of the mason's rate, that was because his input of work, measured in a common unit, was also two-thirds.

> There may be more in an hour's hard work [said Adam Smith] than in two hours' easy business; or in an hour's application to a trade which it cost ten years' labour to learn, than in a month's industry at an ordinary and obvious employment. But it is not easy to find an accurate measure either of hardship or ingenuity. In exchanging indeed the different productions of different sorts of labour for one another, some allowance is commonly made for both. It is adjusted, however, not by any accurate measure, but by the higgling and the bargaining of the market, according to that sort of rough equality which, though not exact, is yet sufficient for carrying on the business of common life.[1]

"Skilled labour," said Karl Marx, "counts only as intensified, or rather multiplied, simple labour, so that a smaller quan-

1. *Wealth of Nations,* Bk. I, chap. 5.

tity of skilled labour is equal to a larger quantity of simple labour."[2] But this proposed conversion of different kinds of work to different quantities of a common kind will not really do. It may rest on circular reasoning—the laborer's rate is two-thirds of the mason's because he does only two-thirds as much "work" in an hour, and we know that he does two-thirds as much "work" because his pay is two-thirds. Or, as in job evaluation today, it may rest upon direct observation of the requirements of different jobs; but this observation cannot provide objective measurement—only subjective assessments that are private to each observer, even though at any one time some consensus prevails. Moreover the choices of the components to be assessed and of the range of points that can be allotted to each component are alike arbitrary. Different panels filling in the same form, or the same panel filling in different forms, will come out with different relative scores for the same jobs, and there is no means of establishing which outcome is better.

Nonetheless, job evaluation is only a painstaking application of the way in which people do continually think and argue about relative pay. Its use persists and extends because it does systematically what otherwise will be done confusedly. Firms find that it removes resented disparities and obviates disputes. In the Netherlands since the Second World War a National Standards Commission has carried out a nationwide job evaluation in a common form—first for the manual jobs, then the clerical—with the object of setting the rate for each job in its fair relation to every other.

Sometimes job evaluation aims at no more than ranking jobs in a hierarchy whose order should be followed by their rates of pay. Here it mingles in practice with another way of

2. *Capital*, trans. E. and C. Paul (London, 1930), Vol. 1, Pt. I, sec. 2.

thinking that, if stated as an abstract principle, is quite contrary—namely, the assumption that far from being reducible to common terms, different jobs have inherently different statuses, some superior, some inferior, and that the structure of pay should conform to this structure of esteem. Though the social stratification of Western societies is changing, jobs do have a ranking by status that corresponds fairly closely to their ranking by pay. A recent tabulation[3] for Britain provides seven groups of occupations:

1. Professional and high administrative
2. Managers and executives
3. Inspectors, supervisors, and other nonmanual—higher
4. Inspectors, supervisors, and other nonmanual—lower
5. Skilled manual and routine nonmanual
6. Semiskilled manual
7. Unskilled manual

Public opinion generally accepts such a table as hierarchical: a given group is thought of as standing higher or lower than another. Generally a group is ranked according to the difficulty of attaining the proficiency that the jobs in it require—whether because the proficiency depends on qualities of mind and character that are inherently rare, or because it can be acquired only through exacting training and long experience. The hierarchy of pay does not, it is true, conform to this hierarchy of esteem completely. There is much overlap and the overlap may run over more than one group—a good many semiskilled manual workers, for instance, earn more than some skilled workers; and some of the semiskilled may be earning more than a good many clerical or technical workers.

3. D. V. Glass, ed., *Social Mobility in Britain* (London, Routledge and Kegan Paul, 1954).

But the maxima of the groups do seem to be arranged one above the other: the highest pay attainable by an unskilled manual worker is generally below that attainable by a semiskilled, the highest for the semiskilled is generally below that for the skilled, and so on up the table.

This agreement in ranking is widely felt to be just. With some possible exceptions such as the priesthood, it is held that a given occupation should be paid less than those of higher and more than those of lower status. One basis of this belief is the sense that if the world's work is to be carried on, each man must stand in his due degree:

> O! when degree is shak'd,
> Which is the ladder to all high designs,
> The enterprise is sick.

Nor, it is felt, can a man usually keep his rightful rung on the ladder if he is known to earn less than one whose rightful place is below him. One criterion for the fair wage is that it shall enable the recipient to keep up a position in the class to which his job assigns him. This criterion has even been set out in a wage-fixing statute by a Labor government in Britain: the Agricultural Wages (Regulation) Act of 1924 required that the rates fixed should "enable a man in an ordinary case to maintain himself and his family in accordance with such standard of comfort as may be reasonable in relation to the nature of his occupation."

Since assessments of the requirements of a job or of the esteem due the man who does it can only be subjective, in practice they lean much on custom. What has long continued must have been long accepted, and what has been long accepted can hardly be unjust.

Custom is in fact a powerful and a distinct influence on

rates of pay. It has set its imprint on the record of wages in earlier years. The wages of builders in southern England can be traced fairly continuously from the late thirteenth century to the present day: one striking feature is how often one and the same rate remains predominant year in, year out. "In many places," Adam Smith said, "the money price of labour remains uniformly the same sometimes for half a century together."[4] For nearly forty years before *The Wealth of Nations* appeared, the predominant rate for the mason and the carpenter in southern England had been two shillings a day; from about 1412 onward it had stood at sixpence a day for a hundred and twenty years. Prices do not behave like that in a stock market or a wheat pit: we cannot suppose that supply and demand came into equilibrium year after year at just the same wage; the sameness must have owed much to custom.

Nor does custom help to settle rates of pay only when they are steady: when they are rising it still bears on differentials. Between 1412 and 1914 the rate for the mason and the carpenter rose fourteenfold, but at one end of the five centuries as at the other, and during almost all the settled periods in between, it was half as much again as the laborer's. There were local differences in England, and though other countries followed the same rule in some times and places they were far from following it in all. Yet the one simple ratio of three to two appears far too widely and too long for us to suppose that it was reached each time by an equilibration of market forces: it must have been what it was primarily because men were following custom.

The force of custom may show itself in such circularity of reasoning as has been mentioned already: the job that

4. *Wealth of Nations*, Bk. I, chap. 8.

once achieves high pay continues to stand high in esteem because the pay is proof that it deserves to. Equally, what costs little may be thought worth little. In Britain the First World War showed how well women could do many jobs that had been thought beyond them. Perhaps the trouble had been that the low rates for their work had been taken as a measure of their capacity: an economist with practical experience of fixing minimum rates in women's trades remarked that "if women's rates are assumed lower than men's by a significant margin, the women are put on to processes which are ill-paid as a market fact."[5]

One other consideration sometimes goes to make up the notion of the fair wage—the worker's needs. We do not usually think we should pay the butcher more for his meat because his wife has had another baby, but when we pay not for the products of work but for work itself we sometimes are ready to pay different sums to two workers doing one and the same job because their needs are different. Where family allowances are a charge on the employer, he usually makes the same absolute or proportionate contribution, in respect of each worker, to a fund from which the allowances are paid out: so the family man costs him no more than a bachelor. But in Japan it is not unusual to add directly to each man's wage an allowance based on the size of his family; and something of the same purpose is served by another allowance based simply on the worker's age. Boards or courts fixing minimum wages have often based their award solely on a calculation of what income a family needs to maintain itself at a level the social conscience will sanction. This is the principle of "the living wage." The Australian arbitrator Mr. Justice Higgins, in his famous Harvester Judgment of 1907,

5. D. H. Macgregor, in a memorandum submitted to the Royal Commission on Equal Pay, 1944–46: Appendix IX to the Minutes of Evidence.

defined the living wage as one sufficient to meet "the normal needs of the average employee regarded as a human being living in a civilized community." A widely accepted justification, if not reason, for paying men more than women for the same work, is that men usually have more dependents. When decisions about wages are centralized—as they have been in one way by the solidarity policy of the Swedish trade unions, and in another by political processes in France—the fixing of a fair wage is seen as the making of a due allowance, and wage settlements appear not so much as the pricing of factors of production as the means to a tolerable distribution of the national income.

THE SUPPLY SCHEDULE OF LABOR

We have been discussing people's ideas of fairness as forces bearing upon rates of pay, but evidently these forces do not have the field to themselves. No matter how strong and unanimous the opinion that a certain rate was fair, the rate could not persist if it was so low that the labor force melted away, or so high that employers would no longer hire. Evidently there is a supply price below which a given labor force will cease to be fully available, and a demand price above which it will cease to be fully engaged. Let us examine these in turn.

The supply price confronts any management that is setting out to increase its labor force. There are various ways of recruiting that will bring in more applicants at the going rate, but if these are not enough the management will commonly consider one way or another of offering more. For several reasons those who are next on the list of potential recruits will be available only at a higher rate of pay. They may live farther away, and need the higher rate to offset the cost and trouble of the journey. They may already be in jobs that pay more than those the first recruits had left. They may be capable of doing the work offered only if they will first make the effort and bear the loss of earnings involved in training for it. They may need higher pay to offset what they, more than the first recruits, feel to be unattractive features of this kind of employment. Each of these obstacles is likely to take the form not of a single cliff but of a continuous if irregular gradient, so that if a given improvement in the offered terms enables the firm to bring in a certain further number of recruits, a bigger improvement would bring it yet more, and so on. We have noted four of these gradients—one in space, from nearer in to farther out; one in alternative opportunity, from lower present pay to higher; one in proficiency, from immediate readiness to a need for protracted training; and one in taste for the work, from liking to aversion.

The combined effect of these gradients is that successively larger numbers of workers will generally be available for a given kind of work in a given place only at successively higher rates of pay. This is expressed by a supply schedule or curve for labor, positively inclined. Our view of its components enables us to see some of the factors that will decide whether in a given instance it will be elastic or inelastic. A plant in a small town, for instance, will find few potential workers living beyond a short distance of its gates; whereas one in a big city is accessible to many more, by reason of both the density of population and the availability of public transport. The rates of pay for different jobs in any one locality, though they vary widely, commonly cluster around a modal value: so an employment that is at present paying a little below the rates in that cluster can, by a small rise, bring its own rate up to that already being received by a larger additional number of workers than if it started some way above or below the mode. But there may be some potential workers for whom the pay provided by alternative opportunities is at present nil, because they are unemployed: insofar as accessible workers are out of work, the supply curve will be virtually of perfect elasticity. In a society, again, where the standard of living is high, education is extensive, and parents generally want to see their children get on, it will be easier to find young people qualified and willing to undergo a given training than in a society where most children are required to earn as much as they can as soon as they can. Maintenance men, who use the same training in a number of different industries, are likely to be in more elastic supply to any one plant than workers whose training is specific to that plant's own processes. Or, to take an example of the fourth gradient, the number of workers available can usually be added to more easily for clean work in normal hours than for jobs that mean getting dirty or working broken hours or night shifts.

The practical import of the supply schedule is often very different in the short run and the long. Where the work to be done and the proficiency required are much the same in one employment as another, a rise in the rate one firm offers may bring a quick response—especially in an industry like building, where many wage earners change employers from time to time in any case, and do not regard a move as taking a plunge. But any period of training means a lag, and for some professions it is long: if a rise in the pay of doctors, for instance, is to call forth a greater supply, it must influence the entrant's course of study as much as ten years before he is ready to practice. The response, moreover, is not merely deferred but is likely to be weakened, because what is offered is not higher pay here and now, but a prospect that terms not less favorable than today's will be offered in ten years' time.

Pay: Conventional and Market Forces

When relative pay is lowered, the difference between the response in the short run and the long is likely to be greater still, for even those who in the nature of their own work would not find it hard to fit in elsewhere may be loath to leave the familiar surroundings in which they feel secure; and others have acquired a proficiency for which there is no ready market outside. The rate needed to attract labor in the first place is higher than that needed to retain it once it has settled in. Much of a firm's labor force is likely, for this reason, to be captive; the firm is a monopsonist in the short run; and the sanctions that check a relative fall in its rates are those less of the supply price than of the unrest that a sense of injustice will bring. This sense is aroused most acutely by the sight of higher rates being paid to certain types of labor only because their supply reacts more sharply. The skilled men are reluctant to go, but it make less difference to the laborers where they work, and if the firm is to keep them it must pay them more. The long-service men stay put, but the rates they are getting will no longer attract an adequate supply of new entrants, so the rates of juveniles must be raised. But it seems an outrage that those who stand low in the scale of esteem, the laborers and the callow youths, should get a rise which those who stand high are denied. So the sense of justice makes the market more perfect, and ensures that all rates will be raised by much the same as those on which the reaction of supply has made itself felt promptly. That reaction, moreover, is not absent elsewhere, but only slow: drivers on the railroads have attained their positions of responsibility through long years of service; they have prestige and a distinctive way of life; yet when their pay has remained for years below that generally received by men of their standing elsewhere, they have been known to leave the railroad.

The supply schedule helps to explain some regional differences. The levels of pay prevailing in different regions of one country have been observed to vary inversely with the natural rate of growth of population there. In the eighteenth century, and very likely for long before, the natural rate of growth was negative in the towns of Britain; Adam Smith remarked that wages were higher in the towns than in the surrounding countryside, and generally decreased as the distance from London increased—"Eighteen pence a day may be reckoned the common price of labour in London and its neighbourhood. At a few miles distance it falls to fourteen and fifteen pence. Tenpence may be reckoned its price in Edinburgh and its neighbourhood. At a few miles distance it falls to eightpence, the usual price of common labour through the greater part of the low country of Scotland."[6] In our own day, rates of pay in Ontario range from 10 to 20 per cent above those in comparable employments in Quebec; and in the United States, rates in the southeast have been 30 per cent and more below those on the Pacific Coast. In country districts where birth rates are higher, or death rates, especially among infants, are lower, many children grow up who can find no work on the land, and the supply price of labor to local industry and the local town is lower than in the regions that can man up their growing industry only by immigration.

One distinct aspect of supply remains to be noticed. So far, we have considered the supply of labor as constituted by the number of persons available, but we have also to think of the supply of work: this requires us to consider the effort that a given number of workers will put in within the year in response to a given rate of pay. Those paid by

6. *Wealth of Nations*, Bk. I, chap. 8.

the hour can vary the number of hours worked; those paid by results can also vary the intensity of effort within the hour. The main issue of principle can be seen if we confine ourselves to variations in hours: at a higher rate of pay per hour, will men choose to work more hours or less? The higher rate makes two differences, which pull against each other. On the one hand, it means that when the worker has put in, say, forty hours in a given week he has already earned more than he would have earned at a lower rate, so that he has less need for a further dollar. On the other hand, a forty-first hour will now bring him more in dollars: any one dollar means less to him, but he can get more of them. On balance, will he have more inducement to work the forty-first hour, or less? There seems to be no reason why the balance should generally come down on one side rather than the other. One would expect that it would come out differently for different people, especially for those with differing family responsibilities; and that for any one man it would vary with the standard of living he has attained. It seems likely that those who are consciously advancing their standard of living to a higher level will respond to a higher rate of pay by working longer hours if they can, but that those who have attained a level of consumption with which they are content will prefer to advance it modestly, if at all, while enjoying more leisure. The two types may be found alongside one another. We know, at least, that over the last hundred years and more the wage earners of the developed economies have used the rising real return to their labor to reduce their hours of work progressively, from sixty a week or more to forty, but that many among them remain very ready to do more work in exchange for a more than proportionally increased weekly wage.

The Economics of Labor

We have seen how the rate of pay fixed for a particular kind of labor has its effects on the number of applicants. It also affects the number of vacancies: just as there is a supply schedule, so there is a demand schedule.

To trace this connection between the rate of pay for a particular kind of work and the quantity of it that employers in the aggregate will wish to hire, let us ask how employers will react to a rise in the rate. This rise we must suppose to occur by itself, not as part of a general upward movement of pay and prices, but as an isolated event at a time when other economic variables are not changing. It must also be a cause and not an effect—that is, it must not be a response to a shortage of labor and the pull of demand, but must impinge upon employers at a time when they are not trying to take on any more of that kind of labor at the going rate—we might suppose, for instance, that an agency of government empowered to fix minimum rates of pay decides on social grounds to raise a particular minimum. In such a situation the variation of one thing at a time enables us to trace that variation's consequences. In the present case, what will they be?

If the labor concerned is direct labor—that is, if a fixed amount of it is required at any one time for each unit of product—then employers can at first do little else than accept the higher cost for the same number of workers as before: that number is fixed by the flow of orders they have coming through their workshops. But the rise in costs will generally have to be covered by higher selling prices. In any one instance, it is true, the employers might have profit margins wide enough to stand some paring, or they might have means

Pay: Conventional and Market Forces

at hand to improve their methods and keep their unit costs down despite the rise in wages; but there can be no counting on such cushions being there, and even when they are, they can absorb one push but not one push after another. Short of fortunate coincidences, then, the selling prices of the products must go up. But in the conditions we are supposing, this is a rise in relative prices, and usually buyers will react to it by taking less of what is now relatively dearer. Sales will be down: there will be less work coming through the shops and fewer jobs for the workers whose pay has gone up—very likely for some others too.

Beyond this first upset lies the possibility of a full adjustment. Though a fixed amount of this kind of labor is needed for each unit of output, and it has to be combined in fixed proportions with other factors that are similarly required, those proportions will generally be different for different products. In the economy as a whole, less of one factor of production can be used in combination with each unit of another, if the output of products that use relatively more of the first is contracted and the output of those that use relatively less is expanded. For any one kind of cake it may be necessary to use a fixed amount of fat with each pound of flour, but a baker issued with less fat than before, relative to his supply of flour, can use his whole supply of both by making more of the kinds of cake that use less fat. This he would have an incentive to do if he were buying his supplies and the price of fat rose relative to that of flour. The same tendency would appear if each kind of cake were made by a different baker: the bakers who made the kinds that used less fat would find their costs going up less and would have to raise their prices less, so that their outputs would not be reduced as much as the others'. This effect is general. A rise in the relative price of one factor of production tends to redistribute resources away from the lines of output that use more of this factor in combination with a given amount of the others, and toward the lines of output that use less. A higher relative pay for one kind of labor tends to reduce the amount of that labor employed in the economy as a whole, even though in each separate line of output the proportion in which the factors are combined is fixed rigidly by the nature of the process performed.

But of course there is often no such rigidity. Given time, the process may be changed. At present, excavation may be done by digging, one man, one spade; if the laborers' pay goes up, it is no use trying to keep down the rise in cost by using fewer laborers and more spades, but it may be possible to use less labor and more capital by going over to mechanical excavators. Even in the short run, moreover, there are many kinds of labor whose relative input can be varied: in the workshop the number of machinists required may be fixed by the size of the output, but there is room for changes in the complement of maintenance men or supervisors; and beyond the workshops are the offices. Generally, any kind of labor whose pay is reckoned part of overhead costs because it does not vary directly with output can, by the same token, be employed in greater or smaller amounts even in the short run. In all these cases, whether the change can be made quickly or only after some time, there is the possibility of varying the amount of one kind of labor that is used to make a given amount of one particular product.

Here again a rise in the relative pay of that kind of labor tends to reduce the relative amount of it employed. The immediate reason is that at the new rate of pay some reduction in the input of that labor will lower costs by more than it lowers output. Underlying this is a relation of great generality—the relation between the input of labor of a given kind and the difference made to output by a unit increase in that input. A firm now has sixteen typists in its office: it could make do with fifteen, and if it wanted a seventeenth it could engage her, so why does it employ sixteen, neither more nor less? There can be only one answer: that though these things are not susceptible of more than a rough estimate, having sixteen typists instead of fifteen makes a contribution to the working of the firm, and ultimately to the output it can achieve with given total outlay, that fully offsets the addition it makes to cost; whereas having seventeen instead of sixteen would not. This answer in turn implies that, at least within the range we are considering, successive increments of input make successively smaller contributions to output. This must be generally so. If it were not so, we could raise all the food the world needs from one acre of ground by putting enough labor to work on it. For each piece of land, in given conditions of agricultural technique and with given equipment, there will be a certain input of labor that will maximize the output of corn per man; and if we raise the input of man-hours by 5 per cent beyond that, the crop will be increased, but not by as much as 5 per cent. The marginal product falls with rising relative input.

This relation holds for all the factors of production, and it sets the terms on which the employer can arrive at the most economical pattern of production—the one that will yield a given output for the lowest possible total cost. The combination of factor inputs for which the total cost of a given output will be a minimum is reached when the employment of the marginal increment of each factor adds to total cost an amount that is just covered by what it adds to proceeds. The employer will not have arrived at that adjustment as long as he can save a dollar by reducing the input of one factor while maintaining output by using more of another factor for an additional cost of less than a dollar. When he has used up all these possibilities of getting the same output for a lower total cost, the increment of output per dollar of expenditure will be the same at the margin of each factor input. If man-hours of one kind are being hired at $2.00 each, and those of another at $2.50, then the inputs must have been adjusted so that what the marginal man-hour of the first kind adds to output is four-fifths of what that of the second kind adds: the marginal physical products of the different factors must be proportionate to their unit prices.

But this principle of proportionality need not be grasped by the employer and consciously applied: because it is the mathematical implication of the principle of cost minimization, employers do in fact act upon it implicitly if they only try to minimize cost. Nor need we even suppose that they are all vigilant to do this, or that if they were they would have the needed knowledge. What the effect of marginal adjustment will be can often be only a matter of judgment. Good managers do have good judgment. But good or bad, vigorous or lethargic, adaptable or conservative, managers come under the test of results. Monopolies can remain inefficient; but to the extent that competition is effective, the firms that are nearer the minimum cost adjustment will do better than the rest, even if they have got there only by accident. Even where it leaves room for substantial differences between firms, competition still checks aberrancy: it eliminates firms that wander too far away from the minimum cost adjustment, or forces them to reorganize. But to the extent that firms are kept at that minimum, albeit within a certain tolerance, the marginal physical products of the factors they use will be proportional to the marginal costs of hiring those factors. It follows that a rise in the unit cost of one factor puts pressure on them to reduce the relative input of it.

When we discussed the supply schedule of a particular kind of labor, we found four gradients which make that price rise with input. We have now discussed the two gradients that make the demand price fall with input. First, as the input of any one kind of labor rises relative to other resources, the outputs of the kinds of products it helps to make rise relative to other kinds, and their relative price will be depressed; so even if each successive increment of input added as much to physical output as the one before, it would add less to the proceeds. But second, it never in fact does go on adding as much, at least past a certain point: the marginal physical product falls as input rises. The demand price that employers are willing to pay for n units of a certain kind of labor cannot long or far exceed the difference that is made to proceeds by having n units instead of $n - 1$; and as input rises, this difference falls for two reasons—a physical unit sells for less, and the increment of physical output is smaller.

This account of the demand schedule partakes more of the nature of abstract analysis, of "classroom economics," than did that of the supply schedule. There it was possible to argue directly from certain facts of everyday observation. Here, though the argument is equally based on observation, the facts are not as clear-cut; they admit of more qualification or exception, and their application to the demand schedule can be reached only by a chain of reasoning. The unwillingness of buyers to take more of a given line of output except at a lower relative price; the possibility of varying the relative inputs of different factors in making one kind of product or group of products; the impossibility, nonetheless, of going on raising output by increasing indefinitely the relative input of one factor alone; the tendencies of employers to work toward the combination of inputs that will yield them a given output at the lowest possible total cost, and of competition to eliminate or reorient those who stray far from that combination—these are the basic observations. Evidently they do not appear entirely on the surface of things, nor are they likely to figure explicitly in the first answers employers give to the economist's questions about their decisions. Yet enough instances appear of them and of their implications, especially where we make comparisons over a wide span. Thus, to follow one line for a moment, the plentiful supply of labor relative to equipment in India explains both why civil engineering there is carried on with a host of hand tools, baskets, and panniers—where the West uses graders, bulldozers, and drags—and why the earnings of the multitudes who work in that way are so low. Some textile mills in India have equipment as advanced as any in the West, but the plentiful relative supply of labor gives them an advantage in using silk-screen printing rather than methods that use more equipment per unit of labor. The opposite condition, a relative plenty of natural resources, appeared in the settlement of the American continent: a carpenter migrating from London to New York in the mid-eighteenth century would about double his real wage; and within the continent, later on, "the frontier territory of Minnesota in 1850 paid rates 70 per cent above more settled Iowa, Missouri, and the East North Central region."[7]

But instances of this kind depend on more factors than they serve to illustrate, and as demonstrations, to say the least, they lack rigor. Perhaps that has been provided for marginal productivity analysis only by the experiments of agricultural chemists on the response of plants to various

7. S. Lebergott, "Wage Trends, 1800–1900," in *Trends in the American Economy in the 19th Century*, Studies in Income and Wealth, 24, National Bureau of Economic Research (Princeton University Press, 1960), p. 452.

combinations of imputs of different fertilizers. Yet if we are in doubt as to how much weight our basic observations will bear, we can ask of each in turn whether its opposite is possible. We need not fear that we are only working through one of those exercises in deduction from hypotheses, where the interest is in the ingenuity of the thought and not in the realism of its starting point. Though we are far from being able to predict the speed and extent of the reaction to a change in the relative rate of pay for a given kind of labor, we can be sure that it exerts a pressure toward a change in the input; and that in general the higher the relative rate at which a given kind of labor is available, the smaller will the quantity demanded tend to be.

THE WHY AND WHEREFORE OF DIFFERENTIALS

We have surveyed a variety of forces that bear on particular rates of pay—forces of convention and of the market, the sense of equity, and the pressures of supply and demand. To those who are in daily contact with the actual fixing of rates of pay it is the conventional forces that are the most apparent. The arguments used about pay are mainly ethical: a wage is claimed because it is fair and just, a differential defended because it is right and proper. There is reluctance to admit that supply and demand are fixing a rate even when they do so most obviously. A recent Royal Commission in Britain thought it "necessary to re-emphasize that the failure of supply to meet the demand for policemen" underlay the whole of their inquiry into policemen's pay; "crime is prevalent, there are not enough policemen to check it, and the broad conclusion is inescapable, namely that police pay must be improved in order to attract more recruits to the service and retain them in it." But the Commission was careful to preface those statements with a defense against the charge of inhumanity: "the disputations of economists upon the validity in particular circumstances of the law of supply and demand, the principle of fair comparison or any other principle governing pay may lead to conclusions which in human terms and in their practical application leave something to be desired."[8]

This prominence of the conventional forces has led some observers to believe that they are in fact paramount—that the rates for different jobs are what they are only because people think that is what they ought to be. The inference follows that if people changed their minds, the rates could change too, and in particular that if only people would accept equal pay as right it would also be feasible.

Suppose surgeons and engineers began to be paid no more than porters and street-cleaners. What would happen? We cannot appeal to the direct test of experience, but we can see what kinds of reactions are probable. On the one hand, the costs and prices of products and services would be changed: some would become cheaper and others dearer. The buyers' reactions to this would create unfilled vacancies in some occupations, and throw men out of work in others. But there would also be shifts in the supply of labor to different jobs. Men would withdraw from occupations in which the relative pay no longer seemed to compensate for the disadvantages, and line up to enter others where the balance between pay and drawbacks had now swung the other way. In particular it is likely that the number of recruits to some of the occupations formerly more highly paid would begin to fall off. It is true there are some people, such as medical missionaries, who complete an exacting training for the sake of the service they can render and not for the exiguous stipend;

8. Interim Report of Royal Commission on the Police, Cmnd. 1222 (1960), par. 148.

and there are some artists who would rather paint in poverty than make a comfortable living in work they like less. But common observation suggests that these people are exceptional. If doctors got no more than street-cleaners, some people would still become doctors, for the sake of the interest of the work and its evident usefulness; but can we believe that the same number would put up with the arduous training, the long years of sustained mental effort as students in which they earn little or nothing, if there were no more pay for them at the end than they could have begun to earn six or seven years before? If not, we must allow that there is a supply schedule to their occupation, and that their pay cannot fall below a certain level without beginning to move down the schedule, reducing the numbers coming forward. When the pay is no more than enough to maintain present numbers, it will still bring to not a few a surplus over their own supply prices; but it has to cover the marginal supply price.

It is significant that the Soviets, who might have tried equal pay, adopted instead under Stalin in 1931 a conscious policy of widening the gap between the higher- and the lower-paid jobs. By 1956 supply schedules had shifted, and Mikoyan could proclaim a change of plan. "In the period," he said, "when we were conducting the industrialization of a peasant country, such a gap was natural since it stimulated a rapid formation of cadres of highly skilled workers which the country greatly lacked. Now, when we have a highly skilled and highly cultured working class replenished each year by people completing seven- and ten-year schools, the gap, although it must remain, will be diminished."[9]

9. Quoted here from M. Yanowitch, "Trends in Soviet Occupational Wage Differentials," *Industrial and Labor Relations Review*, *13* (1960), 166.

These considerations about the likely reactions to the abolition of differentials are reinforced when we ask why differentials are greater in some countries than in others.

A high differential for skill usually goes with restricted access to the means of acquiring it. In underdeveloped economies this access is restricted in various ways: only a part of the children get any schooling at all; because most families are poor they cannot afford to maintain their sons and daughters through years of further education and technical training; barriers of caste, tribe, race, or tongue obstruct entry. Some of these factors may act to keep differentials high within the advanced countries too; in particular, a rate of population growth high enough to get ahead of the growth of the equipment with which qualified labor works will result in a relatively high proportion of unqualified entrants; or the immigration of the untrained may take the same effect, and this may be why the differential for skill was higher in the United States before 1914 than in most other advanced countries. Generally, however, development fosters and in turn is fostered by the extension of education and technical training; there come to be more homes that give the child a literate and knowledgeable company in his early years, and that can afford to pay and wait while he trains; exclusiveness diminishes when newcomers of many types mingle in the centers of growth, and when the struggle for a job of any kind becomes less intense.

The relative strength of the conventional and market forces is also illuminated by the way in which differentials have changed. The conventional forces generally operate to maintain what is customary and accepted; but what stands out in the record of Western countries in the last half-century is the extent to which differentials have narrowed. We have seen how the number of clerical, administrative, and technical workers has risen meanwhile, both because of a relative expansion of private and public services and because within industry itself there are now more men and women in the office for every hundred at the bench. Yet with this has gone a fall in the white-collar worker's relative pay. The most apparent reason for the ability to attract and retain larger numbers at lower relative pay is a shifting of the supply schedule by the increased public provision for education, and the increased ability of families to take advantage of it— far more children of manual workers have been getting the education that is the prerequisite for the white-collar occupations. In the same way, more of them than before have become capable of training for the skilled manual occupations. The effect on the differentials for skill has been enhanced during the last twenty years of full employment by an extension of training within industry itself. Firms have filled vacancies in the higher grades by upgrading, so that their unfilled demand has extended more for the lower grades than for labor as a whole, and the relative pay of those grades has been pulled up accordingly.

In sum, differences in pay seem to owe less to the conventional than to the market forces. It may even be that instead of opinions about what is fair having shaped the pay structure, it is the structure that has shaped the opinions. It is to the supply schedules of labor for different jobs that the pay structure seems to owe its main proportions.

But this is not to say that the relative pay for each occupation is never higher than it has to be to maintain present numbers. One possible reason for a gap between the pay and the marginal supply price lies in the slowness of the reaction of supply, but this can account for a divergence in either direction. Two other reasons make it more likely that the current pay will be the higher. One is the possibility that the

The Economics of Labor

supply curve for some occupations is very steep in the region
of the present margin, by reason of the rare abilities required
or the limitation of training opportunities. Demand may bid
up the pay, but the rise will call forth few additional entrants, or none, even in the long run. If that has happened, as
is likely in a growing economy, a reduction of the pay would
set up an excess of demand but would hardly reduce the supply; and the surplus of the actual pay over the marginal
supply price is a rent where the inelasticity of supply is due
to natural scarcity, and a monopoly gain where it is due to
organized restriction of entry. The second reason is that the
supply schedule is much more effective in raising pay that
has come to be below the marginal supply price than in lowering pay that has come to be above it. In the first case, there
will be unfilled vacancies; in the second, only a waiting list
of applicants. The employer's inducement to change the rate
is greater in the first case; the resistance he will meet with is
greater in the second.

Gaps between the current rate of pay and the marginal
supply price leave a field for the conventional forces to
govern. The case last noted, of an extension of supply failing
to reduce relative pay, is of wide significance in developing
economies. Better education and higher standards of living
extend the supply of labor to the higher paid jobs. Some of
this extension of supply will be matched by an independent
extension of demand, but there is still likely to be an increment of supply for which jobs can be opened only by a fall
in relative pay. Conventional forces, which include the graduate's sense of his own dignity, resist that fall. We have seen
that the relative pay of white-collar workers in Western countries has in fact fallen, but whereas the cause lies in social
changes that have been going on continuously, the actual
movement was concentrated in periods of general rises in pay,

when a relative fall required only a slower rise than in other jobs. We do not know what the pay structure would be like if those who are qualified for a given occupation but find no vacancy in it were able and willing to bring the pay down by offering to work for less. The ultimate change might be much greater than any made by the entrants available here and now, for the number who acquire the qualifications for an occupation is likely to rise with the visible extent of the openings in it.

THE PERSONAL DISTRIBUTION OF EARNINGS: THE LOG-NORMAL

The rates of pay for jobs that we have been study-ing confront workers with a range of opportunities for earn-ing. How much any one worker earns in a year depends on the rate of pay for the job he has taken and also on how much he himself gets done in it—on his personal output, for instance, if he is a pieceworker, or on how many days he works. When actual individual earnings are reported, they prove to fall into a common pattern from which we can learn something about the labor market.

This pattern is the log-normal distribution. When the figures are first reported—let us suppose they are of annual earnings—they are likely to be grouped by intervals whose boundaries might be at, say, $3,000, $3,100, $3,200, and so on. When we draw the corresponding histogram, we find it is skewed, with a mode that comes relatively low in the range—if the lowest earnings were near $3,000 and the high-est near $10,000, we should probably find the mode under $5,500; the grouping below it would be compact, and a long tail would extend into the upper reaches. But suppose that we regroup the data between boundaries set not at equal absolute intervals, as in our example, but so as to mark successive proportionate rises of the same extent—say, of 5 per cent, with boundaries at $3,000, $3,150, $3,307.50, and so on, up to $9,675.30 and $10,159.10—we now find a symmetrical outline of the familiar bell-shaped kind. The change in the intervals amounted to taking equal logarithmic intervals, and when that leads to a curve with the properties of the normal curve of error, we call the distribution log-normal.

The personal distribution of earnings commonly does prove to be log-normal, whether the earnings are those of different workers in the same kind of job or cover a wide range of occupations and industries. In this respect earnings resemble some other social and economic quantities—personal estates, customers' bank deposits, firms' profits, the numbers of employees firm by firm and industry by industry, the populations of cities, the numbers of members in trade unions—all of which have been found to have log-normal distributions. For earnings, the form of the distribution can persist through great changes in the labor market: in Britain, for instance, the distribution of the weekly earnings of industrial wage earners had much the same form in 1960 as in 1906, save that the spread in 1906 was rather wider—and this despite profound social and industrial changes, the upheavals of two great wars, and an elevenfold rise in average earnings. Evidently processes of some generality and persistence are at work.

Statistical theory suggests what they are. It shows how a log-normal distribution will appear if the size of each member is the joint product of a number of influences which are independent of one another and each of which tends to raise or lower the size by a given *proportion* of its present amount. The counterpart of this for the distribution of earnings is (1) that the size of each worker's earnings depends on a number of influences, such as his intelligence, the training he has had, his health, his age, the size of the family he has to support, and the like; (2) that these influences are independent of one another, so that the more intelligent do not also comprise all the more healthy, and so on; and (3) that a given intensity of any one influence takes the same proportionate effect on different workers' earnings whether those earnings are high or low—that if a certain degree of ill-health lowers the laborer's earnings by 10 per cent, for example, it will lower the craftsman's earnings by 10 per cent too. The assumption of independence evidently goes too far, and the fact, for example, that high intelligence and intensive training often go together may account for the higher earnings being sometimes more numerous than a strictly log-normal distribution would allow. But the assumptions need not be rigorously satisfied for the general effect to appear. That earnings are so often distributed log-normally points to the amount of each worker's earnings as being the outcome of a large number of influences which all tend to raise or lower earnings in the same proportion wherever they are present in given strength. In that case the fact of inequality, and its extent, lie beyond the reach of particular acts of policy. These acts change a few out of the many influences, and they may affect the fortunes of particular persons, but the pattern of the aggregate will persist.

This may appear more clearly if we think of the influences that bear on each man's capacity as giving him a certain potential output in each of a number of different jobs. (It is possible to imagine the arrangements of piecework applied generally, so that different men will earn different amounts in the same job according to the output of which each is capable.) Men will now distribute themselves between jobs by each moving toward the job in which the combination of the rate for the job with his own particular output in it offers him the highest earnings. The movement takes its own effect on the relative rates for different jobs, and these relative rates are also being changed meanwhile by shifts in technique and in consumers' demand; but the changing pattern of rates of pay per unit of output job by job impinges only as one among many influences on the assortment of earnings within the potential of any one man, and will not prevent the ultimate distribution of earnings from continuing to take the log-normal form. This would still be so even if some authority decreed rates of pay job by job so as to equalize average earnings in all jobs. One economist has concluded from his analysis of the log-normal distribution of earnings "that whatever the rates of remuneration which either rational choice or irrational prejudice allocate to the units of output in different occupations, such scales of relative rewards exercise no more than a superficial distorting effect upon a basic pattern. This underlying pattern is independent of the subjective feeling of consumers and of entrepreneurs and is determined by objective facts. It depends, in other words, upon the varying relative effectiveness of human abilities when faced with different kinds of productive problems."[10]

10. A. D. Roy, "Some Thoughts on the Distribution of Earnings," *Oxford Economic Papers*, new ser. *3* (1951), 135.

6 THE FIXING OF RATES OF PAY:
COLLECTIVE BARGAINING AND PUBLIC REGULATION

THE ORIGINS OF COLLECTIVE BARGAINING

We have been studying various forces that bear on the rate of pay, but in many countries the actual rate is commonly fixed by a collective bargain and seems clearly to depend upon the bargaining power the parties can apply. What is bargaining power, and how much difference does it make?

Since the worker seeks to acquire it by belonging to a trade union, we may gain some insight into it by considering the needs that the trade union meets. From the end of the eighteenth century until the present day, in one country after another, trade unions have arisen wherever modern methods of transport and manufacture have impinged on a traditional economy. It seems likely that the new methods bring with them new needs or an intensification of old ones. They also bring with them, it is true, some necessary conditions of unionism that may not have been present before—workers who are not isolated but able to keep in touch with one another; a sufficient number who are educated, so as to be able to provide leaders and administrators, or educated outsiders ready to serve; and real wages that are high enough to enable the member to keep up his dues. It is also true that a spurt of industrial development has often been associated with inflation or with war, which itself is inflationary, and men feel more need of a means of pressing wage claims when the cost of living is rising, or are more likely to think that the trade union gives them value for their money when rises are frequent than when pay remains unchanged for years together. But there is also reason to think that trade unions take their rise with industrialism because the changes that industrialism brings in men's working lives make them more conscious of a need to stand together.

Some of these changes affect the personal relation between employer and employed. As firms become bigger, the wage earner no longer works alongside his employer, may cease indeed to see much of him or have any access to him. At the same time, the proportion of the wage earners who can hope to become employers themselves necessarily declines: there is a growing class of permanent wage earners, who cannot identify the employer's prospects with their own and can seek betterment only through raising wages. The pattern and mood of the day's work also change: instead of enjoying the spontaneity of the man who works on his own account or in a small group, and the alternation of spells of indulgence with days of long hours and intensive effort, the factory worker must keep regular hours, maintain a prescribed pace, and take the foreman's orders. Meanwhile, there is a loss of security. Markets are no longer so well insulated by distance: the local worker feels the competition of goods, or other workers, coming in from outside; his own job may depend increasingly on his product finding buyers in markets far away. The fluctuations of such trade break up the protection he has enjoyed through the observance of customary rates of pay, and expose him to cuts in time of slump, with the corresponding need to press claims vigorously when times permit.

But besides these losses of personal contact, freedom, and security, there are other changes that bear more directly on his ability to influence his rate of pay. At all times, if he makes his own bargain with a prospective employer and does not think the terms offered him are good enough, his remedy is to hold out for better. If the employer sticks to his first offer, the outcome depends on which can hold out the longer; though, if he and the employer are near enough of one mind on what that outcome would be, they will settle for terms that seem to each as good as he could hope to get in the end. In several ways industrial development impairs the wage earner's ability to hold out. For one thing, he is now likely to have fewer resources to live on while he is out of work. In the earlier community he was more likely to have had a settled home with a family around him that had other sources of income, and often some land to cultivate; but the labor that comes in to the first mines and factories seldom has such roots in the ground nearby. Migrant labor had always had this disability, that when it reached the place where the job was going it had little means of support with which to bargain about the pay, and that may be why such labor has been so conscious of the need for a trade-union rate, whether it be the masons of fifteenth-century England with their "yearly congregations and confederacies," the wool combers of eighteenth-century England, or the sheepshearers of Australia in more recent years. The labor force of early industrialism is not usually migrant in this sense, but it is commonly uprooted, and lacking in means of support while it is out of a job. "A landlord, a farmer, a master manufacturer, or merchant," wrote Adam Smith, "though they did not employ a single workman, could generally live a year or two upon the stocks which they have already acquired. Many workmen could not subsist a week, few could subsist a month, and scarce any a year without employment. In the long run the workman may be as necessary to his master as his master is to him; but the necessity is not so immediate."[1]

The rise of industrialism also tends to reduce the alternatives open to a worker who does not think a particular offer good enough: when the average size of the firm rises relative to the whole labor force of a region, the number of alternative employers within any one worker's knowledge and reach generally falls. In particular regions there may be a thickening up that more than offsets this: in the industrial conurbations the average worker is in effective touch with more alternative offers of employment than in the small town, even though what firms there are in such towns are smaller. But save for these effects of local concentration, the rise in the average size of the firm is a movement in the direction of oligopsony and monopsony in the labor market.

Industrialization, moreover, generally goes with a growth of population, and there are often times when the applicants increase faster than the vacancies. The growth of population may have set in first, as in Western Europe in the eighteenth century and Asia in the twentieth; or the opportunity of spreading over a rich hinterland may call forth large fami-

1. *Wealth of Nations*, Bk. I, chap. 8.

lies, as in North America; or industrialization itself may bring with it improvements in hygiene and changes in custom that upset the old balance between deaths and births. More jobs are being offered year by year, and in the now advanced countries the trebling and quadrupling of population over the last 150 years has been matched by a trebling and quadrupling of jobs. But it would have been amazing if the match had been exact year by year. Besides times of labor shortage there have been times when it was the jobs that were scarce, and it is these times that have burned themselves into the minds of workers conscious of the swarms about them, the pressure on housing, and the streams of migrants. Even though decade by decade the jobs did in fact keep pace with the applicants in the national aggregate, there have generally been regions where the applicants were in continual excess, or would have been but for migration. But migration heightens the sense of inability to stand out alone; the emigrant sees himself as surplus to requirements at home, and arrives homeless to look for a job among strangers.

If the changes we have been noting had been the only forces at work, the lot of the wage earner would have been harder even than it has been. In fact, though the new forces were powerful, there were others at work to protect the wage earner in his bargain. Sometimes the force of custom was strong, or a neighborhood's sense of the subsistence to which a man was entitled and which in common decency the employer could not deny him; this meant that the pressure of growing population showed itself from time to time in a fringe of complete unemployment rather than in a Dutch auction bringing down the wage of those employed. The better workman, too, did not feel the full force of the pressure of numbers. If all men were interchangeable units of labor supply, the labor market would tend to fluctuate like

The Economics of Labor

a corn market: an excess of one applicant or one vacancy would move the rate in all hirings. But in fact the employer distinguishes between man and man, especially in a neighborhood where each man has his local repute: even when many men are out of work, the good workman may be assured of his job and a ready welcome from another employer if he falls out with his present one.

In discussing the pressure of numbers, moreover, we have already noticed how the rapid and sustained growth of population in the nineteenth century did not bring a cumulation of unemployment, but in the long run the number of jobs rose as much as the number of applicants. This came about through surges of demand that brought actual competition between employers for labor. In the rising phase of the trade cycle there were more jobs available in industry: in the north of Britain that showed itself where the supply and demand for labor met most visibly—in the "mop fair" for farm servants, in which the prevailing rates of the year's engagements went up in a year when the mines and factories were busy. Particular industries in a phase of rapid expansion sent out their recruiting agents. The growth of some occupations was great enough, even within a rapidly growing aggregate, to bring a relative contraction of the supply to others, and domestic service was an example of an extensive occupation—in Britain before 1914 there were more workers in it than in engineering—in which the competition of employers for a short supply raised relative pay.

These forces sheltered the wage earner from the downward pressures of competition when he made his bargain, and sometimes brought competition in on his side to get him better terms. They alone explain why, despite the pressure of growing numbers entering the labor markets of most Western countries in the nineteenth century, money wages on balance rose. They help to explain why by far the greater part of the wage earners did not join a trade union. But that these things are felt to need explanation reminds us of the prevailing disabilities of the wage earner. Especially where industrialization was concentrated locally, many wage earners had reason to believe that they could not bargain each man for himself. To do that, they would have to be able to refuse a job on the terms first offered. Sometimes they could; but too often they knew that if they held off, either another man would take the job or they themselves would be starved out before the employer had lost much.

The remedy was to stand together. They looked to the trade unions they formed to give them bargaining power, which is the power to change offered terms by withholding consent.

ANALYSIS OF BARGAINING POWER

Bargaining power in that sense is confined to the actual process of negotiation, and can be exerted only because terms are negotiated and not announced. There are many dealings in which the buyer or seller does simply announce his terms, and leave it to the other party to take them or leave them. That is so, for instance, in much Western retailing, as distinct from secondhand dealings in the West, or the bazaar in Asia. But it also appears in the labor market, even where collective bargaining is the general rule: an employer advertises a vacancy at a fixed rate of pay, or the members of a profession take what work is given to them at a standard scale of fees. These announced prices and rates of pay are fixed only for the time being, and as supply and demand shift they too will be changed; but at any one time they will not be changed as the result of a negotiation. When negotiation is accepted, it takes place, just as the announced price is fixed, within a certain setting of supply and demand that prescribes limits to the range of possible outcomes. But within those limits the actual outcome depends greatly on bargaining power. This power derives not from the setting but from the loss that one party can impose on the other by withholding its consent to a settlement in the course of negotiations within a given setting.

Each party will commonly enter negotiations with an approximate target. We might ask employers and trade unionists separately, "Suppose the other side notified you of its complete willingness to accept whatever terms you named, what would these terms be?" The answer would provide starting points for the choice of targets. Sometimes these starting points would be far apart, but they would not be the product of mere wishful thinking—for the employers could not go below the rate that they reckoned just high enough to attract and retain the labor force they required, and the trade unionists could not go above the rate that they reckoned just low enough to keep at least the greater part of their members employed. The clearer the requirements of the market— that is, the more competitive the markets in which the employers sell their products and hire their labor—the more likely it is that the two starting points will be close together: there are instances of negotiation in which a sequence of claims, rebuttals, and concessions only provides an approach through an accepted ritual to the outcome both parties have foreseen. But generally the parties have reason to believe that their starting points will lie some way apart. There is, for one thing, a natural bias on each side, the easier to indulge when so much about the future is uncertain in any case: the trade unionists will rate the risk of a given wage imperiling employment lower than the employers do, and the employers will see less risk of a given wage failing to retain the labor force. But bias apart, there can be a difference in the nature of things between the wage that is just low enough to maintain employment and that which is just high enough to maintain the labor force. In the competitive conditions already mentioned the difference will be small. But to the extent that the demand for the product is inelastic, the wage can be pushed up without much falling off in employment; and to the extent that the supply of labor to the particular employers is inelastic, the wage can be pushed down without much falling off in the labor force. Each party, then, in considering its own starting point, must have regard for the fact that the other's is somewhat removed. The fact of bargaining colors the approach to it. In choosing its own target—the rate that it really means to get—each party must move some way toward the center.

Even so, a gap remains. The task of negotiation is to close it. The first method is argument, and here the trade union can help its members by providing skillful advocacy. Even a horse trade proceeds by appeals to reason. The parties to collective bargaining have their consciences too, and can be moved—despite themselves, it may be—by an appeal to the emotions. The parties to a major negotiation commonly find themselves more influenced by public opinion than an outsider might credit. They may also be susceptible to pressure from government. All in all, much depends upon the skill with which a case is presented. Besides that, there is the specific skill of the negotiator, which is basically, perhaps, the ability to sense the other party's real sticking point, so that he himself neither struggles for more nor settles for less than he can really get.

If negotiation closes the gap, as most often it does, the skills of the advocate and negotiator can have done much to decide what the terms shall be on which agreement is reached. If negotiation fails to close the gap, then unless bargaining goes over into arbitration the only resort is to the test of endurance. The negotiators themselves may be put to that test, as they sit on day after day and long into the night. Or they may adjourn, and leave it to their constituents to see which side can hold out longer through a strike or lockout—we may use the word stoppage to cover both.

How bargaining power works can be envisaged as follows. The longer a stoppage has gone on, the harder both sides will generally find it to carry on, for the pressure of some of the losses cumulates, and the resources from which each day's fresh losses can be met will be dwindling. The terms on which each side is willing to settle rather than stay out longer will therefore become more and more favorable to the other side as the stoppage goes on, until a day comes when the convergence is complete and both sides are willing to call the stoppage off on the same terms. If at the outset both held the same expectation of the endurance of both, they would also agree in foreseeing the convergence, and would be willing to settle before any stoppage began for terms they regarded as all they could hope to get in the end. But a side might overestimate its own endurance or underestimate the other's. In that case it would be willing to settle straightaway only for terms less favorable to the other side than that side would expect to get after a stoppage, if its expectations were realistic—and the gap would be still wider if the other side too were overhopeful. So a stoppage there would be. But as it went on, the expected outcomes would be found to be unattainable after all, and each side would become willing to give increasingly favorable terms to the other rather than hold out longer. This willingness might well not be proclaimed, and it is one function of the conciliator to find out how the two sides really feel and reveal their common ground.

This account is abstract. In practice a stoppage is not merely a test of endurance but also, in its way, a continuance of negotiations, which serves to galvanize some elements in them—especially the influence of public opinion. The parties may be moved by considerations less rational than the balance of the cost of going on against the cost of conceding better terms: like countries at war for a strip of desert, they may set the vindication of a right, or the planting of a flag, far above all reckoning of the cost; or they may refuse a concession that would bring them an immediate balance of gain because they feel it would have been wrung from them at the pistol's point. Particularly if between them they are ruining their own industry, neither may want to surrender to sabotage. It is not even clear that the willingness to make concessions will always increase as a costly struggle drags on; greater suffering may generate only grimmer determination. Yet the account we have given does serve to lift out of the welter of events the specific influence on the ultimate settlement of the costs of withholding consent.

For the trade unionists those costs are made up first and foremost of the loss of income for themselves and their wives and children. Many trade unions help their members to meet this loss by issuing strike pay, and unions have often provided this benefit and no other. But there are also many unions, even in Western countries, that have no strike pay; and strikes do sometimes occur and are sustained by workers who are not unionized at all. In these cases leaders can do much to maintain resistance by holding demonstrations of solidarity, collecting funds, and organizing relief.

For the employer the immediate cost of a stoppage is the

loss of the profit, if any, that he could have made by working on the terms for which he could have settled, together with the charges he must incur to keep his plant and cadres intact although not working. Beyond them is the loss, less easy to quantify but often graver because it may continue for years to come, that is inflicted by the impairment of customers' good will and the diversion of trade to competitors. The extent of the costs that a stoppage will impose on an employer varies with the state of his trade. Monday's newspaper must come out on Monday or never be produced at all; but the annual total of most kinds of output can be made up at various times within the year; and when this total will in any case be below capacity, a stoppage of some weeks may not reduce it but only enable it to be produced more economically. During the stoppage, moreover, the employer may be able to keep his customers supplied out of stocks which he is in any case glad to get down. It is otherwise when he is working to capacity: a stoppage then does mean an irrecoverable loss of profitable production and the disappointing of customers. For these reasons the bargaining power of the trade union has sometimes been virtually identified with the state of the employer's order book. But the connection is not complete or invariable. When demand runs high, a stoppage means disappointing customers, it is true, but there is also less fear of their being satisfied elsewhere and staying away. In prosperous times firms have the resources with which to tide them over a stoppage, whereas in depression a firm whose cash position is tight may be acutely embarrassed by any loss of sales. So the state of demand and the extent of the embarrassment a firm will suffer from a stoppage do not always vary together. When demand runs strongly, it is true, the rate of pay that would be arrived at in a perfectly competitive market for the factors of production is higher, and the limits within which negotiations about pay take their own effect are lifted accordingly; but bargaining power will not necessarily push the settlement nearer the upper limit in good times than in bad. In bad times, for instance, when the limits have shifted downward, the repugnance felt to a cut generates in the trade unionists a specially strong will to hold out.

So far, however, the discussion has assumed that the prices employers receive for their products are fixed independently of the settlements made for pay: if once we remove this assumption and allow that a higher settlement may be covered by a rise in prices that would not have come about otherwise, then bargaining power, as the power to change offered terms by withholding consent, does vary with the state of the market. If in a softer market environment employers have less fear of losing business through putting their prices up, the cost to them of meeting a claim will be smaller, and the cost of a stoppage will loom correspondingly larger. But the market environment in this sense depends not on the state of demand alone but on the extent of competition. This in turn depends in part on the area covered by the collective bargain, a question to which we now turn.

THE BARGAINING AREA

In countries where collective bargaining is the predominant way of adjusting rates of pay, the areas covered by the typical bargain differ widely. In Scandinavia, Western Germany, the Netherlands, and the United Kingdom, for example, the typical area is that of the single industry. In France, on the other hand, collective bargaining is predominantly regional; and in the United States more than four-

fifths of the collective agreements in existence in a recent
year had been negotiated with single employers. Why these
differences?

Those who are used to industry-wide bargaining are apt
to put the question in the form, how can any other system
work? For industry-wide bargaining meets needs of both
trade unionists and employers. The trade unionist on the defensive, fending off a cut, feels the need to hold the line
throughout the industry, lest his own employer be undersold
by another who has succeeded in reducing wages. But equally when he is pressing for a rise, the trade unionist may be
told in good faith that it can be granted only if all competing
firms are going to have to pay it. To have a common front
throughout an industry also accords with the unionist's desire for solidarity, and his sense that it is only fair to have
one and the same rate for the job wherever it is done. The
employer who is sensitive to price competition sees the same
advantage as the trade unionist in putting a floor under it
by enforcing a common minimum rate of pay: associated
employers have encouraged and helped trade unions to bring
the nonassociated into line. Employers no less than trade
unionists are sensitive to their flanks when they are on the
defensive: if the unions are pressing claims, and gaining
ground firm by firm, the employers are likely to unite for
mutual defense. It is an immense relief to any one employer
to know that he is now unlikely to be struck unless all his
competitors are struck too; and it is an economy of time and
effort for him to have the negotiations conducted by the
officers of his association. In practice, moreover, he is likely
to keep more executive discretion in his own hands: the industry-wide agreement can of its nature contain only simple
and general provisions, yet the associated employer has met
his obligation to negotiate by putting himself under it, and

what it does not include is left to his "prerogatives of management."

Nonetheless, by no means all collective bargaining has widened out to cover whole industries. The reasons are partly matters of geography and history. Where a number of firms in one industry are concentrated in one region, especially if they are relatively small and closely competitive with one another, one agreement for all is likely. Such regional agreements are made in the United States, for example, in the clothing trades, and in building. But in a vast country such as the United States the parts of one industry in different regions may be separated from one another by differences of outlook and sympathy as well as space. Even in Britain "industry-wide" does not always include Scotland with England and Wales. Much also depends on how collective bargaining took its rise. In the United States it rose in a community where employers had a strong sense of their own independence, a sense that was reinforced by legal sanctions against their combining, albeit combination for collective bargaining was formally exempt. The great extension of collective bargaining, moreover, came from 1933 onward, when the trade unions advanced plant by plant, helped by legislation which gave them bargaining rights not with any two or more employers together but with only one employer at a time. Multi-employer bargaining requires centralization of funds and an effective national executive in the trade union: if, as in France, the members are capable of militant action from time to time but do not remit regular dues, the power of the union resides in the branch and finds its natural arena locally.

There are also some tactical advantages in bargaining with the single employer. Industry-wide agreements are likely to be held back by the capacity to pay of the less profitable section: by bargaining with single employers the trade unionists can get most from those who can give most. But the employer may gain from that too: if he is in difficulties, and can convince the trade union that these are not within his own power to overcome, he can settle for less; if he is prosperous, he commonly likes to be known as one who pays high. In negotiating with one employer at a time, the trade union has the opportunity to support a strike of a part of its membership with the whole of its funds: it can concentrate its thrust on a narrow front, and if it breaks through there, it can fan out by requiring other employers to concede no less. If it strikes one employer, it leaves his competitors at work. But the employer who has confidence in his own abilities will risk that for the sake of being able to make his own bargain in his own way and not having to trammel himself with other men's doubts and difficulties.

In the event, the outcomes of collective bargaining in areas of different size prove to be less divergent than might be expected. The differences of working are more apparent than real. Where bargaining is with the single employer, there may also be pattern bargaining, and agreements that are formally independent may in fact be coordinated by the trade union. Nor can a union make free use of its power to strike employers one at a time: the weapon has too much recoil—the greater the pressure on the employer, the greater the danger to the prospects of those who expect to go on working for him; and in any case experience has shown that if the tactic is pressed home, the employers will associate. Multi-employer bargaining, on the other hand, is consistent with not a little local flexibility: especially in a rising labor market, actual earnings will often rise above the industry-wide rates, and the differences may in effect be negotiated firm by firm. For these reasons it seems likely that insofar as the prices at which firms sell are beyond their effective power to vary merely as a result of the bargain, the coverage of the bargain makes little difference to the outcome: the firms' capacity to pay is given independently and multi-employer bargaining does not seem likely to use it up more or less fully than bargaining with one employer at a time. But we have already noticed the possibility of raising prices solely as a result of the bargain. When this is present the coverage does make a difference. Multi-employer bargaining alone gives each employer an immediate assurance that his competitors will all have to pay the same minimum rates as he, or increase their costs by the amount of the same rise in rates. It is likely that multi-employer bargaining will do more to keep rates up when the pressure on them is downward, and more to raise rates whenever employers are not restrained from passing on the rise in higher prices.

The second effect has received special attention in recent years. The restraint may be absent in any one industry because employers have got into the habit of keeping in step with one another—they follow one of their number as price leader, or, whoever moves first, the rest generally follow—and there is not enough competition from abroad, or resistance from consumers, to prevent them from raising prices in that way. But employers are much more widely able to raise prices to cover rises in pay in the conditions of full employment that have prevailed in the Western European countries since the Second World War. In almost all those countries money incomes, both pay and profits, have risen faster than the real national product, so that prices have risen, often at the cumulative rate of 5 or 6 per cent per annum. Economists analyzing this inflation have attributed much of it to the pull of an excessive monetary demand. But the course of events since 1952 has convinced many of them that another process has been at work—that costs have assumed a capacity for self-propulsion, that rises in pay have taken the initiative, and rises in prices and the expansion of the monetary circulation have been the effect of rises in pay and not their cause. This process of "cost push" is seen to be capable of continuing in the absence of any excess demand. Its essential conditions have been twofold. First, there has been a frame of mind among employers that makes them expect that prices will go on rising, and that higher prices will continue to prove compatible with selling all that can be made. Secondly, the coverage of the collective bargain has been tacitly extended from the industry to the whole economy in the sense that an "annual round" of wage settlements has become an accepted institution—settlements coming at much the same time are made for much the same amount. This spontaneous coordination extends beyond the bounds of each separate industry the assurance that other firms' costs are being raised equally; it makes employers the more ready to negotiate rises; and it strengthens their belief that the authorities will permit, and if need be promote, a commensurate expansion of the monetary circulation. In the Netherlands down to 1959, and in Sweden since 1956, the amount of the general rise has been the subject of a central agreement, though industries have continued to bargain separately.

The institutions of voluntary collective bargaining were worked out in a world where the restraints against raising selling prices were stronger than they have been in the Western European countries of late. Inflation originally due to demand pull has been perpetuating itself through collective bargaining by cost push. The adaptation of collective bargaining to a world of full employment is a major unsolved problem of our time.

EFFECTS OF COLLECTIVE BARGAINING
ON THE PAY STRUCTURE

If these are the workings of collective bargaining, what has been their effect on the structure of pay? Does the record suggest that they have made particular wages or salaries higher or lower relative to the rest?

At the outset it is clear that collective bargaining has made numerous changes in the pay structure because of precepts and tactics that the trade unions have applied. The most general precept of trade unions is that differences of pay, though proper between occupations, are wrong within them: there should be one and only one rate of pay for a given job, irrespective of who does it and where it is done. Basically this rule of "the rate for the job" is a precept of the tactics of defense: if the market is pressing down on rates of pay, a cut accepted at one point will mean competitive undercutting until everyone has to come down. But equally, when the union is pressing for a rise in one sector, it may find that the charge can be borne only if competitors elsewhere are made to bear it too. These tactical considerations are reinforced by the thoughts that the strength of the unionist lies in solidarity, but differences of pay are divisive; and that two rates of pay for the same job cannot both be fair.

By applying this principle of "the rate for the job," trade unions have helped to bring about marked changes in wage structures. They have set their face against different men of a given occupation being paid at different rates within the same plant, save for such differences as are based systematically on some objective feature of a particular operation, such as the complexity of the equipment used for it, or of a particular man, such as his seniority. Trade unions have also worked to reduce differences between the rates of pay for a given occupation in different plants within one region. These have commonly been wide, even between plants that are close neighbors. The first effort of the union is to enforce a common minimum, and this will mean raising the relative rate of pay in the lowest-paying plants. After this, the continuing higher rates in some plants provide arguments for raising the others again; but the claim will be tempered insofar as these other plants are inescapably high-cost plants in other respects—because of location, for example—or are subject to severer competition in their particular product market, so that leveling pay up would threaten loss of jobs there. Generally unions have to accept a rate that is within the capacity of the more constrained sector of the industry, and subordinate the principle of uniformity to the advantage of getting more where more can be got.

The same conflict of considerations has entered into the policy of the unions toward regional differences. On the one hand they have tried to reduce them, and their efforts have been reinforced by the tendency to give the same absolute rise to all regions in times of rising prices, and by the willingness of employers, when they negotiate centrally for several regions, to agree to some leveling up of rates at a time when they would not agree to a general rise. In a number of countries a big change has been brought about in this way since 1914. In that year, for example, the rates for the building craftsman and the engineering fitter in central London were about double what they were only three hundred miles away, in Cornwall: by mid-century these differences and others like them had almost wholly disappeared, save for a continuing "cost of living allowance" for London and sometimes for certain other cities. But on the other hand, when unions have negotiated separately with the employers of different regions they have met with more resistance to raising the lower rates, and the precept of leveling has had to make room for that of advancing wherever one can: the lower rates of some regions do not always forbid a further rise in the others.

The trading relations between different regions of one country in some ways resemble those between different countries, but trade unions in the higher-wage countries have not been able to do much to enforce "the rate for the job" internationally. They have lent general support, directly and through the International Labour Organisation, to the causes of trade unionism and labor legislation in the countries where wages are low. Their international Trade Secretariats try to coordinate action, and the unions of one country have often given help to those of another when battle is joined. But seldom have unionists acted as the American glassworkers did in the 1880s: seeing their own wages imperiled by their employers bringing in European glassworkers under contract to work at lower rates, they sent out delegates who formed some of the glassworkers of England, Belgium, and France into branches of their own American union. The more usual reaction of unionists to competition from the products of low-paid labor has been to demand a tariff "to equalize costs and make competition fair."

The purposes that unions bring to bargaining comprise not only the enforcement everywhere of one rate for each job, but also the fixing of what seem right and proper differences between the rates for different jobs. Sometimes here too the aim has been to level up. The Swedish congress of trade unions, it has been observed, "has followed a generally egalitarian line, a policy of whittling away gradually at almost

every sort of wage differential,"[2] and this has included a de-
liberate holding back of the wages of pulp and sawmill workers in 1937 so that the loggers might get more. International
comparisons suggest that greater centralization of bargaining
usually goes with smaller wage differentials between industries. But more usually the changes in these differentials have
not been an object of policy as much as the changing by-
product of the endeavor of the unions in each industry to do
as well as they can for themselves, and, at the least, keep up
with some other industry that stands close to them.

The differentials between occupations, however, and especially the differential for skill within any one industry,
have been very much an object of union policy. There seems
to be a clash of interests here: if the rise of the total wages
bill that an industry can bear at a certain time is given, the
differential for skill cannot be widened or contracted without
one or the other of the parties to it getting less than they
could have got otherwise. But the clash is felt only if skilled
and unskilled are distinct groups: when the unskilled can
look forward to becoming skilled, a widening of the differential means a brightening of prospects. Cotton piecers expect
to become spinners; men entering steelworks as laborers may
rise to be in charge of a furnace: in such cases it is not usually
a strong purpose of the lower paid to raise their pay relative
to the higher rates. But when there is little movement between grades, the clash is there and is generally felt, whether
the grades belong each to its own occupational union or all
to an industrial one. It is bound to be stirred up even by the
formulation of a wage claim: out of a given rise in the whole
cost of labor to employers, the lower paid will get a bigger
share if all rates are raised by the same absolute amount, and

2. L. G. Reynolds and C. H. Taft, *The Evolution of Wage Structure*
(New Haven, Yale University Press, 1956), p. 247.

the higher paid if they are all raised by the same percentage.

But beyond these effects of trade-union precepts and tactics at particular points, the question remains whether the trade union does generally and inherently get its members higher pay than they would have otherwise.

The record gives no clear answer. In fact it cannot give one, because the presence or absence of trade unionism is only one of many differences that enter into any comparisons of pay in different employments, whether we take different parts of the same industry or different industries, occupations, or regions. In the United States, for instance, the most highly unionized industries in recent years have also been industries with a relatively large amount of capital per worker, a high degree of concentration of output in a small number of firms, and a high rate of technical progress. The wages they pay are in fact relatively high, and in recent years have risen more than the average. How much of this is due to their being highly unionized, or to unions of given strength being able to achieve more in the setting this kind of industry provides, or to factors that have nothing to do with unionism? The often observed absence of association between the strength of unionism and the level of pay is equally inconclusive. In 1892, for instance, when differences in the degree of unionization were greater in Western countries than they are now, Alfred Marshall observed:

> trade unions have been stronger in England than on the Continent, and in America; and wages have been higher in England than on the Continent, but lower than in America. Their strength in England was partly due to that force of character, which was the chief cause of the excess of English over Continental wages. Their weakness in America was partly due to the very

causes that made the wages of the American working man so high; viz. his restless enterprise, his constant opportunities of bettering himself by changing his abode and his occupation, and the abundance of land on which he could settle as an independent owner. The highest wages of all that the world has known have been in some parts of California and Australia; but they were due to causes which excluded the action of Unions.[3]

If pay has risen as fast in nonunionized occupations as in unionized, that may be only because market forces have operated more strongly to raise pay in the former, and if unions had been strong in them, pay would have risen even more; or because the unionized sector did take the lead but pulled the other after it, through the strength of men's attachment to customary parities or the desire of employers to forestall the union organizer.

Yet though we have no controlled experiments and cannot generalize from aggregates, the study of particular phases and industries, with the local comparisons and contrasts they throw up, suggests some lessons of experience. There are two respects in which trade unions do appear to have a differential effect upon the pay for particular jobs.

One is that when they come into action for the first time, they raise the rate of pay relative to other rates; and in subsequent movements it retains, though very likely it does not improve on, this higher ranking. In this impact effect we may well have the measure of the bargaining power of trade unionism. Until the union is formed, the employer may be able to get the labor he needs at a rather lower rate than he would in fact be willing to pay without having to offer fewer

3. *Elements of Economics of Industry*, Bk. VI, chap. xiii, par. 18.

jobs. There is generally some zone of inertia between an upper point at which the rate of pay clearly begins to cut back the number of jobs offered, and a lower at which it clearly begins to cut back the number of workers offering themselves. This zone will be larger, the less elastic the demand for labor and the supply. The demand for labor is inelastic when the buyers' demand for the product is inelastic, or when labor both accounts for a small part of total costs and cannot easily be replaced by other factors. The supply of labor is inelastic when workers cannot readily move to alternative employments, because there are few other jobs for which they are qualified, or there are few such jobs near by and the workers find it hard to move; or because employers agree not to compete for labor. As long as workers make their own bargains and cannot hold out for more than they are offered, the rate of pay may stay near the lower point set by the reaction of supply. It may even be that this reaction is negligible, and the rate is set only by the custom and opinion of the neighborhood or by "the fodder basis," the bare bodily needs of the worker. In all such cases a trade union will be able to raise the rate of pay substantially without adverse effect upon the numbers employed—such seem to have been the effects, for example, of the two waves of unionization of the unskilled in Britain, in 1888–91 and 1910–13. Elsewhere, where the zone may be smaller or the actual rate not so near the lower boundary, the bargaining power of the trade union still has room to raise pay when it is first brought to bear.

The inelasticity of demand also allows trade unions to push up the rates of pay of particular groups who may be relatively highly paid already. Where elaborate equipment is operated by small teams, as in newspaper printing and the process industries such as oil refining, the teams' pay is a small part of the total cost of production, so that a substantial rise for the operator means only a small percentage rise in cost. More widely, this can hold for particular specialists, such as maintenance men, even when they are working in firms whose labor costs as a whole are a high proportion of all costs. In such cases a trade union may be able to push the rate of pay up above the supply price of labor to the job. In the process industries the trade union also has an advantage of bargaining power, in that even a short stoppage is extremely costly to the firm, and the whole training and impulse of management is to avoid it.

A second respect in which a differential effect of trade unionism has been seen is in a stronger resistance to cuts in time of depression. What we know of the movement of wages in times before the rise of modern trade unions shows some cuts in times of bad trade, particularly in employments depending on distant markets, but a remarkable absence of trends descending for ten or twenty years together as a counterpart to the many rising trends. It has been noted that workers who seem incapable of combining to press for a rise will spontaneously unite to refuse work at less than the customary rate, even when jobs are scarce. The "elbow joint" or ratchet effect does not depend upon trade unions. But they do seem to strengthen it: notably in the Great Depression of 1929–32 in the United States the fall in rates of pay was less in the unionized sector than elsewhere. An important use of the elbow joint appears when excess capacity or ease of entry in a price-competitive industry leads to a price war, and firms try to live with cut prices by cutting wages: a union will put a higher and stronger floor under that sort of competition. This has proved one of the strongest inducements to employers to accept and sometimes even foster trade unionism.

The impact and ratchet effects made themselves particularly felt in the rhythmic alternation of good and bad trade that ran through most Western economies from the time of their industrial revolutions until the Second World War. In phases of rising activity the demand curves for particular kinds of labor, especially in the construction and export industries, shifted outward. That might lead quickly to an extension of employment, and employers competing for recruits would raise rates of pay all around. But this effect might follow only slowly if at all, and meanwhile the employer's capacity to pay would be above the prevailing rate. This is the situation that lets a trade union take its impact effect when it begins to bargain, and an established union can take a similar effect when the situation arises in a boom. It can shake the branch as soon as the fruit is ripe: a claim backed by its bargaining power can obtain a rise that otherwise would have come only later if at all. When demand falls, it is the ratchet effect that comes into play. Employers are put under an immediate pressure to cut costs, and one or another of them is likely to take the lead in cutting rates of pay if he can deal with his own work people separately and especially if he can deal with them individually. A trade union can defer a cut, or stave it off altogether, both because it can back its resistance with the threat of a strike and because it can offer each employer an assurance that the rates his competitors pay will be kept up too. The pattern of stoppages in the trade cycle bears these expectations out—a large number of short stoppages in the recovery and boom; in the recession only a few, but those protracted.

Yet it is still hard to tell what the net effect of the trade union has been in the course of the trade cycle. When there is a settled procedure for bargaining, negotiations are not reopened before a fixed term, and employers meanwhile pay no more than the agreed rates: then collective bargaining may bring a rise later than individual bargaining would have done. In recession, employers who have no trade unions to deal with may still be restrained from cutting rates by respect for custom and for the good opinion of the neighborhood and especially of the work people themselves, and by their expectation that any cut they make will only be matched, and very likely more than matched, by their competitors. It is better then not to break the line and start the rush. At least in an industry like building, whose prices need not fluctuate with supply and demand in a produce market, we have seen how the record shows a remarkable absence of falls in rates of pay through centuries before trade unions of the modern kind were there to hold the rates up. In sum, it well may be that the rise of pay from end to end of a sequence of trade cycles has been no greater under trade unionism than it would have been without it. But the average rate of pay over the whole span may still have been higher under trade unionism, because this made the rises come rather earlier, and the cuts come later or not at all—as Marshall put it, because the trade union can "make economic friction act for the workman instead of against him."[4]

CAN THE TRADE UNIONS WIN A LARGER
SHARE OF NATIONAL INCOME?

It may be urged that even if these are the only effects that are brought out clearly by the record, we must not for one moment suppose that they are the only effects actually present. In the eyes of their most active members, trade unions have existed primarily to win a larger share of the product for pay and leave a smaller one for profit: has this

4. *Elements of Economics of Industry*, Bk. VI, chap. xiii, par. 5.

aim been merely delusive? Two considerations suggest that for the most part it has been.

The first is the observed stability of the distribution of the product between pay and profit. We shall be discussing this more fully in the next chapter (pp. 207 ff.); here we need notice only that it appears in a number of countries and persists through the changes of many years. The statistics, it is true, have their margin of error, which generally becomes wider the farther back we go, and is in any case wide enough to cover some substantial variations in the relative sizes of the components. It is also true that some changes in distribution do appear on the face of the record from time to time. Yet what is remarkable when the records of many countries are assembled and compared is the lack of agreement on particular changes, and the extent of agreement on a trend that shows little or no change. In particular, there is often a marked stability in the division between profit and pay as a whole (taking wages and salaries together) of the value added by a particular group of industries. This division varies with the state of trade, the share of profit generally dropping sharply in depression; particular industries, moreover, have their peculiarities; but if we compare a group of industries in years of a similar level of activity, the division of the total value added is generally very steady. This is so despite changes of other kinds meanwhile—in particular, big rises in pay. The implication is that the profit margin in the selling price is in practice not generally compressible by wage rises.

The second consideration sets out some grounds for expecting this to be so. When rates of pay are raised, there can in principle be three kinds of effect. First, the rise in pay per man may only offset a reduction in labor cost per unit of output that is being brought about by rising productivity. In this case, if selling prices and the numbers employed are not changed, total profits will rise in the same proportion as total pay. Second, the rise in pay may raise labor cost per unit of output, and this will be accompanied by a rise in selling price not merely equal in absolute amount to the rise in unit labor cost but proportional to it. In this case again there will be no change in the relative sizes of total pay and total profit. In the third case, too, the rise in pay raises unit labor costs; but here the selling price is unchanged, and the higher unit labor cost is offset by a reduction in the profit margin. Evidently two or three kinds of effect may be present together—a rise in pay may be partly offset by higher productivity and partly covered by a higher selling price, yet still leave something to be found out of the profit margin—but the three cases can be set out separately for analysis. The second seems to be a special one, yet it corresponds with what has frequently happened in practice, especially in recent years. In the first case real wages go up but, as in the second, there is no change in the division of the product. Only in the third does the trade union that pushes through a rise in pay raise pay relative to profit. What prevents this from occurring more often in practice?

There is this obstacle at the outset: if accepting a certain pay claim will reduce the employer's profit for as far ahead as he can see, he will weigh that prospective loss of profit against the cost to him of a strike, and the greater the prospective loss, the more likely he will be to take the strike. Conceivably this reckoning could operate at any level of profit. But in practice the employer is likely to accept the general opinion that high profits can and should be shared, and raising pay has in any case its own attractions for him. Only when the rise would cut into a profit that would generally be reckoned no more than normal, adequate, or reasonable is the employer likely to prefer the cost of a strike to the loss of profit that conceding the claim would mean. Just what level of profits is normal, adequate, and reasonable no one can say but everybody knows: a consensus prevails which no group of experts could formulate in agreed terms but which practical men apply to particular cases. Very likely the consensus shifts from time to time. Whether it moves on its own, or only follows after the facts of the market, we do not know; but at any one time there is a level of profit that employers feel themselves justified by general consent in defending. Below this level again is another that marks the minimum of subsistence for a firm: at anything less, the shortage of finance will drag it further down, or the proprietors will extricate as much capital as they can, to use it on better terms elsewhere. At this lower level, resistance is likely to be stronger still, for what is at stake is survival.

Experience seems to show that trade unions do not generally take the offensive and press a claim when its enforcement would only cut into a profit already no more than is generally reckoned adequate. That will be most unmistakably the state of affairs when there is already unemployment among a trade union's members, and it may be this rather than the expectation of resistance that inhibits action. The trade union needs also to be satisfied that there is no possibility of offsetting higher pay either by higher prices or by greater efficiency, a rare situation in the West in recent years. But where these possibilities really are precluded, and profits are already by prevailing standards no more than adequate, it does not seem that trade unions in practice seek to raise pay by a transfer from profit. As always where there is conflict, a party may feel that it must fight regardless of the cost, and one trade union may risk losses when it feels impelled by considerations of prestige or strategy to keep up with others; it may also be intransigent in opposing a cut even when the present rate can be maintained only by a reduction of profit that it would not take the offensive to enforce. But generally trade unions do not try to raise pay by transfer from profit beyond a certain limit. This is so even where, as in some European countries, many trade unionists regard all and any profit as an abuse: they still cannot abolish it by bargaining.

Beyond the immediate upshot of a struggle, moreover, lies the employer's reaction through the days ahead. We have singled out the case in which there is no present possibility of raising selling prices or increasing efficiency. Situations in real life are less clear-cut, and claims that can initially be met only out of a profit already no greater than is thought adequate can in practice be pushed through. But time will bring changes and openings. The employer will take any opportunity that offers to edge his prices up or lower his costs without lowering his prices; if he can do that at all, it will be by small changes that are made while rates of pay go on unchanged. What the bargain fixed was pay, but these other matters remain within the employer's control. If they give him the chance to restore his profit, he can take it.

Trade-union pressure on profits, indeed, always works under this far-reaching limitation, that collective bargaining controls only rates of pay and not costs or prices. It is only where the market holds selling prices down that pushing up the rate of pay will raise pay by transfer from profit, but it is there that the employer's resistance is strongest. Elsewhere some possibility is open that a rise in pay can be followed by a restoration of the profit margin, through lowering unit costs relative to prices or simply by raising prices. The greater the ease of raising prices, the less reason employers have to resist a claim for higher pay, but equally less is the prospect that pay will rise relative to profit. Where the claim would have to come out of profit, it will not get far; where it goes through readily, it will not come out of profit.

The last sentence may serve to sum up the probable reasons for the observed stability of the division of the product under collective bargaining, but that stability is far from absolute, and the argument must find room for the possibility that where prices and their relation to costs are externally controlled, trade unions can obtain a higher share of the product. They may be able to squeeze profit when they have something to press profit against. From the end of the American Civil War onward, great improvements in transport by land and sea were bringing different regions into closer competition with one another at the same time that increasing supplies of primary products lowered their prices in industrial markets: in what contemporaries came to call the "Great Depression" (1873–96), prices tended downward for a quarter of a century, and to sellers of industrial products any raising of prices must have seemed perilously contrary to the trend of the times. The interwar years in some important respects were similar. When employers generally expect that they will be harmed by competition if they raise their prices or miss any opportunity of getting them down, the market environment is hard; and though employers will be tough bargainers, the bargain will really be about the distribution of the product.

But when the market environment is soft, employers can back away and ride the punch; in the simplest case, they can raise prices in the same proportion as pay. The strongest case of this is presented by the years of inflation under full employment in Western countries since the Second World War. Here in country after country pay has risen at a rate equivalent to, say, doubling every ten years; but profits have risen in much the same proportion. We have already noted the possibility that in this soft-market environment the effects of trade-union pressure are to be seen not in any change in the distribution of the product but only in a general rise of costs and prices.

THE POWER OF TRADE UNIONS TO ALTER
DISTRIBUTION BETWEEN SECTORS

The discussion of the last section was concerned with the factor distribution of income between pay and profit. There remains the possibility that trade unions affect the distribution of the national product between different sectors—for example, that they raise the share of a highly unionized industry as a whole, taking its pay and profit together; or that they raise the incomes of particular groups of workers at the expense of all the rest of the community, including other workers.

One leading possibility appears as a continuation of our discussion of the raising of prices to cover higher pay. We saw that this raising was easier in some periods than others: it may also be easier in some industries than in others. An industry's prices will be beyond its own power to fix to the extent that it is under competition from outside, whether from the same product made in other regions or from other products that the buyer will turn to as substitutes and alternatives. The prices charged by some industries, particularly public utilities, are under public regulation. Competition within an industry itself limits the power of any one employer to fix his own prices to the extent that the product is standardized, and firms are numerous and of similar size. On the other hand there are industries that afford some latitude for the fixing of prices to all employers if they keep in step, or even to each employer separately. An industry may be sheltered from outside competition by the nature of its product, or by tariffs and quotas; the demand for its product within the sheltered market may be inelastic. In an industry like building, most of the output is adapted to the needs of particular sites and customers, and though employers compete by tender, they will all be likely to submit higher estimates when rates of pay are raised for them all. Where one firm is bigger than the rest, it may be able to change its prices with some confidence that the others will follow it; or there may be no one leader but a number of employers who adopt the practice of moving their prices up or down together, whether or not they are organized to discuss and administer the moves. According as the circumstances of a given industry approach these, the employers in it will be able to agree to rises in pay in the expectation of being able to cover them by higher prices without harming their businesses. If trade unions are as strong in the sheltered as in the unsheltered industries, and in the oligopolistic as in the more perfectly competitive, they are likely to raise pay and prices more in the sheltered and oligopolistic. We cannot tell in a general way how this change in the terms of trade between different sectors of the same economy will affect aggregate income and employment in each; it need not much affect the division of the product in either; but we do know that it will raise the relative real pay of as many workers as retain jobs in the sectors that raise their relative prices.

Here the initiative has been taken by a relative rise in pay, and any reduction in the numbers employed has been only an effect of that; but a restriction of numbers may also be enforced directly by the trade union. This is the well-known practice of the limitation of entry to a trade. It takes three forms. One is the requirement that certain kinds of work shall be done only by those having certain qualifications. This may be perfectly reasonable—indeed the government mây enforce requirements of this kind to protect the public— but the effect becomes merely restrictive when kinds of work are included that could be done efficiently by some who lack the stipulated qualification. The second form is the negative counterpart of the first: certain workers are debarred from doing work that they are capable of doing. Women have long suffered from such exclusions: the principle has been accepted that this or that is "not women's work" although in fact women could perfectly well do it; and where men and women have been working alongside one another there has been an invisible but well understood line on the floor of the shop that divides men's work from women's. Similar sweeping exclusions are maintained in multi-racial societies. The third form of limitation is restriction of training. Conceivably a trade union of unskilled men could keep down the number allowed to work in a certain place or occupation—the number of street porters, for instance, in a Chinese town— but the modern instances are not important. If a trade union can seize and hold the exclusive right to do certain work, then even if no training is required it can still restrict entry by charging high initiation dues; but this again has not occurred widely. It is the training of the skilled worker that has provided the most frequent opportunity and means to restrict entry. Access to professional schools may be restricted by the charging of fees over and above the cost of instruction, or by the outright limitation of the number of places. Access to training on the job may be restricted by (1) onerous conditions of apprenticeship, including longer periods of training or more severe trade tests than are really necessary; (2) excluding certain types of applicant, as, for example, entrants over a certain early age; and, above all, (3) enforcing quotas that limit the number of entrants to a fixed total or to a certain proportion of the number of journeymen.

In all these forms of limitation, the conscious motive may be only to "prevent the market being flooded"—that is, to prevent pay being lowered through an extension of supply and through undercutting by those who habitually work for less—and to safeguard job-holders from unemployment. It is difficult to maintain any training scheme without regulation of the numbers passing through it, and such regulation is consistent with an increase in the number of qualified workers. But in some cases the limitation of entry to a trade has the purpose of keeping up higher relative pay by creating a scarcity; and whether intended or not, that is always bound to be its tendency.

THE REGULATION OF WAGES

We have been dealing so far in this chapter only with collective bargaining, but in the whole ecology of pay the place of collective bargaining is restricted. It is predominant only in those countries of northwestern Europe and North America to which the nineteenth century brought economic individualism and economic growth. Australia and New Zealand inherited that tradition, and collective bargaining continues in them, but their predominant method of regulating pay is by arbitration. That is also the predominant method in India. Throughout the countries in which the influence of the Roman Catholic Church on social policy has been strong, particularly in southern Europe and in Latin America, the predominant method is by law and administrative decree. In the Soviet world the level and structure of pay are part of the national plan, and the rate of pay for each job is prescribed in a comprehensive schedule.

Though these other methods extend widely, their working does not need extensive further treatment: the essentials have already been brought out in the discussion of collective bargaining. The main question for all methods of fixing pay is what latitude they enjoy—that is, what the reactions will be to a given rate, and within what limits a rate must lie if it is not to have undesired consequences. Reactions and limits are imposed by the conventional and market forces, and the setting these provide for pay-fixing is essentially the same wherever the worker is free to take and leave jobs. Custom and opinion differ in their content and still more in their effectiveness, but the basic constraints that a lower rate reduces the number of applicants and a higher rate reduces the number of vacancies exist wherever the labor force is not captive and the amount of output disposed of is not independent of its cost. Those who fix rates of pay in different ways may well strike the balance of advantage for a given rate differently, but the expected reactions that enter into the balance will be much the same. How far, for instance, can an intervention raise the pay of some low-paid workers without throwing too many of them out of work altogether, or merely transferring income to them from others no better off than themselves? The answer will be the same whether the intervention comes by the unionization of these workers for collective bargaining, by an arbitral award, or by a minimum-wage law. The circumstances that decide whether a given rise in pay will come out of profit, for example, or will result in higher prices, are much the same, however the rise is made to occur. It is a function of the prices of products and of the factors of production to reconcile two ultimate freedoms—that of people as producers to move their resources into the most attractive of the available employments, and that of people as consumers to lay out their purchasing power on the most attractive of the available products. In any economy that leaves those two freedoms substantially unimpaired, there are market forces that bear upon rates of pay and circumscribe pay-fixing, whatever its procedure.

Nonetheless, different procedures have had their particular purposes. Collective bargaining, it may be said, was developed by communities that relied mainly on the workings of the market, in order to meet some deficiencies in the market's functioning: the workers who needed it most were those who benefited least from the competition of employers for labor and were least able to compare bids before they closed their deal. Where the market did fulfill the functions of bringing a range of potential sellers and buyers into touch with one another and equilibrating supply and demand, the community was disposed to accept the rates of pay the market arrived at. Other communities have felt otherwise. We have seen how the first question about a rate of pay is often not whether it balances vacancies and applicants but whether it is fair; and how the notion of fairness remains influential even in communities that have accepted the individualist principle of the right of each man to make the best use he can of his own resources. In communities that have never accepted that principle, the notion of fairness is naturally more influential still. The teaching of religion and morality is generally that a man should have not what he can get but what he ought to have. During the strike of the Ahmedabad textile workers in 1918, Mahatma Gandhi wrote:

> Pure justice is that which is inspired by fellow feeling and compassion. We in India call it Eastern or ancient justice. Where there is no place for fellow feeling or compassion, it is known as devilish or Western or modern justice . . . There was a time in India when serv-

ants did not ask for higher wages when there was a dearth of servants, and masters did not reduce wages when the supply was plentiful . . . But in most public activities of the West at present there is no place for feeling or mercy. It is considered just that a master pays his servant as he finds convenient. It is not considered necessary to think of the servant's requirements. So also the worker can at will make a demand, irrespective of the employer's financial condition, and it is considered just.[5]

That wages should be regulated by justice rather than by supply and demand is also part of the teaching of the Roman Catholic Church, set out in the encyclicals *Rerum Novarum* (1891), *Quadragesimo Anno* (1931) and *Mater et Magistra* (1961). The employer's part, according to *Rerum Novarum,* is not merely to pay what is agreed upon: "more imperious and ancient than any bargain between man and man is an underlying dictate of natural justice, namely that remuneration ought to be sufficient to support a frugal and well-behaved working man." *Quadragesimo Anno* enlarges this to the principle that "the wage paid to the working man must be sufficient for the support of him and his family." Free competition, it also stated, cannot be "the guiding principle of economic life . . . the public institutions of the nations must be such as to make the whole of human society conform to the needs of the common good, that is, to the standard of social justice."

Those who believe that wages should first and foremost be fair prefer regulation to collective bargaining even when collective bargaining is doing well for the worker. But in

5. M. H. Desai, *A Righteous Struggle* (Ahmedabad, Navajivan Publishing House, 1951), pp. 46–47.

some countries it has been a sufficient reason for imposing regulation that collective bargaining has not been and hardly could be developed. The impact of industrialism on a peasant or tribal society creates the same needs as trade unions have grown up to meet in the West; but in the emergent economies the growth of unions is impeded by the illiteracy of the workers as well as by their poverty and their reluctance to settle in the towns. The remedy is to regulate wages by decree, or, as in India, to provide a system of compulsory arbitration which enables a trade-union spokesman, however little strength he has behind him, to take an employer to court and get a binding award. A further reason for making arbitration compulsory in these societies also commends itself to the employers: the strikes that would otherwise occur from time to time would too often flare up in violence.

The regulation of wages also appeals to those whose aim is the coordinated administration of the economy in the public interest. These are the planners, and they will say that you cannot make a five-year plan and not plan wages. In Britain, Sidney and Beatrice Webb did more than anyone to make the functions of trade unions understood, and it was Beatrice Webb who coined the very phrase "collective bargaining": yet for them it was compulsory arbitration that was "the more excellent way." "I cannot believe," wrote Sidney Webb, "that a civilised community will permanently continue to abandon the adjustment of industrial disputes—and incidentally the regulation of the conditions of life of the mass of its people—to what is, in reality, the arbitrament of private war."[6] Under socialism the "present *competitive* determination of wages" would be superseded "by their assessment by public authority on the basis of the

6. Memorandum appended to Report of the Royal Commission on Trade Disputes and Trade Combinations, Cd. 2825 (1906).

Standard of Life necessary for full efficiency."[7] The structure of pay would be made up of a national minimum and, mounted on that, a differential for each occupation, assessed according to its particular requirements. Each differential must contain "a supplement for scarcity," sufficient to offset the costs of training and any deterrent aspects of the job and to attract "more than common skill," together with "a supplement for the necessary expenses of the professional status," to cover "personal habits and a method of life more costly than the standard prescribed as the universal minimum" when that method of life is necessary for "the fulfilment of particular functions."[8]

It is in agreement with this train of thought that rates of pay in the centrally planned economies have been centrally scheduled. In Babylonia about 2000 B.C. the code of Hammurabi prescribed the wages for agricultural workers, both permanent and seasonal; for ten kinds of craftsmen; for herdsmen and boatmen; for architects, doctors, and veterinary surgeons. In the 1950s rates of pay were officially prescribed throughout Russian industry by a schedule differentiating rates according to grade of labor, zone, and industry: "If Ivan Sidorov is deemed to be in Grade IV, in the central zone, in the automobile industry, then his earnings would be laid down in the appropriate wages regulation, where it is stated that persons of his grade are to earn, let us say, 500 rubles a month."[9] We have already seen that the differentials for the higher grades were widened under the First Five-

7. S. and B. Webb, *What Syndicalism Means*, Supplement to *The Crusade* (London, 1912), p. 152.

8. B. Webb, Minority Report, *War Cabinet Committee on Women in Industry*, Cmd. 135 (1919).

9. Alec Nove, "The State and the Wage-Earner," *Soviet Survey, 26* (1958), 28.

Year Plan to stimulate the supply of skill and, when that supply had risen, decreased again.

These various purposes of pay regulation have their influence on the ways in which regulation works, and there are some lessons of experience to be noted.

It is to enforce a minimum that governments have most often intervened of late. Often their aim has been to help only those who are worst off. One method is to enforce a single national minimum—as has been done by the Fair Labor Standards Act since 1938 in the United States; by the S.M.I.G. (Salaire Minimum Interprofessionnel Garanti) prescribed by the government since 1950 in France; and by the basic wage which has been awarded from time to time since the 1920s by the Commonwealth Court of Arbitration or (latterly) the Arbitration Commission in Australia. The last is an example of a minimum which, though intended originally only to safeguard the weakest, has become in practice a floor on which most of the country's wage structure stands, so that when it is raised, most other rates go up too. The American law, though equally general in form, has affected few other than the relatively small number of wage earners whose current rates were lower than the statutory rate at the time of its first application. When the object is only to help particular groups, an alternative method is to define the groups and to set up for each a board with statutory authority to fix minimum rates in dollars and cents from time to time. This has the advantages of flexibility, both in treating different groups separately and in being able to change the rate without fresh legislation; and of enabling spokesmen of employers and workers as well as of the community at large to be brought into the discussion and determination of the rate. The Australian state of Victoria developed the statutory tripartite wage board in the 1890s;

the United Kingdom followed this example in 1909 in its Trade Board Act, from which has developed a system of Wages Councils that fix minimum rates today for a fifth of all British wage earners. A similar method has been applied by the minimum wage laws of particular states in the United States.

When it was proposed to remedy the poverty of low-paid workers simply by requiring their employer to pay them more, the objection was raised that this would only throw them out of work altogether. The employer of that sort of worker was generally a man of small means, often a sub-contractor who gave the work out but also took part in it himself: he could pay more only if he got a higher price for the product. But the prices of products, it was said, are what the market will bear, and at a higher price less will be sold. The argument would have been more weighty had not trade unions already shown that some rates of pay could be pushed up without apparent detriment to employment. When statutory rates were enforced, it was found that they could often do the same. The reason lay not in any formal fault in the argument from supply and demand but in the practical importance of a possibility that lay within the argument but was not brought out—the possibility that both demand and supply might be inelastic. Where the ill-paid work was only a small part of the total cost of production, or the price of the immediate product was substantially raised by distributors' margins before the product reached the final buyer, or the final buyer himself could not react sharply to a rise in price, there the demand for the work was highly inelastic. That might have been so without the workers being ill-paid: a drop in their rate of pay would have been checked not through its creating unfilled vacancies but through its reducing the number of applicants, as workers went off to jobs where they could earn more. But for some workers no such movement was possible, because few alternative employments lay within their reach and they lacked the knowledge and resources to go farther afield: so the supply of their labor was highly inelastic, and their pay could fall without limit short of the barest subsistence. But the same circumstances that permitted the rate to fall permitted it to be raised.

Minimum-wage regulation has therefore shown its effectiveness. But this must not be exaggerated. The application of the United States federal minimum wage to the lacemakers of Puerto Rico came up against an elastic demand, and the reaction on employment was sharp. In many cases the effects on employment may have been really adverse, but they were mingled with those of other changes: in particular, the kind of labor affected has often been working on hand processes that are in the course of supersession by the factory, and we cannot tell how much, if at all, the minimum wage has accelerated their contraction. Employers no longer allowed to offset inefficient methods by low wages are put under pressure to improve their methods, but that means using fewer workers for a given output. Where minimum rates are set by boards trade by trade, the boards are likely to be conscious of these reactions, and feel their way year by year. They will then only be doing the work of collective bargaining and availing themselves of that latitude which, as we have seen, allows trade unions to keep wages somewhat higher than they would be otherwise over a run of years.

The use of arbitration to regulate wages has often been unintended—the original purpose had been only to supplement the procedures of bargaining by a means of peaceful settlement in the last resort. But compulsory arbitration will not stay in the last resort. Negotiators, knowing that however much they concede in bargaining they are still liable to be taken to court, will prefer to make no concession at all, lest that shift the starting point of arbitration against them: so the bargaining becomes unreal, the parties merely state their cases with declamation and intransigence, and the decision rests with the court. Weak unions will in any case expect to get more from the court than from bargaining. Even where genuine bargaining continues, an awareness of what the court would be likely to award sets a lower limit to the agreement. Where relations are confused and strikes bring riots, the employers may prefer to go to court, because "it does give a settlement." It is therefore understandable that where compulsory arbitration has been instituted, except as an emergency measure in time of war, it has become the main regulator of the whole pay structure.

The arbitrator is likely to bring to bear the layman's views about what is proper, commensurate, and just. His bias will be toward raising pay, for though his awards have statutory backing they can be rejected in practice, and they can be more effectively rejected by the workers than by the employers, for sanctions are much harder to apply against the workers: if he wants his awards to be reckoned sound because they prove acceptable, he must feel for the lowest rate that the workers are likely to be willing to tolerate, and take care not to go below that. But he will also have regard for the capacity of the employers to pay, and through this will implicitly take some account of the effects of a rate of pay on the number of jobs available. His wish to make his awards consistent with one another will involve him in some job evaluation. But save insofar as this leads him to new findings, he is likely to feel that equity calls for the maintenance of customary differentials, and he is not likely to initiate great changes in the pay structure. He may change it in another sense, by resisting movements that would otherwise come about under market pressures, but these movements may still reassert themselves through employers paying "overaward rates" where demand runs higher. The arbitrator's effect on the general level of pay in money is another matter. One means to consistency is to generalize a rise, so that one test case decides the amount of an "annual round." Each particular award gains in acceptability to the extent that it is only part of a general movement, and employers have a corresponding assurance of being able to cover it by higher prices. A system of compulsory arbitration therefore promotes the rise of the general level of pay in money.

The object of much administrative pay-fixing, on the other hand, has been to hold rates of pay down. The public regulation of wages that was common in Europe before the rise of individualism had as one of its objects the assigning to each occupation of its due degree, and the repressing of any tendency of the workers "to get above themselves." "Because a great part of the people," said an English ordinance of 1349,[10] "and specially of the workmen and servants has now died in this plague, some, seeing the necessity of lords and the scarcity of servants, will not serve unless they receive excessive wages"; and the ordinance went on to forbid employers to give, or workers to receive, higher wages than had prevailed before the plague. A French ordinance at this time of the Black Death attempted not to prevent the rise of wages but to limit it to one-third. In Florence the woolen manufacturers abolished freedom of wage contract and set up a committee to fix wages.

In more recent years the need to check the rise of costs and prices under excess demand during the Second World War and under full employment since has brought instances of

10. The Ordinance of Labourers. Quoted here from Bland, Brown, and Tawney, *English Economic History, Select Documents*, p. 164.

the administrative regulation of maximum wages. In the United States the Economic Stabilization Act of October 1942 required pay and prices to be held at the levels they had then reached, and the National War Labor Board was empowered to veto any change in wage rates. After the outbreak of war in Korea in 1950 a statutory order forbade any rise in rates of pay in the United States pending authorization by Stabilization Boards set up for wages and salaries. In the Netherlands, at the end of the Second World War, employers and trade unionists instituted a national wages policy of which one object was to regulate the movement of the general level of wages in the interests of the orderly development of the economy, and a Board of Mediators was given statutory power to validate collective agreements—in effect, pay could be raised only with the Board's permission, and it was an offense for employers to pay more than the permitted rates.

The lesson of experience is that maximum-wage regulation is exceedingly hard to enforce. In minimum-wage regulation the workers generally want to comply, and if enforcement is needed it is only against certain employers; but a maximum wage is something both parties want to evade—the workers, obviously, to earn more; but also the employers, to retain their labor. Evasion, moreover, can take many forms. Wage books can be in perfect order, but the hours of overtime can be inflated; workers can be promoted to higher-paid grades; various benefits such as free transport and free meals can be added to the stipulated wage. In both war and peace employers and trade-union leaders may accept the need to adhere to a national plan; but those employers who want to raise their output may be unable to recruit without offering more, and once bidding has begun others will find their labor force melting away. Maximum-wage regulation is therefore unlikely to succeed without effective control of the deployment of labor. The United Kingdom, which did have such control during the Second World War, dispensed with wage regulation.

Experience has shown that the administration of rates of pay through a centrally planned schedule is not wholly impracticable, but only if it allows deviations and is prepared to follow as well as lead. One overriding condition is that there shall be no independent trade unionism or political source of opposition. Given this condition, the only reactions that decide the viability of a particular rate are those of workers choosing and changing jobs and of managers trying to fill vacancies and raise output. As long as the number of vacancies does not exceed that of applicants in the aggregate, an entirely arbitrary schedule of job rates could survive: there would be a line, perhaps invisible, of applicants for jobs whose rates were above the current supply price of labor to the job, but the excess supply would not increase the number of vacancies by reducing the rate, and those not lucky enough to get in would simply have to take some other job, if they were to have a job at all. The deployment might make a poor match of workers' qualifications to job requirements, but jobs would be filled. It is otherwise if aggregate vacancies exceed applicants: there will be some jobs now that cannot be filled unless the terms are made more attractive. Russian experience shows that this brings the ingenuity of managers into play to evade the schedule. For pieceworkers this was not difficult: though attempts were made at the center to enforce common minimum norms of performance, most piece rates have in practice to be set job by job, and managers had only to set a loose rate to ensure that the pay envelope would be big enough to attract and retain the desired kind of labor. For timeworkers evasion was less easy, but something could be done by artificial upgrading—in a number of industries no one was left in the two lowest grades—and by contriving bonuses. These things not only pulled the actual structure of earnings away from the official schedule but brought distortions and anomalies into it, and also brought about a creeping and unplanned rise in the general level of money pay, of a kind familiar in Western countries under full employment. The endeavor has since been made to prune some of the anomalies, and also to restore the connection between the schedule and actual earnings, but to do this Mahomet has had to go to the mountain, and it is the schedule that has had to be adjusted to the facts of the market.

7 THE GENERAL LEVEL OF REAL PAY

When money wages are compared with the prices
of the things wage earners generally buy, we get a measure
of real wages. For a refined measure of that kind we need a
broadly based average of actual earnings, and an index number of the cost of living based upon a wide sample of family
budgets and embracing a wide range of outlay, from houseroom to haircuts and from bread and meat to movies and mo-
toring. Such particulars are available only for recent years,
and if we are to look farther into the past we must be content
with a rougher measure, in which some more or less representative rate of pay is compared with the cost in the produce
market, not the retail shop, of an assortment of some of the
staples of consumption—the bread grains, for example, meat,
cheese, beer, candles and firewood, canvas, and woolen cloth.

The Economics of Labor

The basketful of such things that a representative day's wage will buy in Western economies today is probably five or six times as big as it was before the Industrial Revolution. A ratio and contrast of the same magnitude stands between present-day real wages in the Western and the underdeveloped economies. Before the Industrial Revolution such glimpses as we catch of real wages show some big ups and downs but no progressive trend. How can we account for these movements and variances?

There is evidence that the dominant influence on real wages in the earlier stages of Western economies was population pressure, and it remains dominant in some underdeveloped economies today. The familiar Malthusian connection between population and the standard of living runs through diminishing returns in agriculture: save as technique advances, a greater number can raise more food from a given area only under penalty of getting less per man. But a growth of population in some countries had little power to raise the output of food at all. We have seen that the wage earners were commonly a small part of the whole occupied population. But it was a part that expanded rapidly when population grew, for the other occupations—on the land, and among the small masters of the workshops—did not take up more manpower readily: the landless men could fill no niche in the established order, but became an overspill, with only their hands to offer for hire. More children were growing up in the villages than could inherit their fathers' holdings; the younger sons must find what work they could with loom or forge in the cottage, or take themselves off to seek employment in the towns. If they found jobs, they would be producing personal services or workshop manufactures, the output of which would be increased. They would need to exchange most of it for that part of the output of foodstuffs and raw materials that was sold off the farm. But this agricultural surplus would not grow much. The technique of the times and the forms of landholding did not allow many more men to be used either to work the cultivated area more intensively or to break in the waste; when more cloth or pans or planks were given in exchange for a sack of corn the real income of the farmers rose, but that imparted no effective stimulus to raise the output of farming as a whole. So the terms of trade between the workshop and the farm turned against the workshop: a day's work in loom-loft or forge or saw-pit commanded less food in exchange. As population grew, the wage in terms of food was forced down more than the output of food per head of the whole population.

In southern England we can trace the variations on this theme from the end of the thirteenth century, insofar at least as the wages of mason and carpenter are a guide to wages generally. The first movement is in reverse. In 1349–50 the Black Death carried off, it is thought, about a third of the manpower of the country; the land and equipment, no smaller than before in the aggregate, were now half as big again per worker; real wages rose. It may be because the plague recurred that the rise went on, but through the fifteenth century real wages traversed a plateau that was high even by recent standards: the same crude measuring rod applied throughout makes the real wage of the building craftsman higher then than it was ever to be again in southern England until 1880.

But by 1520 a great change had set in. In the rest of that century the craftsman's money wages were to double, but the prices of basic consumables rose fourfold. This extraordinary impoverishment, moreover, did not afflict the wage earners of England alone: reckonings of the same kind show the building craftsman suffering to very much the same extent at this time in France and Alsace, in Münster, Augsburg, and Vienna, and in Valencia. In all these places, and in the region of Stockholm too, the records show that the terms of trade between workshop and farm turned against the workshop. Generally the prices of manufactured products like bricks, iron, lead, and cloth rose in much the same proportion as the craftsman's money wage, but farm produce rose twice as much. About 1600 the man who brought to market a bag of nails he had made in order to exchange it for corn was getting half as much corn as his predecessor would have gotten a hundred years before. The generality of this effect suggests a general cause, and the most probable is a growth of population.

At least the same effect of falling real wages appears again in southern England at a time when we know from more direct evidence that a rise in population was setting in. For about a hundred years after 1650 real wages had been recovering, not fast or steadily but on the whole progressively: about 1750 they turned down again, and within the half-century (if we measure them by prices at wholesale) they fell by a third. What is writ large in the records of pay and prices can be watched as it goes on in the microcosm of one English village.[1] Before 1750 few villagers had come to the overseers of the poor for relief, and those that did often had means of support and only needed a helping hand—a widow whose spinning wheel needed replacement, an orphan boy who could get a place in a farmer's house if he could have his clothes provided. But in 1752 for the first time a workless man was relieved; by the end of the century the annual cost of relief had risen from under a hundred to nearly three

1. Tysoe in Warwickshire. The particulars here are taken from M. K. Ashby, *Joseph Ashby of Tysoe, 1859–1919* (Cambridge, Eng., Cambridge University Press, 1961).

thousand pounds, and forty men or so were "roundsmen"—workless men who were sent the round of the farms to pick up jobs for a pittance, but had their bread money made up by a dole. The picture of rural overpopulation and debilitation has its counterparts in the underdeveloped countries of more recent years.

But the growth of population from 1750 onward saw a new possibility open. The growth was rapid in Ireland as well as in Britain—probably in both islands the population doubled in less than a hundred years. In Ireland the food for more and more stomachs was found by subdividing holdings and growing more potatoes, until disease destroyed the crop of 1846. Then famine and pestilence killed hundreds of thousands, and a great emigration of the remainder began: by the end of the century the population of 1846 had been halved. In Britain it was otherwise: revolutionary methods in agriculture had enabled much more food to be raised from the acre, and many acres hitherto waste to be brought under cultivation; revolutionary methods in transport and industry enabled increasing numbers to produce manufactures and export them in exchange for food grown overseas. Population continued to grow, but productivity was rising too. By 1850 it was productivity that was taking the lead. A bigger output of manufactures per head now meant more food per head. International trade made the density of population in the one island irrelevant to the standard of living its workers could attain, save in time of war.

The forces that underlie this story have renewed their interplay in the emergent countries of our own day. A rise in population sets in for reasons little connected with the beginnings of economic growth: the most usual is the reduction of the death rate by the withdrawal or extirpation of some disease. There follows pressure on the food supply, and a fall in real income that may be concentrated on an overspill of landless men, or may be more diffused if the structures of the family and of land tenure allow the work and produce of the farm to be shared by increasing numbers. If industries are developed to absorb the overspill, the real incomes of those who work in them depend upon the size of the agricultural surplus: unless that rises, the expansion of industrial employment may be compatible only with a worsening of the terms of trade between workshop and farm, and the endeavor to keep wages up relative to peasant incomes may only stop the expansion of industrial employment. The rise of productivity in industry, even the setting up of the most efficient plants the advanced countries can design, provides no way out unless the products can be exported in exchange for food. But granted the opportunity to exchange manufactures for food on constant or improving terms, at home or abroad, a rising population can provide itself with a rising income per head, and real wages can rise as industry expands and productivity advances with technique and organization.

FLUCTUATIONS OF REAL WAGES

The dependence of real wages on the terms of trade between workshop and farm has set its mark upon their fluctuations until recent times.

Up to the late eighteenth century the staple foodstuffs were seldom moved long distances, within countries or between them, simply because they were too costly to transport by wagon and pannier and sailing ship, or could in any case not be preserved during the journey. Men depended for most of their food on the crops grown within a few miles of them. They were therefore exposed to all the vicissitudes of the local harvest, and could be famished while there was plenty only fifty miles away. But better transport would still not have availed when the harvest failed throughout a whole region. Then there was just less to eat everywhere: but it was the wage earner who had to tighten his belt most. Those to whom the crop belonged could take what they wanted at the source, subject only to their need to sell some part for cash; the others were rationed by price. But the wage earner had only a small margin out of which to raise his outlay on food, and it was not then the practice to vary money wages with the cost of living. For centuries in England the highest year's price of corn in any decade was commonly not less than double the lowest. At some times this would have meant a meager subsistence in the lean years and an ample diet in the fat ones; at others, what was no more than enough at the best of times dropped below the level of subsistence in the hard times.

The consumption of a great part of the labor force of the world still varies from year to year with the harvest. The remedy, that of making good a shortage in one place by fetching more from another, is open only to those whose standard of living is already high, for what they find it cheaper to import would still be dear to the worker in an underdeveloped country even if it could be delivered at the same price to him there.

Up to the present day the movements of real wages have been influenced by another sort of fluctuation in the availability of primary products. We have seen how an adverse movement of the terms of trade between workshop and farm provided the lever with which population pressure pressed real wages down: but these terms of trade have changed for other reasons. Since the early nineteenth century, when international markets for some of the staple foodstuffs and raw materials began to form, the prices of these primary products have moved in alternating phases of some twenty to twenty-five years. Until 1848 they tended downward; then on balance they rose until the end of the American Civil War, or perhaps until 1873 and the breaking of the boom after the Franco-Prussian War. They fell next, substantially, through the years termed the "Great Depression," until the mid-1890s. From then until the First World War they rose again; in the interwar years they came down; from the late 1930s they lifted sharply until 1951 and the end of the Korean Conflict. The movements of other prices show some sympathy, so that the price level as a whole reveals what Kuznets has designated "secondary secular fluctuations." But for the present purpose what is important is that the swings of the prices of primary products have generally been wider than those of other prices, so that the quantity of primary products that a given cargo of manufactures would command in exchange has generally risen during the phases of falling primary product prices, and conversely.

This brought a corresponding fluctuation in the rate of rise of real wages. The movement of money wages, as it can be traced in a number of Western countries from the middle of the nineteenth century, shows some sympathy with that of the general price level: money wages rose substantially in the periods of rising general prices, and more slowly, sometimes hardly at all, in the other periods. But they moved with the prices of manufactures rather than with those of primary products: hence real wages, insofar as primary products entered into them, rose faster in the periods when the prices of those products were falling, even though money wages rose slower then. The old relation between workshop and farm was now appearing in the international market. The changes in relative prices marked changes in the relative rate of growth of supplies. The periods of falling prices of primary products were those in which these products were becoming more abundant. The steelworker can be thought of as having been paid by being given part of the steel he had helped make: how big a real wage that brought him depended greatly on how much grain and meat he could barter it for from time to time.

But the extent to which primary products make up the real wage has declined as the real wage has risen. The scanty records of household budgets down to the end of the eighteenth century suggest that outlay on foodstuffs used to make up not less than 60 per cent of wage earners' total outlay. For British wage earners just before the First World War the proportion was still put at 60; but budgets collected in the 1950s have brought it down to 35. In the budgets of urban wage earners and clerical workers in the United States in 1953 the proportion was just over 30 per cent.

SUBSISTENCE WAGES WHERE
ENTERPRISE IS NOT EXPANSIVE

Evidently the steelworker's real wage also depended on how much steel he received. This in turn may be considered to depend on two factors: the output of steel per worker, and the share of this that he retained. If this formulation is not merely an identity, it suggests that the wage depends in practice both on the size of the output and on certain forces that decide how this will be divided, and that a rise in the output will generally bring a rise in the wage. But that begs a question. In much of the world's history the laborer has earned no more than will keep him and his family alive, and in some places that is still so today. We do not have to look far for a possible reason why the wage is no higher: there is population pressure, and a margin of hungry jobseekers is always there to be taken on at a subsistence wage. The demand for labor may extend, but that will not raise the wage. Higher productivity offers a way out from population pressure only if there is some assurance that this pressure will not still keep wages down. The level at which they stick need not be a bare subsistence: custom, or the social conscience, or a tacit agreement of the workers themselves, may set a higher minimum. Yet as long as there are always more men standing ready to take a job at the one unchanged rate, the effect will be the same—output per man may rise, but the real wage will not.

How likely is this to occur in practice? We can readily envisage situations in which it will. Suppose, for instance, that a tropical island is devoted almost entirely to growing sugar, and that the industry is organized in estates which provide the only considerable channel of employment for wage earners on the island. Malaria used to be endemic, but now modern insecticides have suppressed the mosquito, and population is rising. The increment is bound to provide a supply of laborers ready to fill any vacancy at the going wage. It may be that their competition for jobs pulls that wage down, and the lower wage makes it worth the estates' while to take more men on: but unless this goes so far that the whole increment has been absorbed for the time being, the possibility remains of getting more workers without having to offer more. As long as this is so, an increase in the profitability of the industry will extend the demand for labor, but not raise the wage. The price of sugar may rise in the world market, and this will raise the average value product per worker, but the part retained by the worker will be a constant absolute amount. It is not necessary to postulate any zone of inertia in the matching of the demand for labor with the supply: the workers may always be getting the full demand price for the number employed, yet except insofar as more are employed (if more are), the workers still have no part nor lot in the rise of the real income of the island. That rise will be concentrated on the profits and rents of the estate owners.

This situation is possible, but it depends on two conditions that are not widely found in practice. The first is the horizontal supply curve of labor. This may actually be present less often in the emergent than the advanced economies. In some emergent economies when more children survive they can be absorbed within the family, through which they have access to land, and are assured of a subsistence within the way of life and locality in which they have grown up. In that case the supply of wage earners to industry can be extended at any one time only if recruits can be attracted from successively better supplied households and remoter villages. It is in the advanced economy, where the family is less extensible and the land is completely taken up already and worked with economy of manpower, that the man without means of support save by wage earning is more likely to be found. The capacity of traditional societies to absorb increments of population varies from region to region and is bound to have its limits everywhere. But when it is extended to the limit of great impoverishment, the effect may be a check to the growth of population rather than an extrusion of manpower—debilitation does not make a labor supply.

A horizontal supply curve of labor is often precluded by another circumstance: men differ in their aptitudes, and the kind of man who will make a useful wage earner may be in limited supply even when nondescript labor is plentiful. Men differ in their bodily strength, their education, and their attitude to work, in an emergent even more than in an advanced society. The supply of footloose labor for irregular and temporary employment is one thing; that for steady work, with the household settled near the factory, quite another. These considerations help to account for the distinction between permanent and temporary workers in Indian mills, and the permanent workers' getting wages well above the level of incomes in the villages. It is possible for more coolies to be always available at the going wage, while the supply curve of more qualified labor is inclined positively.

The second condition responsible for the outcome in the island is that the supply of enterprise was inelastic. When the profits of sugar-growing rose, the estate owners did not bring more land under cultivation and recruit labor to work on it, for virtually all the land was under cultivation already; and for the same reason the high rate of return could not attract competitors from outside. But we also tacitly assumed that the funds which high profits made available for new investment did not induce the estate owners, or enterprisers who borrowed from them, to develop new activities—to set up a factory for utilizing by-products of the sugar cane, or build a hydroelectric plant in the hills, or create a tourist industry. That could well be: the estates might be owned by patrician families, with a traditional way of life, glad enough to draw more money from the accepted source but looking down on other ways of making it. More generally, the incomes that provide the main potential source of funds for investment in an economy may be concentrated in the hands of a group—landowners, or merchants, or employers in an established industry—who are traditionalists and not innovators, who like sumptuous living but also like to take things easy, and do not judge one another by their success in expanding their activities and fortunes. To the extent that this is so, a rise in the rate of return will not stimulate enterprise, and so extend the number of jobs to be filled and bid up wages, but profits can rise while wages remain at a customary level.

For rising productivity to enable a growing labor force to find work at rising rates of pay, enterprise must be responsive to the rate of return. There must be a supply price of capital and enterprise such that, as long as the current levels of productivity and pay offer a return to investment above that supply price, new investments will be undertaken and new jobs created. When the supply of enterprise is elastic in this sense, a lag of pay behind productivity will bring an extension of the demand for labor. However fast population is growing, there cannot be a jobless overspill unless, at the current levels of productivity and pay, the rate of return is so low that all extension of enterprise is checked. As long as the rate of return is high enough to allow enterprise to extend at a greater rate than population, pay will rise.

REAL WAGES AND OUTPUT:
THE CAPITAL–OUTPUT RATIO

In the Western economies whose population has been growing during the past hundred years, pay has in fact risen. The labor force has grown often at the rate of 10 per cent or more each decade, and though a fluctuating rate of unemployment has been severe at its worst, there has been no cumulation of excess labor: over spans in which the number of applicants has doubled, the number of vacancies has about doubled too. But meanwhile pay also has risen, not of course merely in money, but essentially in real terms. There are some countries whose statistical records enable us to trace the general movements of wage rates and prices, and compare wages with other components of the national income, from some time in the last half of the nineteenth century. These records indicate a rise between the early 1860s and the eve of the Second World War that amounted to multiplication by 2.5 or more in France, the United Kingdom, and the United States, and by more than 5 in Sweden. The indications are not comprehensive and cannot be exact, but they do serve to establish orders of magnitude.

Above all, they establish beyond all doubt the fact that real wages have risen greatly. This is evidence that the supply of enterprise has in fact been elastic, that investment and promotion and development have gone on fast enough to outpace the rise in population and to extend the demand for labor faster than the supply. The state of affairs that Marx observed in Western Europe in the 1840s gave him grounds to expect that as time went on real wages would be held down to the subsistence level or even forced below it, while profits rose. This expectation has not been fulfilled. Despite an ever-increasing supply of labor, real wages have risen with the general rise in productivity.

We can go further than that. The two rises have followed roughly parallel trends: the proportionate share of the product accruing to employed labor has not changed widely or cumulatively.

Before looking at the evidence we must clear up some questions of formulation. Wages themselves are only one part of the return to labor as a factor of production in its most comprehensive sense: there are also salaries, and the earnings of those who do not work under a contract of employment. These last, the self-employed, comprise professional men like lawyers, doctors, and consultants, with craftsmen who do repair and contract work, and—often the most numerous—small shopkeepers and farmers. The incomes in this "sector of unincorporated enterprise," as the statisticians term it, are mixed, in that some part of them must commonly be imputed to the equipment, stock-in-trade, or land owned by the worker; but with few exceptions, the greater part is a return to labor. The share of the national product that goes to any one group of workers will naturally depend, among other things, on their relative numbers. Generally, in the course of recent economic growth, the relative number of salary earners has risen, and that of the self-employed has fallen. The first change tends to lower the share of wages, the second to raise it, but neither necessarily marks a change in the wage per wage earner relative to the rates of return per unit of other factors of production. But one way of eliminating the effect of shifts in relative numbers is suggested by the identity:

$$\text{Share of wages in national income} \equiv \frac{\text{Number of wage earners}}{\text{Number of occupied persons}} \times \frac{\text{Average wage}}{\times \text{Average national income per occupied person}}$$

The two elements farthest to the right make up by themselves a wage–income ratio whose observed movements provide a compact indication of the behavior of wages as the return per unit of a factor of production, relative to other such returns. When the records allow, a similar ratio may be calculated for wages and salaries taken together.

The course of the wage–income ratio can be followed in several countries through much of the past hundred years. It shows some sharp cyclical movements, and probably also some gradual changes persisting through longer periods; it also shifts through the two great wars. But in comparison with the other changes that have taken place meanwhile, with the growth of population and output, the transformation of technique, the rise of new industries and occupations and the decline of old, the impacts of war, the doubling and redoubling of price levels—in comparison with these expansions and upheavals, the trend of the wage–income ratio is conspicuous for its stability. In Sweden, to take a strong example, the average money wage-rate in 1913 was 3.5 times what it had been in 1861; the national income in money, reckoned per head of the occupied population, had been rising meanwhile along a trend of nearly 2.5 per cent a year; and the standard of living had risen to an extent indicated by a trebling of the real wage-rate. Yet the wage–income ratio was no different in 1913 from what it had been in 1861. Those happen to be two years when the ratio was at a cyclical low point, and there had been five intervening years when it had been more than 15 per cent above that. Yet the trend is level: if money income per occupied person was rising along a trend of nearly 2.5 per cent a year, so were money wage-rates.

For the 1950s we have records from a number of countries that enable us to combine wages with salaries, and compute the ratio of average pay per employee of all kinds to average income per occupied person. Within agriculture the pay–income ratio generally differs a good deal from that in the rest of the economy, and the relative size of the agricultural sector also differs from country to country, so it is the pay–income ratios for the rest of the economy, exclusive of agriculture, that can be compared most closely. In eight countries for which estimates have been made—Australia, France, the Netherlands, New Zealand, Sweden, the United Kingdom, the United States, and Western Germany—the pay–income ratios in 1950–57 all lie fairly near the common level of 0.75, and save for a decline in the Netherlands and a rise in Sweden the movements from year to year are small. This similarity between different economies in the same decade reinforces the impression of stability made by the absence of upward or downward trends from one decade to another within one country.

It seems, then, that real pay has risen in the course of economic growth because the forces that determine the rates of return to the various factors of production have raised the return to labor in much the same proportion as the returns to productive factors generally. But if we try to give that conclusion more precision we come up against a further complication. We have made allowance for changes in the numbers of other types of occupied persons working alongside the average wage earner: we have yet to allow for changes in the amount of capital he works with. The amount of capital per man varies widely. It rises in the course of economic growth. In the United Kingdom, for example, it may have about doubled between 1870 and 1914. It is very different between countries at different levels of productivity: the amount of capital per worker in manufacturing was reckoned to be about 2.5 times as great in the United States as in the United Kingdom in the 1950s. But unless the rate of return to capital falls when the quantity of capital per worker is, say, doubled, the total amount allocated to capital out of the output per worker must also be doubled. Can this leave the worker with as big a proportion of the product as before?

It can, on condition that when the capital per worker is doubled, the output per worker doubles too. Let us take a simplified case in which labor consists solely of the one category of "workers," and the product is divided exclusively between wages and profit. Suppose that, when output per worker in unit time was $100, capital per worker was $350, and that at 10 per cent, capital received $35 while the other $65 of the output went to wages. Over a span within which the purchasing power of the dollar remains unchanged, the amount of capital per worker rises to $700: then at 10 per cent, as before, capital receives $70. But if meanwhile the output per worker has risen to $200, wages can amount to $130, and the division of the product remains as before, while real wages have doubled. It is useful to put the identity in general terms. If the quantity of capital is C, and the annual output or product is P, then the capital–output ratio (c), as it is usually termed, is C/P. If this ratio is a constant over time, we can write:

$$C \equiv cP$$

Suppose also that the rate of return on capital is r, so that total profit is rC. Then total wages will be $P - rC$, and the share of wages in the output will be

$$\frac{P - rC}{P} \equiv 1 - rc.$$

Evidently the division of the output will be steady if r and c are both steady, or if their changes offset one another.

What do we know of their actual behavior? Our knowledge of r is necessarily obscured by the errors in the available estimates both of aggregate profit and of the total capital on which it is earned; in international comparisons there may also be differences of coverage. What estimates we have indicate sharp cyclical changes, among others, but little sign of any progressive rise or fall in the rate of return on risk capital as a concomitant of economic growth. We should be surprised to find this rate of return, on the average of any decade and of any large assortment of concerns, higher than 15 per cent or lower than 5 per cent. As for c, the evidence again has its margin of uncertainty, and as far as it goes it indicates changes from time to time that have sometimes been big. But we can take a range of from 3 to 4.5 as representative of the values of c generally indicated: that is, if we include in capital not only equipment but building, stocks, and work in progress, then this total stock of capital has generally come out as equivalent to between three and four and a half years' current output. If improvements in technique and management result in output per man rising faster than capital per man—that is, if the capital–output ratio is reduced—then comparative stability in the rate of return to capital will go with an increased share of pay in the product. A recent study, for instance, indicates that over the span 1919–57 capital per man in the United States (excluding governmental activity and income from abroad) was increased by a factor of about 1.5, whereas output per man was increased by about 2.5; that is, the capital–output ratio was reduced by a factor of about 1.5 ÷ 2.5 or 0.6—actually, it seems, from about 4.5 to 2.6.[2] Around 1919 the share of labor of all kinds in total income was given (allowing for rounding off) by

$$1 - rc = 1 - 0.06 \times 4.5 = 0.72 \text{ approx.}$$

That is, the average rate of return on capital was about 6 per cent, and pay made up 72 per cent of total income. By 1957 the expression had become (again with rounding off)

$$1 - rc = 1 - 0.07 \times 2.6 = 0.81 \text{ approx.}$$

The rate of return on capital has gone up, from 6 to 7 per cent in the round figures used here, or, more nearly, by a tenth, so that the total compensation of the capital with which the average man was working will have risen by a factor of 1.5 × 1.1 or 1.65, against the multiplication of his output by about 2.5. This implies that real pay per man rose more than output per man; in fact, it was raised by a factor of about 2.8. The share of labor in the product was also

2. J. W. Kendrick, *Productivity Trends in the United States* (Princeton, National Bureau of Economic Research, 1961).

thereby raised. Initially, we may write—in terms of the division of output *per man*,

Share of labor (72) + Share of capital (28) = Output (100).

Multiplying 72 by 2.8, and 28 by 1.65, we get 202 + 46 = 248, that is, the original output raised by the already-mentioned factor of about 2.5. The share of labor has risen from 72 to over 81 per cent.

The record of a number of periods and countries thus composes a picture of the distribution of the product during economic growth, in which variations such as we have just studied occur around a central tendency of considerable uniformity. As the quantity of capital per worker is increased, the accompanying advance of technique prevents the product per unit of capital from falling, so that the product per worker rises in the same proportion as the quantity of capital per worker. As long as this is so, a stable rate of profit implies a stable share of pay in the product, and conversely. In fact, there has been such stability: if far from complete, it has nonetheless been pervasive.

But we must recognize that our account of the central tendency has been merely descriptive: it has not solved problems, only posed them. Why has the supply of enterprise apparently been sufficiently elastic to prevent the rate of profit from rising progressively despite the growth of population? Why has the rate of return on risk capital been in the region of 10 per cent rather than, say, 25 per cent? The capital–output ratio seems to owe its relative stability to a balance between the lowering of output per unit of capital by decreasing returns to investment under constant technique and the raising of output per unit of capital by technical advances. Has this balance been merely adventitious, or does it mark an equilibrium of forces? In the presence of a certain rate of growth of population, maintenance of the central tendency requires a certain rate of investment, which requires a certain rate of saving. Why should it be just this rate of saving that comes out of the current distribution of income? In the preceding chapter we discussed the factors that help fix a given rate of pay, and argued that marginal productivity was one of them. But what assurance is there that the levels of pay implicit in the central tendency will not be above or below the marginal product of labor?

These questions have not been neglected. The theories of capital and interest, and of risk, enterprise, and profit have tackled some of them. They all enter into the theory of growth, and economists who have constructed models of growth have shown how possible answers can be combined. These analyses are highly germane to the explanation of the observed movements of wages and salaries. Yet they belong to realms of discourse beyond the scope of this book. Here we can take up only the question that belongs most closely to the economics of labor—what relation is there between the fixing of rates of pay by the macroeconomic process we have just been discussing and the tendency to equality between pay and the marginal product in microeconomic adjustments?

THE COBB-DOUGLAS FUNCTION

The formal theory of distribution shows that there need be no conflict. All the activity of an economy can be regarded as being carried on in one great enterprise that combines the services of a number of broadly classified factors of production—in the simplest and most abstract case just two, labor and capital. The enterprise has a single composite product. Various combinations of the productive factors can be used to make it, and to each set of inputs there corresponds a certain output. These relations are summarized in a production function, which shows how much product will be yielded by any set of inputs of the factors. If each factor iş remunerated at a rate equal to its marginal productivity, a certain aggregate payment will be allotted to it: but why should these payments in the aggregate exactly distribute the whole product, neither more nor less? Formal theory has shown that they will do this if the production function is of such a kind that changing all the inputs in a given proportion will make the same proportionate change in output. If output is reckoned in physical terms, this seems only what is to be expected. One production function of this kind is the Cobb-Douglas. Let there be two factors of production, labor and capital, whose inputs are L and C, and let the quantity of product they yield be P. Then the Cobb-Douglas production function is of the form

$$P = a\,L^k\,C^{1-k}, \qquad (0 < k < 1).$$

As long as the technical conditions relating inputs and outputs are of this form, the marginal productivity of a factor will be a constant proportion of its average productivity, whether the relative input of that factor is large or small. The marginal productivity of labor, for instance, will be a constant proportion of the output per worker. If the factor is paid according to its marginal productivity, the total payment to it will be a constant proportion of the whole product.[3] In each case, this proportion will be k.

3. $$\frac{dP}{dL} = a\,k\,L^{k-1}\,C^{1-k} = k\,\frac{P}{L}$$

$$L\,\frac{dP}{dL} = k\,P$$

The General Level of Real Pay

From recent statistical materials we can assign a magnitude to k. We have seen how the payment accruing to labor in its most comprehensive sense comprises not only wages and salaries but a large part of the incomes of the sector of unincorporated enterprises. The statistics of national income now brought together by the United Nations for a large number of economies show that this sector varies widely in its relative size from one economy to another, with corresponding inverse variations in the shares of wages and salaries in national income. But when we add these forms of income together, we get a great deal of uniformity. Out of twenty-five countries for which we can do this through 1950–57, in sixteen the total share of labor so reckoned lies between 81 and 87 per cent. These sixteen include economies very different from one another in other respects—the United States and Ceylon, for instance, Sweden and Brazil, the United Kingdom and Japan. Some deduction is due for the return to capital included in the mixed incomes of the sector of unincorporated enterprises. We do not know how much. But perhaps a round figure of 75 per cent will give the order of magnitude of the share of labor in its most comprehensive sense. This is the sort of value we can assign to k.

Doing so, we can say that as long as the aggregate production function is of the Cobb-Douglas type, and the technical relations that it expresses remain unchanged, the marginal productivity of labor will be three-quarters of the average output per worker, and if the rate of pay for labor as a whole is equal to its marginal productivity, its total pay will be three-quarters of the national income. These proportions of three-quarters remain unchanged whatever the inputs and however great or small the amount of capital per worker. In these conditions, therefore, the fixing of pay by forces that check divergences between pay and marginal productivity is consistent with the observed behavior of pay as a share in the product.

But the conditions include unchanging technical relations. What happens when these relations change? We have seen how a progressive improvement in technique is implied by the observed absence of any progressive rise in the capital–output ratio as the quantity of capital per worker has risen. But if this is the form that technical progress has taken, it can leave the internal or distributive properties of a Cobb-Douglas production function unchanged.[4] For then the function changes over time, so that a given historical increase in the quantity of capital per worker is associated with an equal proportionate increase in the output per worker, and it can change in this way by a progressive rise in its constant term a, without any necessary change in k. Improvements in technique of this kind raise the total output yielded to a given set of factor inputs, but not the proportionate division of the output between the factors.

This is far from establishing what relations have actually underlain the observed course of events, but it does show that a progressive technical advance is not necessarily inconsistent with stability in the distribution of the product between the factors of production, when the forces determining factor prices act to check divergences between those prices and the corresponding marginal productivities.

4. We have $P = aL^k C^{1-k}$, or $\dfrac{P}{L} = a\left(\dfrac{C}{L}\right)^{1-k}$, and this is required to change its form over time so that if $\dfrac{C}{L}$ is varied meanwhile in the proportion λ, $\dfrac{P}{L}$ will vary in the same proportion. But this will be so if a changes to $a\lambda^k$.

The General Level of Real Pay

As far as the central tendency holds, the rise of real pay depends on that of productivity in the whole economy. If productivity rises faster or slower from time to time, so will real pay. But the central tendency does not hold completely—it marks out a trend, about which the actual course of events describes its variations, so that real pay rises now slower and now faster than productivity. There are two kinds of reasons for variations in the rate of rise of real pay.

It is probably with the first that we are confronted in the slower rise of productivity in the thirty years from the 1880s to the First World War than in the thirty or forty years before. An index of real wages made by deflating average money wage-rates by the cost of living shows a point of inflection in the mid-1890s in a number of countries, with a slower rise afterward, or even little rise at all on balance for nearly twenty years, down to 1914. This calculation depends a great deal on the prices of foodstuffs and raw materials in the world markets, and it fixes the point of inflection in the mid-1890s because it was then that these prices ended a twenty-year fall and set off on a rising course. Statistics of output suggest that the slowing down in growth came earlier and more gradually. Its underlying causes seem to have been the working out of the impact effects of the techniques of iron, steel, and steam. In 1880, to take one example, the tonnage of British shipping under sail had been half as great again as that under steam, but by 1883 the steam tonnage drew level, and by 1895 it was more than twice as great. Replacing a sailing ship by a steamship made a great advance in productivity at one bound. When that had been achieved, further advances depended on improvements in the steamship. These were made, but took only gradual effect. The example may serve to typify the great gains brought more widely by the building of the railroads and the application of steam power to machines of iron and steel, and likewise the pause that followed. Great new technical developments lay ahead: electricity, the internal combustion engine, the man-made fibers, the new chemical industry, a new agricultural revolution. Many of these were in the early stages of application before 1914, but as yet they had not risen far enough to replace the flood tide of innovation that was ebbing as they rose. Meanwhile there was no such slackening in the growth of population. Because of previous changes in the age and marital structure of the population, the entrants to the labor market may increase faster or slower than the population as a whole, and in Britain they were particularly numerous in the opening years of the twentieth century. In the United States a similar effect was produced by very high rates of immigration.

If this reading of history has the gist of the matter in it, it reminds us that there is at no time an assured balance between the rate of growth of the labor force and of the forces we have comprised under the title of the extension of enterprise. No doubt reactions run from each to the other. It has been remarked that some of the periods of most rapid growth in productivity have been periods of rapid growth in population too, and the growth in population may stimulate enterprise in several ways—by increasing the number of those who have to strike out on a line of their own, by holding down real wages relative to output per head, and by diffusing a general sense that increases of capacity will be warranted. Conversely, a rise in productivity may stimulate the growth of population—regionally by encouraging immigration and generally by lowering the death rate or promoting earlier marriages. But such reactions take time, and many other forces are at work. At any one time the current rate of growth of the labor force on the one hand and of technique, equipment, and enterprise on the other must be substantially independent of one another. As the balance between them sways, so the rate of rise of real pay will vary.

We noticed that it will also vary by reason of distributive changes. The internal proportions of the central tendency are not immutable. With a given rate of rise of output per worker, the real wage may rise now somewhat faster, now somewhat slower, or within a year or two it may be displaced in either direction.

The immediate means is a changed relation between money rates of pay and the selling prices of final products. Much of the present argument has dealt directly with real pay, whereas in the actual world real pay emerges only from the relation between money rates of pay and prices which themselves are set, at least proximately, by separate decisions. If the central tendency is to hold, and real pay is to move parallel to output per head, prices and money rates of pay stand in a necessary relation to each other. If either takes a particular course, the other must adapt itself to it, so that the quotient of the two will yield the required real pay. If output per head is rising at 3 per cent a year, and real pay is to move parallel to it, then if money pay rises by 5 per cent a year, prices must rise by about 2 per cent, and if money pay does not rise at all, prices must fall by about 3 per cent.

But the ease with which prices and money rates of pay can be raised depends on factors that are partly common to both and partly distinct. A strong light is thrown on the common factors by full employment. This swells the membership and funds of trade unions, but when the trade unions are strong everywhere, they are the more likely to succeed in wage claims because each employer has an assurance that labor costs are going to be raised all around, and prices are likely to follow. In the same conditions, employers are the more ready to agree to rises in money pay because they anticipate little disadvantage from raising their prices. But some factors are distinct. Trade-union vigor has undergone changes from time to time over and above those that go with the level of employment. Resistance to wage cuts is spontaneously stronger than support for wage claims. Public policy may be exerted more or less powerfully to hold or raise money wages. Prices, for their part, may be pressed down by more competition from other regions. Monetary and fiscal measures that change the flow of effective demand take their effect on the markets for final products before this gets through to the labor market. Once any trend of the price level has set in, it reinforces itself by the expectations that it forms in employers' minds: to raise the price of one's own product seems dangerous, however good the particular case for it, when price reductions are the acknowledged order of the day, but harmless when everybody is doing it.

It is by the momentary conjunction of such factors as these that some of the observed variations of the relation between real pay and productivity seem to be explained. We have already seen something of the possibilities, in our discussion of what the bargaining power of the trade union can do to reduce the profit margin. Generally, when the resistances to price-raising are weak, pressures that would push money rates of pay up will have much their own way, but they will carry prices up with them and will not gain at the expense of profit margins. But when the resistances to price-raising are strong, the possibility does exist of a stronger pressure raising money pay relative to prices—that is, raising real pay relative to productivity. A strong case appears when market forces are actually pressing prices down: the inherently dogged resistance to cuts is then likely to make any reduction in money pay smaller than the contemporary reduction in prices. These different conjunctions are found in the rising and falling phases of the trade cycle, but perhaps they may also be traced in the secondary secular fluctuations we noticed earlier: a distributive shift in favor of pay is less likely when the long-term trend of the price level is upward. A striking instance is the remarkable constancy of the division between pay and profit in the Western economies through the years of full employment after the Second World War.

There remains one other possibility, which is suggested by a marked rise in the wage–income ratio in several countries between 1914 and 1924. Money incomes of all kinds generally rose rapidly during the First World War and in the postwar boom, and then dropped back. But other incomes dropped back more than wages, so that the wage–income ratio rose—in France, Germany, the United Kingdom, and the United States perhaps by as much as a fifth, in Sweden by as much as two-fifths. Moreover, this seems to have been not a fluctuation but a lasting displacement of the prevailing level. One contributory cause has been the reduction by rapid inflation of the relative size of incomes that are fixed in terms of money or can be adjusted only slowly: in particular, the share of rent is likely to have been generally reduced. But for Britain, at least, the record suggests another possibility—that the average rate of return on risk capital was reduced. The way in which this could have come about we have already suggested: in the slump that followed the postwar boom profits were caught between the hammer of deflation and the anvil of labor's resistance. But the effect persisted, at least until it was overlaid by the Great Depression that set in during 1929. The persistence may only have marked a lag in the reaction of the supply of risk capital to a reduction in the rate of return on it. But it also raises the question whether there may not be a conventional element in the rate of return used to guide decisions on pricing and on the claims of proposed investments. At any one time a consensus may prevail on what rates of return are "attractive," "reasonable," or "inadequate." War, inflation, and deflation break the consensus up: the old bench marks are lost, and when a new consensus forms, it may be about a new level. But whatever the explanation, a displacement of the general level of the return to risk capital evidently carries with it the possibility of a shift in the general level of real pay.

Here as elsewhere, however, the static relations of distribution are entwined with the dynamic relations of growth. The displacement that makes a rise in real pay possible today may slow down the rise tomorrow. If the required rate of return on risk capital were really conventional and nothing more, then a reduction of the rate the consensus accepts would not reduce the supply. But though a reduction of the actual rate fails to generate sufficient pressure to restore current profit margins, it may still reduce new investment, either because the reward no longer seems worth the trouble or because existing profits do not provide enough funds for plowing back. In that case the rate of growth of the economy would be slowed down. Unhappily there seems to be no equilibrating mechanism here. The initial maladjustment is a particular rise in pay relative to profits, and the effect is that real pay is lower than it would have been otherwise on the aggregate of a run of years. The corrective would be a reduction in money pay relative to prices, but there seems to be no way in which a slower rate of growth of the economy tends to bring this about, save insofar as the restraint of development leaves more men without jobs, and this in turn exerts a restraining influence on wage claims.

THE CENTRAL CONTROL OF TOTAL PAY

The dynamic processes we have been considering include a feedback from the aggregate of current changes in pay to the particular changes made job by job. Some aggregates are matters only of statistical summation: the day's total of road accidents can be reckoned up, for instance, without the accumulating total having affected what happened at any point during the day. But even where each rate of pay is negotiated separately, the aggregate of pay is not just a total we may add up if we choose, but forms part of the system of economic forces. An analogy is provided by commodity markets: the total quantity of butter sold day by day is made up by many transactions that appear independent, but if it proves to differ from the total supply reaching the market there will be a rise or fall of stocks, and a change in price that will come back to the shops and affect subsequent purchases. One housewife may now find herself constrained to buy less, because others have been buying more. In much the same way, the cumulated change in pay as a whole forms part of the circuit that governs the changes in pay job by job.

Nonetheless, until recently the total of pay was not itself an object of policy in the Western economies. Persons and unions took action to raise or lower particular rates of pay, and governments intervened to restrain or reinforce such action or initiate it themselves; but it was no one's business to act upon the sum total of pay. As governments came to take increasing responsibility for economic affairs, they became concerned with aggregates such as the balance of payments, the quantity of money, effective demand, and the level of employment. But not until the coming of full employment, during the Second World War and the years since, did the total of pay generally present itself as an object of policy.

It did so then because the course of particular negotiations began to contribute to a rise in money incomes greater than that in the real product, and checking inflation was seen to require the restraint of particular rises within bounds set by the permissible increase in the total. Two ways of achieving this have been tried. One is to leave negotiations to follow their various existing procedures, but prescribe certain "guidelines," which though they allow some differentiation in special circumstances will ensure, if generally observed, that the total rise in pay will not exceed the anticipated total rise in the available real product. The other way is to coordinate negotiations explicitly. A major step, which has been taken in the Netherlands, Denmark, and Sweden, is to arrange that the principal collective agreements shall all have the same date of expiry: the total effect of a year's new settlements is now not a consideration that can appear only after the event and as the year goes on, but demands attention at the outset of all negotiations. A natural further step is to conduct an initial negotiation centrally and reach a framework agreement, laying down a pattern to be observed in the particular negotiations that follow. Such an understanding between the national organizations of employers' associations and trade unions was reached in the Netherlands through the Foundation of Labor from the end of the Second World War down to 1959, and in Sweden since 1956 has been expressed in agreements running for two years at a time. But no procedure has been wholly successful: the problem of controlling the rise of pay in the aggregate without assuming control of its movements in detail remains unsolved.

The General Level of Real Pay

It has called for new policies and improvised procedures in the Western economies, because they had developed institutions only to adjust particular rates separately, and had been content to let the whole be arrived at simply as the sum of the parts; but in the Soviet world it has been the whole that has been fixed first, and the institutions of central planning have been available to do this. Whereas in the West the share of labor in the product has largely been left to be settled by market forces, in the Soviet Union it has been a direct object of policy and has been intended to be settled by authority.

In principle, the procedure has been simple. The product is to be divided between what is paid out to workers on the one hand and what is used in the public sector on the other— in investment, social services including education, the administrative work of government, defense, space research, and the like. The division is made in two ways. The more direct is to budget for a certain total bill of wages and salaries, and keep this total down so that consumption by households may be kept down. But however big wages and salaries are in money, the real income available to households can be kept down by taxation and by higher prices—which amount to much the same, for the main tax is on turnover. The second way of adjusting the share of labor is therefore to finance the public sector by taxes that raise an industry's value product at market prices above its wage bill. In the event, should the monetary purchasing power accruing to households prove greater after all than the output, at market prices, assigned to them, then the safety valve is a rise in prices. The major determinant of the share of labor is thus the direction of resources, through the production programs, toward households on the one hand and the public sector on the other.

The political authority that sanctions the plan thereby approves or imposes a particular division of the product and general level of real pay. It may have been at times that certain programs in the public sector were pushed as far as possible, subject only to maintaining the existing level of real pay; or even that this level was deliberately lowered somewhat to release more resources for such programs. At other times a need to reduce discontent and encourage workers by more tangible rewards may have been politically paramount. But in whatever way the decision was reached, it would fix the size of the total wages fund for the period of the plan. The planners must then allocate this fund among the different branches of activity, according to the output scheduled for each and the labor required for that output. No doubt it would have been from budgets prepared branch by branch that the overall plan was compiled in the first place, and when the basic decisions had been taken at the highest political level the task of the planners would be only to make adjustments in the allocations already envisaged. But in principle the whole is fixed before the parts, by a centralized decision concerning the total real income to be made available to labor.

What is at issue may be illustrated by the simplified accounts for the Soviet Union in 1955 that appear on the next page. Out of the total product of 1100 bns. (as reckoned here), 218 bn., or about a fifth, were saved; of the remaining 882 bn., 215 bn. were absorbed by government, and the remaining 631 bn. went to consumption by households. This consumption was largely financed by the allocation of 588 bn. to wages and salaries.

But under this planning procedure, just as under the income policies of the Western economies, there has been difficulty in practice in keeping the payments of wages and salaries man by man within the intended bounds. The Soviet

The General Level of Real Pay

	Government		Enterprises and Farms		Households		Total Economy	
	Expenditure	*Receipts*	*Expenditure*	*Receipts*	*Expenditure*	*Receipts*	*Expenditure*	*Receipts*
			(Billions of rubles)					
INCOME ACCOUNT								
Gross product		120		902		78		1100
Wages and salaries	120		468			588		
Social transfers	60	22	22			60		
Taxes and profit deductions		488	436		52			
Purchase and repayment of state bonds	12	31			31	12		
Subsidies	77			77				
Balance = gross disposable income	392		53		655		1100	
	661	661	979	979	738	738	1100	1100
INCOME USE ACCOUNT								
Gross disposable income		392		53		655		1100
Consumption	251				631		882	
Balance = gross saving	141		53		24		218	
	392	392	53	53	655	655	1100	1100

Source: Adapted from *U.N. Economic Bulletin* for Europe, May 1957, Table I, p. 91.

Union, having retained few controls on the movement of labor between jobs, has found it hard to combine the central planning of the wage fund with the play of supply and demand in the labor market. We have seen how managers competing for labor have outrun their allotted funds. Between 1947 and 1956 no general rise in money wage rates was planned, but the actual rise averaged some 27 per cent. Here as in the West the result has been an undesired rise in the prices of consumers' goods.

Up to now we have treated real pay simply as the physical quantity of a representative assortment of goods and services that can be bought by the sum of money that constitutes a wage or salary. But in many employments and economies the worker is not recompensed simply by a pay packet. His material well-being depends on more than the size of the basketful his pay will buy.

There are in fact three elements to be comprised in any full account of what he gets in return for his work. The first is what the employer hands over to him individually. This is part of the cost the employer incurs if he employs an extra unit of labor, and avoids if he does not; and it is actually remitted to the worker (save for taxes or agreed contributions deducted at the source) and is not merely made available to him in the way of an amenity of which he may or may not choose to avail himself. The sum due may include not only payment for work done or for time spent at work but also for time taken to travel to and from work; for permitted absence, whether for sickness, a national holiday, or days of unemployment within a guaranteed week; and for time taken off within the nominal hours of the working day —tolerated tardiness at the start, time for washing up at the close, breaks for refreshments. Generally payment is due at the end of the period paid for, but some may be deferred, such as allotments to holidays with pay and pension funds; and in India a substantial part of annual earnings commonly consists of a bonus declared, or negotiated, once or twice a year. The greater part is reckoned in money, but sometimes part is transmitted in kind, through the provision of meals, or fuel and other household supplies, and of lodging or a house free of rent or at a reduced rent.

The cost of a particular worker to his employer often also contains a second element: for each worker he employs, or each increment of his wages bill, the employer makes a contribution to an insurance fund or a fund for social benefits. He may be obliged to do so by law, or may have set up a scheme of his own volition or in agreement with the trade unions. The insurance funds may cover industrial injuries, sickness, medical treatment, and unemployment. The funds for social benefits exist especially to provide family allowances: part of each man's wage is withheld by his employer and remitted instead to a national fund which is paid out to married men according to their family obligations; in effect, within a given wages bill the bachelors are made to transfer part of their earnings to the married, and the parents of small families to those of large ones. Thus in France in 1955 a married unskilled worker, if he had two children, received half as much again as an unmarried one, and if he had five children, 2.4 times as much. This element is evidently part of the pay received by workers as a whole, though how much of it goes to any one worker does not depend on the work he does.

The outlay some employers incur on behalf of their workers contains a third element, in the form of benefits and amenities made available to the workers generally, though not allocated periodically or in fixed amount to any one of them. Some of these benefits consist of payments of money —such as "severance pay," or compensation for discharge on grounds of redundancy—which are paid out to particular workers, but are made only occasionally and are not provided for by regular allocations attached to wage payments. But the greater part of the outlay is for amenities such as canteens, recreation rooms, sports grounds, and clubs. Some amenities are to be regarded only as improvements in working conditions—air conditioning in offices, for example, or pit-head baths for the miner: they add to the balance of advantage in a particular job, but the worker avails himself of them only insofar as he is doing that job, and they are not a part of his consumption out of working hours. But the amenities with which we are concerned here are enjoyed out of working hours, and are of a kind on which the worker would be spending his own money if they were not provided by the firm. What the firm spends on them we can therefore regard as part of the cost of labor to it. But how far they should be reckoned part of the pay workers receive is uncertain. They may provide one man with what he would otherwise spend much on, and another may not use them at all. Because they do not give the workers the freedom that a cash payment carries with it to choose what form one's consumption shall take, they seem likely to be worth less to the average worker than they cost the firm.

The real wage is made up of all three elements: what the worker receives in money and kind, what is paid on his behalf to funds, and what use he makes of the amenities made available to him.

Since the First World War the second element has grown, for three reasons: in times of inflation the immediate needs of workers with families to feed have been met in this way without as great a rise in pay having to be given to all; public policy has approved in principle of some socialization of the wage, or has used employers' contributions as part of the finance of social insurance; and as real wages have risen, trade unions have found increasing room in their claims and agreements for "fringe benefits." But a general tendency has impinged in different ways on different countries. Some finance social insurance by contributions from workers, employers, and the taxpayer, some from a payroll tax, some from general taxation. Where a general system has been set up by law, as in Great Britain, a smaller part of the contributions appears as a cost of labor than where, as in the United States, more has been left for the trade unions to negotiate with the employer. Differences between countries also arise from the sheer size of the provision that is made. In many European countries it is large. In France, for example, in employments within the general scheme of social charges, paid-out wages and salaries amounted in the 1950s to rather less than three-quarters of total labor costs, and the difference was made up of allocations to workmen's compensation, social insurance, and, above all, family allowances. Within a single country industries differ by tradition, or according to the nature of their work, in the extent of the difference: against the proportion of three-quarters just mentioned for France generally, that on the French railroads has been put at little more than half, by reason of the extent of holiday pay, medical services, housing allowances, free travel, and the like. A European survey[5] of the extent of all benefits and charges other than the money payments currently transmitted to the worker for hours actually worked found that in the 1950s these other elements of labor cost amounted to from 40 and 50 per cent of the paid-out wage in Italy and Yugoslavia, from 30 to 40 per cent in Austria, France, Greece, and Turkey, from 20 to 30 per cent in Belgium and Western

5. I.L.O., *Labour Costs in European Industry*, Studies and Reports, new ser. 52 (1959).

Germany, and between 10 and 15 per cent in Denmark and the United Kingdom.

The development of various forms and channels of remuneration reveals two features which differentiate the contemporary contract of employment in many countries from a simple payment for a piece of work done, and which enter into the rise of the standard of living of the worker without taking much effect on the measurable real pay.

The first is that employment confers status. The domestic worker of the eighteenth century, working in his own cottage, with his own equipment, and in his own time, was a subcontractor rather than a wage earner. The first workers in the mill lacked the freedom that detachment had preserved and were subordinated to the requirements of the firm, but without becoming members of it. Yet as the provisions of the contract of employment have been expanded, the worker has attained rights as well as duties: safeguards against arbitrary treatment, limitations on the power of the employer to dismiss him, benefits accruing by reason of continued association and not of particular work done. Such provisions have their analogies within the family and the state, and impart to employment something of the status that belongs to membership of a community.

The second feature is that the contract of employment has been used as part of the administrative machinery of social benefits and social insurance. The extent to which this has been done varies more widely from country to country than the extent of social benefits and social insurance themselves. These may be administered not only through employment but through voluntary societies and through government itself or the agencies it sets up; and they may be financed not only by employers' and workers' contributions but by voluntary subscriptions and the general fund of taxation. The lines may be drawn in various places between what the worker is paid for particular pieces of work, is allotted as a member of a productive association, and is entitled to as a citizen. This makes it difficult to compare the levels of real pay in different countries, or measure the rise of real pay in any one.

There is, however, one further component of the rise of real pay that is in a way measurable—the increase of leisure. To call leisure part of pay may seem sophistical, and certainly it is not part of the cost of labor to the employer. If the working week is simply reduced by an hour without raising the hourly rate, one cannot say that pay has risen, even though the workers may prefer the new arrangement. But at least in recent years a reduction in hours has usually been negotiated only when the hourly rate has been raised enough at the same time to keep up weekly money pay, and then the extra leisure constitutes the rise. The miner who took a shift off used to be said to be "buying daylight": when workers negotiate a reduction in weekly hours from 42 to 40 without loss of pay—that is, with a 5 per cent rise in the hourly rate —we can think of them as first getting the 5 per cent rise on all 42 hours, and then using the whole rise to buy two hours of leisure. In any case we cannot compare the real wages of two workers by looking only at the quantities of goods and services their money earnings will buy, without regard to how long they have to work to get the money.

The general rise in the real return to labor in the developing economies during the last hundred years and more has in fact been taken out partly in the form of more leisure. One way in which more leisure could have been enjoyed was through fewer members of the household going out to work at all. When the head of the house earns little, the wife often has to go out to work too, and the children have to earn what they can in part-time work before they leave school, and begin full-time work as soon as the law allows. As the head comes to earn more, this pressure is relieved. At higher levels of pay, too, preparation can be made for earlier retirement. For these reasons we might expect rising real pay to bring a falling participation rate: a lower proportion of the population of working age will be gainfully employed. But this has not happened: the records of a number of countries show that the participation rate has been remarkably steady. Probably this means not that the factors that lower it have not been operative but that they have been offset by others. Among these may well be the release of women from household duties by a reduction in the size of the family and the mechanization of domestic work. More women have had the education to fit them for nonmanual jobs, and more jobs both manual and nonmanual have been opened to women. It may well be also that the place of poverty in making people add all they can to family income has been taken by the opportunity a higher standard of living gives of rising higher still—of acquiring a better house, for instance, or a car.

Though the opportunity to enjoy more leisure does not seem to have been generally used to lower the proportionate number of persons who go out to work, it certainly has been used to lower the number of hours the average person works in the year. Before the Industrial Revolution the hours we hear of were long everywhere, savagely long by modern standards, not less than twelve hours a day in summer and ten in winter, and that for six days a week. Such hours can have been made supportable only by a leisurely pace of work, a good many tolerated breaks, and sometimes also a good many days of festival. The early factories brought added reasons for working long hours: in some places to make full use of intermittent water power while it was available, and more generally to spread the costs of mill and machinery

over as big an output as possible. But the bringing of workers together in factories also gave an opportunity of regulation that was lacking before, and it was used at first on
grounds of humanity to protect women and children from
the exhaustion of long hours. Meanwhile, as collective bargaining grew up, it began to regulate hours as well as wages.
The clerical worker, much more highly paid relative to the
manual laborer then than now, took out some of his advantage in shorter hours, which are still widely accepted as belonging naturally to his occupation. But in Britain some
manual workers were able to negotiate the 9-hour day and
54-hour week about the middle of the nineteenth century.
That was to remain standard practice down to the First
World War, save only for the adoption of earlier stopping
times on Saturday. But meanwhile employers had begun to
discover the inefficiency of long hours, and by 1890 some
were introducing the 8-hour day. It was that day, and the
5½-day week, that characterized the interwar years, though
in France and the United States the 40-hour week was adopted as a palliative for the unemployment of the 1930s. Since
the Second World War the 40-hour week has become typical
of industrial practice in the Western countries. The Soviet
Twenty-Year Plan of 1961 promised a transition within the
next ten years to the week of 36 hours completed in either
six days or five.

Meanwhile annual holidays with pay, which were usual
in a modest way for clerical workers before 1914 but had
made only a sporadic appearance for manual workers, have
become the general practice, and have been widely extended
to not less than two weeks, besides certain days of national
holiday.

The reductions of working hours have been achieved not
gradually but in particular jumps, separated by long periods

of little change. When the jumps have come, no doubt there has been an element of fashion in them. Yet there is no reason to doubt that the reductions have marked a decision about the alternative uses of resources: rather than use all their increased command of resources to get more goods and services, people have chosen a smaller increase of goods and services together with some increase of leisure. No doubt more extensive education has increased the demand for leisure by developing the capacity to enjoy it. But also, goods and leisure are complementary: it is useless to have more amenities unless one has time to enjoy them, and such enjoyment depends a great deal on equipment, especially for housing and travel. It is therefore likely that for some time in the future, as in the past, the rise of real pay will take the form both of more leisure and of more goods and services.

BIBLIOGRAPHY

ABBREVIATIONS

AER	*American Economic Review*
BOUIS	*Bulletin of the Oxford University Institute of Statistics*
BSGF	*Bulletin de Statistique Générale de la France*
CJEP	*Canadian Journal of Economic and Political Science*
EA	*Economie Appliquée*
Econ	*Economica*
Economet	*Econometrica*
EHR	*Economic History Review*
EJ	*Economic Journal*
ER	*Economic Record*
IJLE	*Indian Journal of Labour Economics*
ILR	*International Labour Review*
ILRR	*Industrial and Labor Relations Review*
IRRA	Industrial Relations Research Association, proceedings
IRSH	*International Review of Social History*
JASA	*Journal of the American Statistical Association*
JEH	*Journal of Economic History*
JPE	*Journal of Political Economy*
JRSS	*Journal of the Royal Statistical Society*
LLJ	*Labor Law Journal*
MLG	U.K. *Ministry of Labour Gazette*
MLR	*Monthly Labour Review*
MS	*Manchester School*

251

Bibliography

OEP	*Oxford Economic Papers*
QJE	*Quarterly Journal of Economics*
RE	*Revue Economique*
RECI	*Review of Economic Conditions in Italy,* Banca di Roma
REP	*Revue d'Economie Politique*
RES	*Review of Economics and Statistics*
Sank	*Sankhya*
SCB	U.S. Department of Commerce, *Survey of Current Business*
SEJ	*Southern Economic Journal*
SJPE	*Scottish Journal of Political Economy*
SR	*Social Research*
SS	*Soviet Studies*
ST	*Sociologie du Travail*
VS	*Volkswirtschaftliche Schriften*
WA	*Weltwirtschaftliches Archiv*
WS	*Wirtschaft und Statistik*

GENERAL SOURCES

A. The Classics (in chronological order)

Smith, Adam, *The Wealth of Nations* (1776), Bk. I, chap. 8.
Mill, John Stuart, *The Principles of Political Economy,* 1848.
Marx, Karl, *Capital* (1867), *1*.
Walker, Francis A., *The Wages Question,* 1876.
Marshall, Alfred, *Principles of Economics* (1890), Bk. VI.
——— *Elements of Economics of Industry* (1892), Bk. VI, chap. 13.
Clark, John Bates, *Distribution of Wealth,* 1899.
Taussig, F. W., *Principles of Economics* (1911), Bk. V, chaps. 47, 48.
Moore, H. L., *Laws of Wages* (1911).

B. Modern Texts

Cartter, A. M., *Theory of Wages and Employment,* Homewood, Ill., Irwin, 1959.
Douglas, P. H., *The Theory of Wages,* New York, Macmillan, 1934.
Hicks, J. R., *The Theory of Wages* (1932), London, Macmillan; New York, St. Martin's, 1935.

Bibliography

Reder, M. W., *Labor in a Growing Economy*, New York, Wiley; London, Chapman & Hall, 1957.

Reynolds, L. G., *Labor Economics and Labor Relations* (1949), 2d ed. New York, Prentice Hall, 1954.

Robertson, D. J., *The Economics of Wages and the Distribution of Income*, London, Macmillan; New York, St. Martin's, 1961.

Sellier, F., and A. Tiano, *Economie du Travail*, Paris, Presses Universitaires de France, 1962.

C. History: Regional and Sociological Studies

Bogart, E. L., *Economic History of the American People*, New York, Longmans Green, 1930.

Dube, S. C., *Indian Village*, Ithaca, Cornell University Press; London, Routledge & Kegan Paul, 1955.

Durkheim, E., trans. G. Simpson, *The Division of Labor in Society*, Glencoe, Ill., Free Press, 1947.

Hughes, T. L., and D. E. T. Luard, *The Economic Development of Communist China, 1949–1960* (1959), 2d ed. London, New York, Toronto, Oxford University Press, 1961.

Marshall, T. H., *Citizenship and Social Class*, Cambridge, Eng., Cambridge University Press, 1950.

Nove, A., *The Soviet Economy*, London, Allen & Unwin, 1961.

Ogden, C. K., ed., History of Civilization Series, New York, Knopf; London, Kegan Paul, Trench, Trübner, c. 1925.

Phelps Brown, E. H., *The Growth of British Industrial Relations*, London, Macmillan; New York, St. Martin's, 1959.

Shann, E. O. G., *An Economic History of Australia*, Cambridge, Eng., Cambridge University Press, 1930.

Smith, T. C., *The Agrarian Origins of Modern Japan*, Stanford, Stanford University Press, 1959.

Tawney, R. H., *Land and Labour in China*, London, Allen & Unwin; New York, Harcourt Brace, 1932.

CHAPTER BIBLIOGRAPHIES

The books cited in the bibliographies for each chapter have been selected, from a wide field, with the following points in mind:

1. Their coverage, taken all together, of the main questions discussed in the relevant chapter.

2. Some extension, so far as possible, of the geographical range—and here attention is called to the United Nations *Economic Survey of Europe* and *Economic Survey of Asia and the Far East* (published yearly) and to the *Studies and Reports* of the International Labour Organisation (Geneva).
3. Readability.
4. Ease of access.

For each chapter, the bibliography is arranged in an order that corresponds roughly to the sequence of discussion in the text, but one book may refer to more than one part of the discussion. Where there are works of application to the whole chapter, they have been put at the beginning.

For Chapters 5, 6, and 7, much of the material is to be found only in journals; therefore, under each of these chapters there is an additional bibliography of articles. Most of the articles are studies, mainly quantitative, of the forces bearing upon wages.

Chapter 1 is omitted from the following list because it requires no bibliography.

A. Chapter 2

Finley, M. I., *Slavery in Classical Antiquity*, Cambridge, Eng., Heffer, 1961.

Mireaux, E., trans. I. Sells, *Daily Life in the Time of Homer*, London, Allen & Unwin, 1959.

Stampp, K. M., *The Peculiar Institution*, New York, Knopf, 1956.

Clapham, J. H., and E. Power, *The Cambridge Economic History of Europe*, Cambridge, Eng., Cambridge University Press, 1952: vol. 2 (ed. M. Postan and E. E. Rich), see especially chap. 6.

Unwin, G., *The Gilds and Companies of London* (1908), 3d ed. London, Allen & Unwin, 1938.

Andrieux, A., and J. Lignon, *L'Ouvrier d'Aujourd'hui*, Paris, Rivière, 1961.

Moore, W. E., *Industrial Relations and the Social Order* (1946), rev. ed. New York, Macmillan, 1955.

Hare, A. E. C., *The First Principles of Industrial Relations*, London, Macmillan, 1958.

Webb, S. and B., *Industrial Democracy* (1897), 2d ed. London, Longmans, 1919.

Bibliography

Perlman, M., *Labor Union Theories in America, Background and Development*, Evanston, Ill., Row, Peterson, 1958.

Hoxie, R. F., *Trade Unionism in the United States* (1917), 2d ed. New York, Appleton, 1928.

Galenson, W., *Comparative Labor Movements*, New York, Prentice Hall, 1952.

Clegg, H. A., *A New Approach to Industrial Democracy*, Oxford, Blackwell, 1960.

Tillyard, F., *The Worker and the State* (1923), 3d ed. London, Routledge, 1948.

B. Chapter 3

Moore, W. E., and A. S. Feldman, eds., *Labor Commitment and Social Change in Developing Areas*, New York, Social Science Research Council, 1960.

Slotkin, J. S., *From Field to Factory: New Industrial Employees*, Glencoe, Ill., Free Press, 1960.

Kerr, C., J. T. Dunlop, F. H. Harbison, and C. A. Myers, *Industrialism and Industrial Man*, Cambridge, Mass., Harvard University Press, 1960.

Elkan, W., *Migrants and Proletarians*, East African Institute of Social Research, London, New York, Nairobi, Oxford University Press, 1960.

Myers, C. A., *Labor Problems in the Industrialization of India*, Cambridge, Mass., Harvard University Press, 1958.

Okochi, K., *Labour in Japan*, Science Council of Japan, Division of Economics, 18, Tokyo, The Council, 1958.

Ginzberg, E., *Human Resources—the Wealth of a Nation*, New York, Simon & Schuster, 1955.

Williams, Lady, *Recruitment to the Skilled Trades*, London, Routledge & Kegan Paul; New York, Humanities Press, 1957.

Anstett, M., *La Formation de la main d'oeuvre qualifiée en union soviétique de 1917 à 1954*, Paris, Rivière, 1956.

Nove, A., *The Soviet Economy*, London, Allen & Unwin, 1961.

Vernon, P. E., *The Measurement of Abilities* (1946), 2d ed. London, University of London Press, 1956.

Crook, G. H., and M. Heinstein, *The Older Worker in Industry*, Berkeley, Institute of Industrial Relations, University of California, 1958.

Bibliography

C. Chapter 4

Thomas, B., ed., *Economics of International Migration*, London, Macmillan; New York, St. Martin's, 1958.

Clark, C., *The Conditions of Economic Progress* (1940), 3d ed. London, Macmillan; New York, St. Martin's, 1957.

Jaffe, A. J., *People, Jobs, and Economic Development*, Glencoe, Ill., Free Press, 1959.

Haber, W., et al., *Manpower in the United States*, Industrial Relations Research Association, 11, New York, Harper, 1954.

Schumpeter, E. B., ed., *The Industrialization of Japan and Manchukuo* (New York, Macmillan, 1940), Pt. 2.

Reynolds, L. G., *The Structure of Labor Markets*, New York, Harper, 1951.

Adams, L. P., and R. L. Aronson, *Workers and Industrial Change*, Ithaca, Cornell University, 1957.

Ornati, O., *Jobs and Workers in India*, Ithaca, Institute of Industrial and Labor Relations, Cornell University, 1955.

Beveridge, W. H., *Unemployment* (1908), new ed. London, New York, Toronto, Longmans Green, 1930.

Kloosterboer, W., *Involuntary Labour since the Abolition of Slavery*, Leiden, Brill, 1960.

Grad, A. J., *Land and Peasant in Japan*, New York, Institute of Pacific Relations, 1952.

Parker, H. M. D., *Manpower: A Study of War-time Policy and Administration*, London, H.M. Stationery Office, 1957.

Schwarz, S. M., *Labor in the Soviet Union*, New York, Praeger; London, Cresset Press, 1953.

D. Chapter 5

Dunlop, J. T., ed., *The Theory of Wage Determination*, New York, St. Martin's; London, Macmillan, 1957.

Taylor, G. W., and F. C. Pierson, eds., *New Concepts of Wage Determination*, New York, London, Toronto, McGraw Hill, 1957.

Fogarty, M. P., *The Just Wage*, London, Chapman, 1961.

Wootton, B., *The Social Foundations of Wage Policy*, London, Allen & Unwin; New York, Norton, 1955.

International Labour Office, *Job Evaluation*, Studies and Reports, New Series, 56, Geneva, 1960.

Bibliography

Glass, D. V., ed., *Social Mobility in Britain,* London, Routledge & Kegan Paul, 1954.

Abegglen, J. G., *The Japanese Factory,* Glencoe, Ill., Free Press, 1958.

Myers, C. A., and G. P. Shultz, *The Dynamics of a Labor Market,* New York, Prentice Hall, 1951.

Aitchison, J., and J. A. C. Brown, *The Log-Normal Distribution, with special reference to its Use in Economics,* Cambridge, Eng., Cambridge University Press, 1957.

Articles: grouped according to subject as treated in text, but listed in chronological order.

The Supply Schedule of Labor
Robbins, L. C., *Econ,* no. 28 (1930), 123.

Schoenberg, E. H. and P. H. Douglas, *JPE, 45* (1937), 45.

Mosback, E., *WA, 82* (1959), 133.

The Demand Schedule for Labor
Lester, R. A., *AER, 36* (1946), 63.

Machlup, F., *AER, 36* (1946), 519.

Lester, R. A., *AER, 37* (1947), 135.

Reder, M. W., *JPE, 54* (1947), 450.

Stein, J. L., *RES, 25* (1958), 182.

The Why and Wherefore of Differentials
Oxnam, D. W., *ER 26* (1950), p. 1.

Salkever, L. R., *ILRR, 6* (1952–53), 299.

McCaffree, K. M., *RES, 25* (1953), 30.

Routh, G. C. A., *Econ, NS 21* (1954), 201.

Muntz, E. E., *ILR, 71* (1955), 575.

Phelps Brown, E. H., *Econ, NS 22* (1955), 349.

Reder, M. W., *AER, 45* (1955), 833.

Marchal, J., and J. Lecaillon, *QJE, 73* (1958), 166.

Fogarty, M. P., *EJ, 69* (1959), 55.

Yanowitch, M., *ILRR, 13* (1959–60), 166.

——— *SS, 11* (1960), no. 3.

IRRA, 13th annual meeting (1960), pp. 250 ff.

Bibliography

The Personal Distribution of Earnings: the Log-normal
Gibrat, R., *BSGF, 19* (1930), 469.
Roy, A. D., *EJ, 60* (1950), 489, 831.
———*OEP, NS 3* (1951), 135.
Goldsmith, S., et al., *RES, 36* (1954), 1.
Denison, E. F., *AER* (May 1954), p. 254.
Solterer, J., *Ordo, 10* (1958), 271.
Lydall, H. F., *JRSS, A 122* (1959), 1.
——— *Economet, 27* (1959), 110.
Lydall, H. F., and J. B. Lansing, *AER, 49* (1959), 43.
Lebergott, S., *AER, 49* (1959), 328.
Mayer, T., *RES, 42* (1960), 189.
Kendall, M. G., *JRSS, A 124* (1961), 1.

E. Chapter 6

For the origins of collective bargaining, see the bibliography of Chapter 2. See also the first two references in the bibliography of Chapter 5.

Ford, P., *The Economics of Collective Bargaining*, Oxford, Blackwell, 1958.

Kornhauser, A., R. Dubin, and M. R. Ross, eds., *Industrial Conflict*, New York, Toronto, London, McGraw Hill, 1954.

Sturmthal, A., ed., *Contemporary Collective Bargaining in Seven Countries*, Ithaca, Cornell University, 1957.

Reynolds, L. G., and C. H. Taft, *The Evolution of Wage Structure*, New Haven, Yale University Press; London, Oxford University Press, 1956.

Levinson, H. M., *Unionism, Wage Trends and Income Distribution*, Michigan Business Studies, 10, no. 4, Ann Arbor, University of Michigan, 1951.

Slichter, S. H., J. J. Healy, and E. R. Livernash, *The Impact of Collective Bargaining on Management*, Washington, D.C., Brookings Institution, 1960.

Tiano, A., *L'Action syndicale ouvrière et la théorie économique du salaire*, Paris, Génin, 1958.

Tavitian, R., *La Part des Salaires dans le revenu national*, Paris, Génin [1959].

Bibliography

Bradley, P. E., ed., *The Public Stake in Union Power*, Charlottes-ville, University of Virginia Press, 1959.

Nigam, S. B. L., *State Regulation of Minimum Wages*, Bombay, Calcutta, Asia Publishing House, 1955.

Walker, K. F., *Industrial Relations in Australia*, Cambridge, Mass., Harvard University Press, 1956.

Johnston, T. L., *Collective Bargaining in Sweden*, London, Allen & Unwin, 1962.

Bergson, A., *The Structure of Soviet Wages*, Cambridge, Mass., Harvard University Press, 1944.

Nove, A., *The Soviet Economy*, London, Allen & Unwin, 1961.

Articles: grouped according to subject as treated in text, but listed in chronological order.

Analysis of Bargaining Power
Hansen, A., *AER, 11* (1921), 616.
Riches, E. J., *ER, 9* (1933), 226.
Yoder, D., *JPE, 48* (1940), 222.
Spielmans, J. V., *JPE, 52* (1944), 319.
Knowles, K. G. J. C., *BOUIS, 9* (1947), 285.
Ross, A. M., *AER, 37* (1947), 793.
Lindblom, C. E., *QJE, 62* (1948), 396.
Forchheimer, K., *BOUIS, 10* (1948), 9.
Woodbury, R. M., *ILR, 60* (1949), 451.
Nash, J. F., *Economet, 18* (1950), 155.
Ross, A. M., and D. Irwin, *ILRR, 4* (1950–51), 323.
Rees, A., *JPE, 60* (1952), 371.
ILR, 72 (1955), 78.
Schelling, T. C., *AER, 46* (1956), 281.
Harsanyi, J. S., *Economet, 24* (1956), 144.
Hammett, R. S., et al., *JPE, 65* (1957), 126.
Wagner, H. M., *SEJ, 23* (1957), 380.
Stevens, C. M., *QJE, 72* (1958), 77.
Reder, M. W., *ILRR, 13* (1959–60), 349.

The Bargaining Area
Seltzer, G., *JPE, 59* (1951), 319.
Chamberlain, N. W., *ILRR, 10* (1956–57), 3.
Guigni, G., *ILRR, 10* (1956–57), 424.

Bibliography

Levinson, H. M., *LLJ, 9* (1958), 669.

Lohse, L., *MLR, 81* (1958), 1230.

Sellier, F., *ST, 4* (1960), 289.

Knowles, K. G. J. C., and E. M. F. Thorne, *BOUIS, 23* (1961), 1.

Proksch, A., *ILR, 83* (1961), 229.

Maher, J. E., *ILRR, 15* (1961–62), 3.

Taira, K., *ILRR, 15* (1961–62), 33.

Effects of Collective Bargaining on the Pay Structure

Ross, A. M., *QJE, 62* (1948), 263.

Lester, R. A., and A. M. Ross (reply), *QJE, 62* (1948), 783.

Ross, A. M., and W. Goldner, *QJE, 64* (1950), 254.

Rees, A., IRRA, 3d annual meeting (1950), p. 203.

———— *AER, 41* (1951), 389.

Turner, H. A., *MS, 20* (1952), 227.

Sobotka, S. P., *JPE, 61* (1953), 127.

Bronfenbrenner, M., *AER* (May 1954), p. 293.

Scherer, J., *ILRR, 9* (1955–56), 213.

Maher, J. E., *AER, 46* (1956), 336.

Beck, J. W., *ILRR, 11* (1957–58), 231.

Ulman, L., and A. Rees (reply), *AER, 48* (1958), 408.

Lurie, M., *JPE, 69* (1961), 558.

Can the Trade Unions Win a Larger Share of National Income?

Phelps Brown, E. H., and S. V. Hopkins, *OEP, NS 2* (1950), 226.

———— and P. E. Hart, *EJ, 62* (1952), 253.

Denison, E. F., *SCB* (June 1952), p. 16.

Burkhead, J., *JASA, 48* (1953), 192.

Sultan, P. E., *RES, 36* (1954), 67.

Johnson, D. G., *RES, 36* (1954), 175.

AER (May 1954), pp. 279–321.

Beck, J. W., *SEJ, 22* (1956), 457.

Rothschild, K. W., *WA, 78* (1957), 157.

Beck, J. W., *SEJ, 23* (1957), 285.

Cheek, B. M., *ER, 33* (1957), 191.

Bibliography

Solow, R. M., *AER, 48* (1958), 617.
RE (1959), p. 1.
Weitzmann, I., *VS, 34* [1958].
Ozanne, R., *QJE, 73* (1959), 177.
Shrimali, P. D., *IJLE, 3* (1960), 22.
Phillips, J. D., *RES, 42* (1960), 164.
Marchal, J., et al., *REP, 70* (1960), 321.
Raabe, K. H., and G. Hamer, *WS, 12 N.F.* (1960), 257.
Simler, N. J., *RES, 43* (1961), 369.

Power of Trade Unions to Alter Distribution between Sectors
Garbarino, J. W., *QJE, 64* (1950), 282.
Cullen, D. E., *AER, 46* (1956), 353.
Perlman, R., *ILRR, 10* (1956–57), 26.
Meyers, F., *ILRR, 12* (1958–59), 434.
Hildebrand, G. H., *AER* (May 1959), p. 399.
Weinstein, P. A., *JPE, 68* (1960), 379.
Schwartzman, D., *CJEP, 26* (1960), 428.

The Regulation of Wages
Webb, S., *JPE, 20* (1912), 973.
Hammond, M. B., *QJE, 29* (1914–15), 98, 326, 562.
Sells, D. M., *ILR, 8* (1923), 191.
Riches, E. L., *Econ, NS 5* (1938), 316.
Hetherington, H., *ILR, 38* (1938), 472.
Pierson, F., *AER, 30* (1940), 72.
Brown, W. M., *AER, 30* (1940), 98.
Stigler, G. J., *AER, 36* (1946), 358.
Hamberg, D., *SEJ, 15* (1949), 321.
Isaac, J. E., *ILR, 63* (1951), 149; *69* (1954), 570.
Oxnam, D. W., *ILRR, 9* (1955–56), 610.
Peterson, J. M., *JPE, 65* (1957), 412.
Gulick, C. A., *IRSH, 2* (1957), 351; *3* (1958), 1.
Lubin, I., and C. A. Pearce, *ILRR, 11* (1957–58), 203.
Badenhoof, L. S., *MLR, 81* (1958), 737.
Peterson, J. M., *ILRR, 12* (1958–59), 406.
Lester, R., and J. M. Peterson (reply), *ILRR, 13* (1959–60), 254.
Douty, H. M., *Econ, NS 27* (1960), 137.

Bibliography

F. Chapter 7

Lewis, W. A., *The Theory of Economic Growth*, London, Allen & Unwin, 1957.

Kuznets, S., *Six Lectures on Economic Growth*, Glencoe, Ill., Free Press, 1959.

Rostow, W. W., *The Process of Economic Growth* (1953), 2d ed. Oxford, Clarendon Press, 1960.

Kuznets, S., *Secular Movements in Production and Prices*, Boston, Houghton, 1930.

Meade, J. E., et al., *The Economic and Social Structure of Mauritius*, London, Methuen, 1961.

Kendrick, J. W., *Productivity Trends in the United States*, Princeton, National Bureau of Economic Research, Publications, 71, 1961.

Wisert, F. M., *Fringe Benefits*, London, Chapman & Hall, 1959.

Long, C. D., *The Labor Force under Changing Income and Employment*, Princeton, Princeton University Press, 1958.

Northrup, H. R., and H. R. Brinberg, *Economics of the Work Week*, National Industrial Conference Board, Studies in Business Economics 24, New York, 1950.

Articles: grouped according to subject as treated in text, but listed in chronological order.

> *Variation in Real Wages in Undeveloped Economies*
> Gilboy, E. W., *RES, 18* (1936), 134.
> Coleman, D. C., *EHR*, 2d ser., *8* (1955–56), 280.
> Phelps Brown, E. H., and S. V. Hopkins, *Econ, NS 23* (1956), 296; *NS 24* (1957), 289; *NS 26* (1959), 18.
> Rostow, W. W., *EJ, 66* (1956), 25.
> Helleiner, K. F., *CJEP, 23* (1957), 1.
> Hobsbawn, E. J., *EHR*, 2d ser., *10* (1957–58), 46.
> Habakkuk, H. J., *JEH, 18* (1958), 486.
> Hager, E. E., *AER, 49* (1959), 310.
>
> *Fluctuations of Real Wages*
> Lewis, W. A., *MS, 20* (1952), 105.
> Phelps Brown, E. H., and S. A. Ozga, *EJ, 65* (1955), 1.
> Lewis, W. A., and P. O'Leary, *MS, 23* (1955), 113.
> Maynard, G., *EJ, 68* (1958), 737.

Bibliography

Subsistence Wages where Enterprise is not Expansive
Spengler, J. J., *AER, 41* (1951), 343.
Eisner, R., *AER, 42* (1952), 43.
Kuznets, S., *AER, 45* (1955), 1.
Fellner, W., *EJ, 67* (1957), 16.
Kaldor, N., *EJ, 67* (1957), 591.
——— *Sank, 18* (1957), 173.
Samuelson, P. A., *AER, 47* (1957), 884.

Real Wages and Output: the Capital-Output Ratio
Phelps Brown, E. H., and S. V. Hopkins, *OEP, NS 2* (1950), 226.
Phelps Brown, E. H., and B. Weber, *EJ, 63* (1953), 263.
Handfield-Jones, S. J., and B. Weber, *OEP, NS 6* (1954), 101.
Power, J. H., *AER, 45* (1955), 197.
Fellner, W., *EA, 9* (1956), 283.
Gordon, R. A., *AER, 46* (1956), 307.
Swan, T. W., *ER, 32* (1956), 334.
Wooden, D. G., and R. C. Wasson, *SCB* (Nov. 1956), p. 8.
Maywald, K., *EHR*, 2d ser., *9* (1956–57), 89.
Solow, R. M., *RES, 39* (1957), 312.
Power, J. H., *EJ, 68* (1958), 34.
Lomax, K. S., *JRSS, A 122* (1959), 185.
Williams, F. M., and E. J. Eaton, *AER, 49* (1959), 584.

The Cobb-Douglas Function
Cobb, C. W., and P. H. Douglas, *AER Supplement, 18* (1928), 139.
Schultz, H., *JPE, 37* (1929), 505.
Douglas, P. H., *AER, 38* (1948), 1.

The Rate of Rise of Real Pay: Dynamic Processes
Keynes, J. M., *QJE, 51* (1937), 209.
Harrod, R. F., *OEP*, no. 2 (1939), 1.
Sayers, R. S., *EJ, 60* (1950), 275.
Phelps Brown, E. H., and P. E. Hart, *EJ, 62* (1952), 253.
Phelps Brown, E. H., and S. J. Handfield-Jones, *OEP, NS 4* (1952), 266.

Bibliography

Coppock, D. J., *MS, 24* (1956), 1.
Long, C. D., *RES, 42* (1960), 140.

The Central Control of Total Pay
Chapman, J., *RES, 36* (1954), 134.
Zoeteweij, B., *ILR, 71* (1955), 148.
Roberts, B., *Econ, NS 24* (1957), 191.
Pels, P. S., *ILR, 75* (1957), 437.
Bussey, E. M., *MLR, 81* (1958), 982.
Isaac, J. E., *QJE, 72* (1958), 115.
Lohse, L., *MLR, 81* (1958), 1230.
ILR, 79 (1959), 1; *80* (1959), 319, 391.
Haas, B., *MS, 28* (1960), 177.
Holzman, F. D., *QJE, 74* (1960), 167.
Ruban, M. E., *SS, 13* (1962), 237.

Supplementary Elements of Real Pay
Chapman, S., *EJ, 19* (1909), 353.
Vannatelli, C., *RECI, 6* (1952), 385.
Robertson, D. J., *SJPE, 2* (1955), 1.
Dunlop, J. T., and M. Rothbaum, *ILR, 71* (1955), 347.
MLG, 65 (1957), 277.
MLG, 65 (1957), 330.
Zeisel, J. S., *MLR, 81* (1958), 23.
McCormick, B., *ILRR, 12* (1958–59), 423.
Cohen, S., *ILRR, 13* (1959–60), 64.
Moser, L. N., *EJ, 72* (1962), 320.

INDEX

Ability, 156; distribution of, 73–75; limitations of, 72–75; and supply curve for labor, 151

Absenteeism, 54, 60

Accidents, 45–46; liability for, 48

Advancement, 58

Africa, 10, 73, 117, 118; division of, 79

Agricultural Wages (Regulation) Act (*1924*, Britain), 131

Agriculture: techniques, 27, 108, 208, 211. *See also* Farmers; Farming; Land; Peasants

Ahmedabad textile strike, 195

Alsace, 210

Amenities at work place, 57–58, 243–44

America, 10, 146

America, North, 79, 161, 193; glass workers' union, 177. *See also* United States

American South, 20

Anglesey, 78

"Annual round" of wage settlements, 174, 203

Apprentices, 22, 28; ratio to masters, journeymen, 25, 193; sale of, 17, 65

Apprenticeship, 16; age of entry, 100; in China, People's Republic, 70; duration of, 60, 66; in guilds, 65–66; limitation of numbers, 39, 66, 192; of slaves, 16, 65

Arabs, 78

Arbitration, 166, 203

Arbitration, compulsory, 45, 193, 199, 201–02; as regulator of the pay structure, 202

Arbitrators, principles followed by, 202–03

Aristotle, 10

Arnot, R. P., 177 n.

Ashby, M. K., 210 n.

Asia, 10, 81, 160

Asians, in Africa, 68

Athens, ancient, 17, 20, 64

Augsburg, 210

Australia, 10, 80, 222; compulsory arbitration, 45, 133–34, 193, 199; sheepshearers' union, 160

Austria, 245

Authority, personal and executive, 51–53, 55

Babylonia, 15, 16, 28, 65, 116, 198

Badlis, 94, 108

Bargaining, individual, 159–60, 163, 181

Bargaining area, 169–84

Bargaining power, 33–34, 159–60; analysis of, 163–69

Belgium, 177, 245

265

Index

Index

Index

Index

Index

Index

Index

of, 170–71; productivity, 88, 105,
224; recruitment for, 105–06;
training for, 71; in underdeveloped economies, 55 et seq.

Manpower, in wartime. *See* Direction of labor

Marginal analysis, 142–45; and
macroeconomics, 227. *See also*
Cobb-Douglas function

Marginal productivity, 227 et seq.

Markets, 11, 23, 26, 159. *See also*
Labor markets

Marshall, Alfred, 16, 59, 179, 184

Marx, Karl, 37, 128, 220

Masons. *See* Building workers

Masters. *See* Employers

Mater et Magistra (1961), 196.

Maximum wages, 203–05; ease of
evasion, 204

Mechanics, "base," 18

Merchants: control of producers,
23; employing outworkers, 24;
restriction of competition between, 23

Merit rating, 128

Mexico, 58; service occupations in,
84–85

Migrants, 27, 159. *See also* Immigrants

Migration, 77–82 passim, 161, 208,
211, 232; and cyclical variations,
80; major movements, 77–78; restrictions on, 81–82; seasonal, 53,
107.

Mikoyan, Anastas I., 149

Military service, 117

Miners, 45; "buying daylight," 247;
loss of independence, 24

Minimum wage boards, 201

Minimum wages, 44, 140, 193–98,
204; and efficiency of production,
201; and family needs, 133–34;
as floor to wage structure, 199;

and level of employment, 194;
national minima in Australia,
France, and U.S.A., 199; for particular groups, 199; and product
prices, 200; and unemployment,
200–01

Minnesota, 146

Mitbestimmung. See Codetermination

Mobility of labor, 98, 111–12

Monasteries, possession of slaves,
13

Monopolies, 144

Monopsony, in the labor market,
137

Moore, Governor H., of New York,
11 n.

Moore, W. E., 63 n.

"Mop fair," 162

Münster, 210

Myers, C. A., 57 n.

Nago, 115

National income: average per occupied person, 222; distribution
of, 134, 220, 226–27, 235; distribution in Soviet Russia, 239–42;
distribution and trade union action, 184–90; uniformity of
shares, 229

National income statistics, 185

National wages policy, Netherlands, 204

National War Labor Board
(U.S.A.), 204

Negotiation, wage: influence of
market conditions, 164; process
of, 164–67. *See also* Bargaining
power

Negroes, importation into the New
World, 15

Netherlands, 222; bargaining area,
169; central wage agreement, 174;

Index

Index

Index

Index

Index

Index